Nature, Production, Power

Nature, Production, Power

Towards an Ecological Political Economy

Edited by

Fred P. Gale and R. Michael M'Gonigle

University of Tasmania, Tasmania, Australia, and University of Victoria, British Columbia, Canada

Edward Elgar
Cheltenham, UK • Northampton, MA, USA

Published by
Edward Elgar Publishing Limited
Glensanda House
Montpellier Parade
Cheltenham
Glos GL50 1UA
UK

Edward Elgar Publishing, Inc.
136 West Street
Suite 202
Northampton
Massachusetts 01060
USA

A catalogue record for this book
is available from the British Library

Library of Congress Cataloguing in Publication Data

Nature, production, power: towards an ecological political economy / edited by Fred P. Gale and Michael M'Gonigle
    p. cm.
    Includes bibliographical references and index.
    ISBN 1-84064-317-X
    1. Environmental economics. 2. Sustainable development. 3. Human ecology. I. Gale, Fred P. II. M'Gonigle, R. Michael.

    HD75.6.N415 2000
    333.7--dc21

                                                              00-028846

ISBN 1 84064 317 X

Printed in the United Kingdom at the University Press, Cambridge

Contents

List of Tables

List of Contributors

Laurie Adkin is Associate Professor, Department of Political Science, University of Alberta, Edmonton, Alberta, Canada.

Arun Agrawal is Assistant Professor, Department of Political Science, Yale University, New Haven, Connecticut, United States.

Gar Alperovitz is Lionel R. Bauman Professor of Political Economy, Department of Government and Politics, University of Maryland, College Park, Maryland, United States.

Ted Benton is Professor, Department of Sociology, University of Essex, Colchester, United Kingdom.

Alex Campbell is Special Assistant, Civil Society/Community-Building Initiative, University of Maryland, College Park, Maryland, United States.

Ken Conca is Associate Professor, The Department of Government and Politics, University of Maryland, College Park, Maryland, United States.

Fred Gale is Associate Lecturer, School of Government, University of Tasmania, Tasmania, Australia.

Mary Mellor is Professor in Sociology and Chair, Sustainable Cities Research Institute, University of Northumbria at Newcastle, Newcastle upon Tyne, United Kingdom.

Michael M'Gonigle is Professor of Law and Eco-Research Chair of Environmental Law and Policy, Faculty of Law and School of Environmental Studies, University of Victoria, Victoria, British Columbia, Canada.

Michael Northcott is Senior Lecturer in Christian Ethics and Practical Theology, University of Edinburgh, Edinburgh, Scotland.

Ellie Perkins is Associate Professor, Faculty of Environmental Studies, York University, North York, Ontario, Canada.

Haripriya Rangan is Lecturer, School of Geography and Environmental Science, Monash University, Melbourne, Victoria, Australia.

Thad Williamson is a Graduate Student, Department of Government, Harvard University, Cambridge, Massachusetts, United States.

Acknowledgements

Without the involvement of a large number of individuals, this publication would never have seen the light of day. The editors would like to thank our contributors for their enthusiasm and cooperation in writing their chapters, commenting on the chapters of others, and making revisions based on those discussions. The book's coherence is much improved by the stimulating debates that have taken place, especially those that occurred at the contributor's Victoria Workshop, which was held in Victoria, in May 1999. The authors would like to acknowledge with thanks, also, the contributions of those who participated in an earlier, online Virtual Workshop (held in the spring of 1998) on the same theme.

Financial support was received from the Eco-Research Chair of Environmental Law and Policy, University of Victoria and the Canadian Social Sciences Humanities and Research Council (SSHRC). The former funded the costs of the Victoria Workshop, enabling our contributors to spend three days on Vancouver Island in in-depth discussions on their chapters and the larger questions raised by the project. The SSHRC Fellowship enabled one of the editors to devote his full-time attention to managing the production process and preparing the manuscript for publication.

We would also like to thank Emily Walter for her excellent tape recording of the proceedings of the Victoria Workshop. We owe an especial thanks to the Eco-Research Chair's Administrator, Liz Wheaton, who looked after our contributors' accommodation and travel arrangements, and who took care of many other tasks with her customary graciousness.

Preface

The purpose of this book is to conceptualize a new ecological political economy (EPE). This is a daunting task. Many analytical perspectives exist today – from ecological economics to ecofeminism, from eco-Marxism to social ecology – that share some values and assumptions, but which also differ over others. As a result, to attempt the integration into a single, or overarching, school of thinking is dangerous. Both theoretically and practically, the quest for integration can lead to the creation of a meta-narrative that homogenizes differences, overlooks specific details in the pursuit of overarching ('totalizing') comprehensiveness, and in practice colonizes divergent identities. The project must be approached cautiously, and self-reflectively.

However, it must be approached, as integration can draw together disparate strands that had previously gone unnoticed, and so take theoretical understanding to a higher level of explanatory power. At a practical level, the greater coherence that results can better mobilize civil society in the pursuit of alternative futures. These are the primary motive forces of this book, and we have undertaken it by drawing together a variety of perspectives. Each contributor has been asked to elucidate what, from his or her perspective, constitutes some of the central elements of ecological political economy. Today, much of the work of the critical theorist is to deconstruct past, and proposed, ideologies. Yet a corollary to this is the commitment to theoretical construction, without which we are left with, at best, a deference to contingency. At worst, in the age of economic globalization, this deference translates all too easily into capitulation to a corporatist future. In the commitment to creating alternatives, it is necessary to develop theoretical arguments that offer new understandings of the dynamics of social organization that can translate into practical guidance, and action.

Concerned with 'the nature and causes of the wealth of nations', political economy claims to be 'scientific'. Its goal has long been 'to comprehend society as a whole, its total development, in terms of the relations between its constituent parts – the relations of production, social and political relations' (O'Connor, 1976). Claims to an explanatory single truth or explanatory variable are, of course, suspect. In the social sciences, however, political economy addresses, in a systematic fashion, the larger processes of social self-maintenance and reproduction. Outside the academy, most are woefully unaware of the existence or operation of these dynamics – and are largely unconcerned. Thus, as O'Connor (1988) has memorably noted, are many Northern environmentalists 'sub-theoretical'. And so, environmental erosion spreads, all the while being treated as just another policy issue. But it is not, and we must look beyond.

In this book, the contributors do just this, and the result is, we hope, a rich diversity of theoretical work under the broad rubric of 'ecological political economy'. The central problematic confronting each author was to conceptualize the ideas, institutions and dynamics of unsustainable development. This unites an otherwise diverse group of Canadian, American, Asian, British, Australian and European scholars. This geographic diversity is matched by an equal diversity of research backgrounds in common property theory, Marxism, ecofeminism, theology, critical theory, international political economy, economics, environmental science and ecology. Based on this critical conceptualization, the constructive task was to map out the transformative potential of the myriad social struggles occurring at the local, national, regional and global levels; and above, below, within and beside the market.

To impose any 'order' on this theoretical diversity invites challenges, and we have largely resisted doing so. In our view, the chapters prepared for this book could be classified in terms of their central theme into four different categories. Consequently, we have divided the book into four sections, each of which focuses on a different 'level' of analysis. In Part One, the central focus is on 'community'. Despite their different perspectives on this complex concept, M'Gonigle, Northcott and Agrawal all chart how communities in different regions of the world are struggling to gain greater control over their locales and the natural resources therein. M'Gonigle sees communities as crucial actors in the ongoing struggle between 'centre' and 'territory' – an ongoing, unresolvable dialectic that traverses spatial and power relations. Northcott describes how a specific local community, located in Scotland on the Island of Harris, is resisting modern 'development' by rejecting the establishment of a superquarry. An outcome, he suggests, of the rediscovery by the islanders of their indigenous, religious culture. Agrawal, meanwhile, cautions us not to 'essentialize' communities as inherently ecological, and directs our attention to the need for detailed analyses of each community's situational context and institutional specificity.

While each study in this book is strongly theoretical, three of our contributors (Adkin, Benton and Mellor) made political economy, and its necessary rethinking, their explicit starting point. These studies are brought together in Part Two. Again, the diversity in theoretical perspective and approach is striking. Adkin argues for the necessity of linking ecological political economy to a philosophy of human needs and to a political discourse of radical democratization. Such linking, she contends, creates the potential for the development of 'affinities' among struggles or identities, and hence a strategy of collective action. In the absence of such linkages, she views EPE as a highly 'contingent' discourse in political and social terms. Benton takes a less post-structuralist approach, arguing for an 'open' historical materialism, one that historicizes Marxist theory, creating theoretical space for recognizing and integrating the contributions of other important critical thinkers such as Gramsci, Althusser, Foucault and Habermas. Mellor reconstructs our question from a materialist ecofeminist perspective, arguing that the relations of reproduction are central to any ecological political economy, warranting a shift in focus away from the production of goods and services through the market to their 'provisioning' by families and communities.

The modern state is a central theme in Part Three. Rangan – following a critique of the two 'faces' of the local/global environmental discourse (one of which essentializes communities as inherently ecological; the other, as inherently anti-ecological) – presents a positive example of the state's progressive ecological potential as a regional actor. Drawing on her research in India, she describes how the state government of West Bengal supported the establishment of Joint Forest Management, an approach that increased accessibility of goods and services, providing both social and ecological benefits. Conca, while recognizing the vital role that the state must play in any future ecological society, discusses how the analytic focus on the nation-state, which currently 'frames' national and global policy discussions about environmental problems and solutions, profoundly distorts our understanding. An ecologically informed political economy would, at a minimum, deconstruct the statist frame, making visible the 'sustainable middle' – the large heterogeneous population that lies between those who massively under-consume resources and those who massively over-consume them.

In Part Four, the focus shifts to the 'system' of production relations. Once again, the diversity of the contributions is evident. In their chapter, Alperovitz, Williamson and Campbell present a critique of both socialist and capitalist systems of production, identifying how the structures intrinsic to each system lead to inevitable environmental problems via resource over-exploitation and pollution. The authors outline a strategy for building 'ecological norms' from the bottom up, a strategy aimed at improving local economic stability, generating a local civic culture, democratizing capital and reducing inequalities. The authors then document a large number of civil society experiments under way in the United States to achieve this. The focus of Perkins' chapter is trade and exchange. She notes that the existing system of 'free trade' lacks effective 'feedback' mechanisms to constrain capitalism's expansionist logic. She sets out a definition of sustainable trade, viewed as 'sustainable exchange' among production regions, in which decisions are made democratically and ecologically. This focus on the 'system' of production relations is continued in Gale's chapter on the 'socionatural web', a unified space constituted by the natural and social processes of production, transportation, display and consumption. Gale contends that states and corporations are ineffective guardians of the socionatural web, because each benefits too greatly from a 'conversion regime' based on the private factory, the free market and proprietary technology rights. He details how (global) civil society institutions, such as the Forest Stewardship Council, are using eco-certification and labelling schemes to regulate production and consumption through the entire commodity chain.

The diversity of backgrounds, disciplines and contexts represented by the contributors to this book does not, as already noted, make a synthesis desirable. Indeed, on reading the chapters, one is struck by the breadth of analytical concerns that underlie contributors' responses to the central challenge. A notable reflection of this breadth is the fact that each author, despite some common citations, draws on different theoretical literature, citing different examples to make their case. But if a synthesis is not possible, nevertheless, the authors clearly share many similar concerns, critical approaches, and broach an array of common themes. These are perhaps best stated as questions for further discussion and elaboration. Is an 'ecological political economics' possible and desirable? What epistemology adequately mediates between the natural world of biophysical processes and the social world of production and power? What are the key ontological units and actors – 'nature', 'community', 'state', 'region', 'market', and 'co-operative', 'private firm', 'state-owned enterprise' – that would constitute the ecological political economy? And how are these units related (that is, via 'production', 'provisioning', 'centre-territory dialectic', 'intentional structure', 'networks', 'democratic discourse', 'state administration', 'socionatural web' and so forth)? These questions, though large, also require practical answers. Whether such answers will be forthcoming depends on the degree to which analysts embrace a research agenda that fully integrates nature, production and power relations. Given the significance of the quest, it is our hope that they will, and that the studies in this book assist in this important task.

Fred Gale and Michael M'Gonigle
June 2000

PART ONE

Ecological Political Economy and Community

1. A Dialectic of Centre and Territory: The Political Economy of Ecological Flows and Spatial Relations[1]

R. Michael M'Gonigle

I'd like to share a revelation that I've had during my time here. It came to me when I tried to classify your species. I've realised that you are not actually mammals. Every mammal on this planet instinctively develops a natural equilibrium with the surrounding environment. But you humans do not. You move to an area and you multiply and multiply until every natural resource is consumed and the only way you can survive is to spread to another area. There is another organism on this planet that follows the same pattern. Do you know what it is? A virus. Human beings are a disease, a cancer of this planet. You are a plague (*The Matrix*, 1999).

The 'restless formation and reformation of geographical landscapes' that is triggered by the dynamics of capitalist development has been the most important discovery arising from the encounter between Western Marxism and Modern Geography (Soya, 1989).

It is trite to note that one of the signal developments of the late twentieth century has been the collapse, at least at the level of practical 'geopolitics', of the capitalist/communist polarity. At the same time, contrary to those who interpret the end of the Cold War as the universal triumph of a liberal political economy – the end of history – recent events point to the continuation of conflicts which are every bit as fundamental. Many of these conflicts – competition between the great religious 'civilizations' (such as Islam and Christianity), nationalist and ethnic wars, global environmental decline, and Southern poverty – are actually larger than the historical conflict between capitalist and socialist ideologies. Indeed, they pose a variegated challenge to the globalizing trajectory of the whole 'Western' mode of historical and cultural development.

An ecological political economy addresses this larger trajectory. Indeed, it can well be argued that the task of a new political economy is a universal one, inter- as well as intra-cultural. In keeping with the call by some postmodern geographers for a 'spatialized ontology' (Soya, 1989) that accommodates spatial diversity (Benko and Strohmayer, 1997), the signal characteristic of ecological political economy is, by definition, its attention to *physical* or *spatial* relations in both the natural and social worlds. This integration has long been a concern for exponents of 'social ecology' (Bookchin, 1980; Light, 1998). In this chapter, we examine these spatial relations in terms of two opposing tendencies or, to put it another way, two idealized forms of social organization that exist as a dynamic tension, or dialectic, in all human relations and societies. I call these tendencies Centre and Territory.

AN ECOLOGY OF SPATIAL RELATIONS

Unlike specific (Western) concepts such as capitalism or communism, these terms, centre and territory, can be applied to the full range of human cultural experience. The terms resonate with typologies that have long existed in the literature of political economy (for example, Harold Innis and Immanuel Wallerstein) and regional planning (for example, John Friedmann). Drawing on these traditions, these terms highlight the relationship between the character of institutional space and the physical flows of energy through that space. At one dialectical pole, centre is manifest in hierarchical organizations built around the imperatives of concentrated power, sustained indirectly by non-local resources (or flows of energy).

In contrast, territorial forms of social organization are rooted in forms of social power which are dispersed and on-the-ground, and are maintained by local resources and direct production. The (increasingly global) crisis of the West, including the impacts of both its capitalist market economy and its statist concentration of power, can be analysed from this dialectical perspective as a diffused yet pervasive manifestation of centre-over-territory.

In the above formulation, centre and territory have both a physical component (geographic spatial relations), and a social component (institutional relations). It would, however, be inaccurate to reduce them to discrete, concrete, either/or dichotomies. Quite the contrary, unlike the largely physical concepts of 'cores and peripheries' that are utilized by dependency theorists, centre and territory are social tendencies that intermingle in various degrees and manifestations in the many places and acts of everyday life. That is, they exist as omnipresent tendencies in all forms of social organization and cultural consciousness. Centre, for example, is manifest in the fluorescent lights in the corporate office tower, but it also exists in the authority of a local mayor or a traditional aboriginal chieftain. Territory is manifest in the town hall meeting in the remote village, but exists in the urban neighbourhood association as well. Thus, territorial forms permeate the big city, while centrism pervades even the most remote places.

These terms describe not specific structures but dynamics that exist at all scales. Territory might be characterized as the social/natural process of 'living in place'. This is not the same as 'community', which is a complex mixture of both dynamics. Nor is it captured by the geographical terms 'regional' or 'local'. Territory does not privilege a particular form of organization (for example, the agricultural village) over another (for example, nomadic tribes), nor is there a single design for the ideal territorial institution in the future. At the same time, a territorialist society necessarily fosters self-reliance (with a collective awareness of the centralist tendencies of large-scale, inter-regional trade), egalitarian social relations (with the collective control of the hierarchical division of labour and power) and ecological stability.

In the 1999 hit film, *The Matrix*, the viewer is told that the Earth was virtually destroyed by the mindless virus of human growth and conquest. The film neglected to distinguish what aspects of human organization were implicated in the destruction; nevertheless, the character of what replaced human society was instructive. A centralist totalitarian system had been created, but it existed only as a 'virtual', that is, completely non-physical reality. Inside and outside the movie theatre, the momentum of centralist power does indeed dominate industrial society today. Yet a completely centralist society could never be created and sustained in the future, except by escaping its own physicality. However great may be the efficiencies and technologies created by industrial economies of scale, still these economies subsist on physical resources that come from, and go, somewhere. In this light, the significance of the tension between centre and territory can be seen in the evolving character of the dialectic itself, a dialectic that is never resolved. It is, instead, a perpetual fact of social life.

Unlike a traditional class analysis, these terms do not describe a simple bipolarity. On the contrary, their unique dialectical character stems from the complex interplay of geographical (horizontal) with institutional (vertical) spatial relations. For example, a large city seems to be the quintessential centralist creation. Yet it can be more or less territorial depending, on the one hand (from a geographical perspective), on how it uses resources. What is the extent of its dependence on physical imports? How self-consciously efficient is it in the internal use and distribution of these resources? How does it utilize its own internal resources, through recycling and reuse? What, in short, is its 'ecological footprint'? On the other hand, from an institutional perspective, how equitable and participatory are its processes of economic production and political decision making? How stratified are its internal production relations?

How open, and innovative, are its processes of planning and development? Similarly, a rural area might be more or less centrist according to how dependent it is on high-volume extractive industries, and exports, and how its internal relations are shaped to reflect this.

It is also important to note that centre is not equivalent to 'bad', and territory to 'good'. Big cities are places of great cultural diversity and excitement, while, as Marx famously noted, rural life can sometimes be characterized by its 'idiocy' (although such idiocy he attributed to the artificial separation of 'town and country'). Technological centralism (including, most notably, the division of labour) is undeniably wealth-generating, while political centralism can be useful for fostering inter-regional equity. Certainly, the black poor in rural Alabama were grateful for the federal Civil Rights Act in the 1960s, and the peacekeeping force that was deployed in East Timor was a product of a 'centrist' institution. Nevertheless, the legitimacy of centrist structures can ultimately be assured only when their own successes also support, not erode, territory. An important justification of centrist hierarchy (and the flows that it demands) thus exists in its support for territorialist non-hierarchy. This is the logic of ecological federalism.

Pressing questions arise from the application of these 'generative principles' (Harvey, 1996, p. 59) to the pursuit of social sustainability. On the one hand, if 'human nature' includes characteristics of greed and the will to power (as liberal theorists assert), one might enquire as to how the universal tendencies to centre power have historically been held in check by territorial institutions. On the other hand, if the prospect of ecological overshoot looms before us, one must ask how (or if) centralist institutions might now be re-formed to support and protect, rather than erode, territorial values and processes. The practical challenge of an ecological political economy is thus to inform the pursuit of a better balancing in this tension; it is not to seek its final resolution in some ultimate institutional configuration.

In the operation of this dialectic over the historical evolution of Western social systems, two fundamental trends can be identified, which have served to erode territorial forces, and thus put in place a self-reinforcing spiral of centrist growth. These trends are (1) the growing dominance of *hierarchical institutions* that (2) are *sustained by increasingly distant resources*. This is the hallmark of the 'progress' that has taken Western society out of the 'dark ages' – organizing the world to maintain the continuous flow of resources to, and up into, the papal institutions in Rome, the Norman Crown in Westminster and the corporate offices in New York and Tokyo. In the process, countervailing structures and processes fell by the way, a process of 'development as enclosure' where private rights of institutional accumulation displaced communal responsibilities of collective self-maintenance.[2]

Horizontal Relations

The attention to horizontal spatial differentiation conjures up those political economies that view capitalism as a global system of geographic power relations (such as dependency theory) between highly developed 'core' areas and less developed 'peripheries'. While this is a useful characterization of capitalist dynamics, many other centralized hierarchies have arisen, and been maintained, over space and time, without the assistance of large-scale market exchanges. Imperial forms of conquest that utilize bureaucratic forms of territorial control, production and distribution long predated the liberation of market forces in the West. As theorists of a 'world system' (for example, Gills and Frank, 1991) argue, such patterns of hierarchical social growth mark a variety of civilizations over many millennia. In this light, capitalism must occupy a subsidiary position in our historical understanding. Thus, a centre-territory dialectic draws our attention to the generalized *dynamics* of various modes of organizing power rather than to simply the specific *structures* in which these dynamics may be embedded at any time and place, including the market and the state. While still addressing the hugely important character of capitalism and liberal democracies, this shift expands the focus of critical inquiry as well as the range of alternative futures.

This perspective helps clarify many of the similarities between capitalist and state socialist societies. Most significantly, it draws attention to the inevitable failure of state-centred, bureaucratic management as the vehicle for challenging capital. In the process, it identifies the limits of a Left vision that relies on this management for a social base of production, while it also provides a guide to look to alternative forms of place-based economics and politics. There is much work to be done here. For example, many critical geographers who are attentive to spatial relations nevertheless continue to ignore the ecological economic literature, and thus scarcely explore the critical implications for political economy of physical energy flows across space (Benko and Strohmayer, 1997; Harvey, 1996).

Vertical Relations

With regard to the second vertical axis of institutional space, ecological political economy has close connections to the debates that have long been concerned with the tension between face-to-face community and organizational hierarchy. Spanning the political spectrum over many centuries, this debate exists across a range of thinkers. It includes conservatives (from Edmund Burke to Robert Nisbet and Amitai Etzioni), liberals (especially contemporary theorists such as Charles Taylor and Michael Sandel), and radicals (from the sixteenth-century Diggers to

nineteenth-century anarchists to twentieth-century social ecologists). In this
varied company, the institutional implications of 'local' and 'place' let alone
'community' are not simple, although all share a concern for the role of place-
based 'organic' forms of embedded authority as compared with more
institutionally centred 'rationalist' structures of top-down control. From an
ecological perspective, at stake are the directions in which energy, resources,
wealth, culture, authority and power all flow – and are recycled.

Overall, a basic contradiction can be seen to beset all forms of centralist
growth. In short, the rise of central power is, and always has been, sustained
by the territorial structures that precede that rise, and it cannot survive
without them. Human wealth depends on natural processes; administered laws
depend on collective customs. Yet, given the values, ambitions and inequities
embedded within hierarchy, most such systems are driven to grow, although
the motive forces and internal dynamics for this growth vary widely. By the
nature of the physical flows that sustain hierarchy, centralist institutions can
grow only by consuming the very territorial processes (both environmental
and social) on which they depend and, in doing so, await their own demise.

This is the story of countless civilizations past that have risen, only to fall.
In analysing the history of 'Western' institutions, this approach draws
attention to a great variety of manifestations of centre power. It includes, for
example, the impact of writing-based over oral practices, of bureaucratic laws
over local customs, or of patriarchal forms of authority over egalitarian ones.
It also helps explain the age-old conflict between religious institutions of
monotheistic transcendence and 'more primitive' beliefs in spiritual
immanence (M'Gonigle, 2000). While attentive to materialist imperatives, the
recognition of such a variety of centralist forces describes a history that is
decidedly less economically deterministic than other critical (especially
Marxist) analyses. However, the result is still one of system contradiction
where the 'internal' dynamics of growth generate expanding 'external' social
and environmental imbalances that, together, produce system crisis.

IMPLICATIONS FOR POLITICAL ECONOMY

Approaching ecological political economy from the territorialist perspective
orients the discipline in a discernible manner economically, politically and
epistemologically.

An Ecosystem-based Economics

A territorial economic analysis draws directly on ecological economics and its explanation of the entropy-generating nature of all material production (Georgesçu-Roegen, 1971). This analysis highlights the inevitable social and natural erosion associated with high levels of economic activity, and particularly with those biophysical 'flows' necessary to sustain centrist structures of all types, including corporate capitalism. By drawing attention to the thermodynamic costs inflicted on the natural world by any economic system based on high levels of continuous production, ecological economics points to the inevitable need to reorganize the factors of production on some form of 'steady-state' basis.

Centrist hierarchies can, of course, be sustained by such flows over long periods of time, and have been. But they can only be so when they have a proportionally large territorial base from which to draw. In other words, centrist sustainability decreases with increases in scale, in particular, with increases in the relative scale of centrist to territorial structures. To maintain their stability, centrist structures must 'import sustainability', and are thus inherently imperialistic. In the late twentieth century, one motive force for globalization stems from the diminution of territorial resources from which centrist structures might draw their wealth. This is the age of a few 'last places left'. Past centrist successes thus create the conditions for future centrist decline. This is the fundamental contradiction of economic globalism.

Nevertheless, from an ecological viewpoint, it is not only the accumulation/growth-driven character of modern capitalism that is the problem, but any form of growth-oriented, 'high throughput' (productivist) economy. This recognition challenges Marx's belief that greater worker wealth in a socialist state could, with the widespread redistribution of wealth, overcome the basic capitalist contradiction (falling demand) that occurs when a small segment of society owns the vast proportion of wealth. Instead, to this day, nature has been immiserated and poisoned to provide the vast flow of resources and energy that has allowed a large segment of society, including many workers, to rise above industrial revolution conditions and share in the wealth that productivity-driven growth has created.

In the author's home, British Columbia, for example, the labour economist, Richard Schwindt (1996), calculated that the rents gained from the liquidation of the province's old growth forests were distributed 67 per cent to labour, 27 per cent to corporations and 6 per cent to government. The serious pursuit of environmental sustainability is thus a most disruptive social objective, attacking as it does the foundation of contemporary social wealth. In those 'developed' countries where it has been achieved, it threatens the material basis for existing levels of social equity.

As a result, perhaps even more than with traditional socialist thought, this understanding points to the imperative of achieving high levels of substantive equity between genders (Mies, 1986), races, regions and cultures as the prerequisite for reducing the pressures for more unsustainable throughput. In turn, as the emerging literature on 'green governance' indicates, ecological transition is fundamentally dependent on the invigoration (largely through the activities of new social movements) of new forms of democratic and cooperative participation that can, at all levels, tackle the embedded cultural dependence on linear flows of energy/power.

An ecologically based economic transformation must address both spatial dimensions – horizontal/physical and vertical/institutional. Ironically, an ecological political economy is not so much opposed to the market mechanism *per se* as it is concerned with the spatial context within which the market operates. This is the lesson of Polanyi's famous critique (1944) of the liberation of the market from social control. Fundamentally, an ecological political economy points not to the need to do away with markets but (again) to shift every entropy-generating (Hornborg, 1998) economic system away from encouraging more linear growth to creating alternative structures of circular economy. This is the distinction between 'sustainable development' (which seeks to tack environmental constraints onto an otherwise unrestructured process of capitalist, economic growth) and the more reconstructive path of 'developing sustainability' (where new, ecologically based institutions are fostered including those based in market transactions).

This sounds distinctively unradical. Certainly, the processes of ecological transformation are diverse; despite its weaknesses, the market can, and must, play a role. Today, from whatever political perspective, everyone is dependent on high levels of economic flow. As a result, the challenge of ecological reconstruction is radical if only because it is both so immense, and so personal. After all, every pension fund – including those of Northern environmentalists, labour leaders, and critical academics – is invested in the high throughput growth economy, including so-called 'green' funds with their minimal screening criteria. Tangible support for developing real economic alternatives is virtually non-existent.

The (economic) direction for developing sustainability is not difficult to discern, beginning as it does with the basic need to reduce throughput. For example, it implies a clear strategy for 'world cities' – circumscribing their colonizing lines of material supply, and placing greater reliance on their own circular processes. There is a now vast technical literature on this transition, a literature that focuses on such concepts as resource efficiency, materials recycling, dematerialization, industrial ecology, demand management, smart growth, urban green governance and so on. This shift to limited input circularity applies to a vast range of sectors, from organic agriculture to preventative health, from community development to fisheries conservation.

As noted above, with decreased throughput comes the necessary attention to increased equity, growth in throughput having been the historical safety valve for class differentiation. Nevertheless, as advocates of demand management, for example, will argue, an important role exists here for market pricing – as long as prices are able to reflect 'full cost accounting'. For this sort of change to work, however, that ideal mechanism of linear resource colonization – market exchange – must be re-submerged in a larger structure of conscious political control.

This re-submergence underlies, for example, the promise of 'ecosystem-based management', although environmental advocates rarely appreciate this (M'Gonigle, 1998a). This idea takes as its starting point the need both to maintain ecosystem integrity and to constrain human activity within that context; that is, what is possible economically (and socially) is a function of what can take place within functioning ecosystems. For example, in traditional forestry, the level of cut is set economically (by what the industry needs), and environmental side effects are constrained with restrictive standards. In ecoforestry, both the level of cut, and forest practices, are determined by what works within the maintenance of the 'structure, composition and function' of the forest ecosystem.

Although economy/ecosystem relations have always been mutually constitutive (Harvey, 1996, p. 185), an ecosystem-based approach represents a fundamental philosophical shift in the reference point for resource production, limiting such production according to the surplus that a healthy ecosystem (that is, an ecosystem that maintains its 'integrity') can give up. In this light, an ecological 'community' would embody those forms of cooperative social organization that can, over a long term, support processes of local ecosystem self-maintenance and self-reproduction.

Many innovations in ecological production embody such a 'circularity' in production. For example, the 'precautionary principle' requires that potential environmental impacts, rather than being addressed as an afterthought (an 'externality') of production processes, are addressed in the basic design of the production system, for example, through the use of 'closed loop' processes (M'Gonigle, 1999a). The outcome of this is 'clean production', which can also be seen as embedding management objectives within the production process.

Where this approach is applied at a level of multiple industries (for example, where the waste of one industry is used as an input to another), the currently fragmented conception of industrial production gives way to the spatially based approach of 'industrial ecology'. By fostering such an approach to economic production, regulation shifts from trying to *manage the unmanageable* (attempting to constrain production with external rules) to *unmanaging the manageable* (facilitating new enterprises that are inherently self-regulating).

Community-based Politics

If a territorialist analysis points to an alternative to the productivist economy, so too does it offer a redirection for the centralist state, and a new progressive politics. Again, this redirection is, to a great extent, spatial in nature, going beyond individual policies, programmes and even legislative reforms to address a *constitutional reconstruction* that can begin to shift the dynamics of state power.

Historically, the rise of the state has been achieved through the continuing displacement of local cultures and their 'sovereignty' – the state's primary objectives being to enclose territory, to secure economic flows to the centre and then to control potentially countervailing territorial power. The very character of this state is centralist.

For example, the founding work of English liberal theory, Thomas Hobbes's *Leviathan*, was a product of the chaos of civil war, and it elevated stability under an all-powerful sovereign – power at the centre – as the greatest good of the emerging state. Democracy was far off in the historical future. Instead, concern about the potential for the abuse of state powers led political theorists to focus primarily on dividing governmental authority *vertically* (that is, the three branches of legislative/executive/judicial authority). There was not comparable appreciation for the economic and political benefits for distributing power *horizontally*. Despite philosophical references to social contracts and popular sovereignty, private power and public authority flowed from the top.

In this light, the differences between communist, socialist and capitalist states are differences of degree. In a recent newspaper account, the Russian aboriginal group, the *Chukchis*, explained what happened to their traditional way of life herding caribou, both under the Soviet system, and after its collapse:

> 'Nature itself commands that an aboriginal person should live in nature. Every cell in your body feels good only when you're in nature' (says Mikhail Pleshkov). Much of the reindeer-herding tradition was destroyed by the Soviet Union, which collectivised the herds and placed them in the hands of a few bureaucrats. The younger Chukchis were sent to boarding schools, where their language and customs were discouraged. When the Soviet system disintegrated in 1991, the herds were quickly sold off or split up. 'The Soviet system broke the connection between the generations,' Mr. Pleshkov said. 'We have very few older people who can teach reindeer herding . . .' (York, 1999, p. A15).

This same history has been told countless times in Canada, replete with stories of residential schools, beatings for speaking a native language, sorrow at villages depleted of young people, and pain at a generation unable to learn directly a territorial culture and way of life.

Historically, of course, critical theorists have demonstrated how the activist state has, at best, worked to ameliorate some of the most egregious effects of private economic power (for example, through social welfare legislation) without challenging the overall momentum of centralist power. The continuing failure even to slow, let alone redirect, this momentum points to the inherent limits of solutions that depend largely on bureaucratic regulations to constrain the very sources of economic flow on which those agencies themselves depend. For a larger redirection to occur, the issue is necessarily a constitutional one of state function and design that can provide an ecologically based counterbalance to extractive centralist powers.

Elucidating what this counterbalance might look like – from ecosystem-based participatory governance (applicable equally to 'world cities' and resource regions) to new forms of federal association – is a major challenge of ecological political theory. This challenge has urgent global significance in order to offer an alternative to the *de facto* constitutional process that is redefining the state within the neo-mercantilist framework of the World Trade Organization (M'Gonigle, 1999c).

In this light, a huge diversity of social movements share common cause – from feminist demands for the recognition of non-patriarchal institutions of informal (that is, non-cash) economic production, to the advocates of community-based development in urban ghettos, to the demands for indigenous rights by forest dwellers and artisanal fishers. The rootedness of such groups in more autonomous local spaces strikes deeply at the current configurations (and conceptual foundations) of state power, and their goals have provoked reactions that range from indifferent neglect to violent suppression. Nowhere in the upper echelons of centrist power are the beneficial transformative possibilities of such movements appreciated.

Nevertheless, such movements need not be 'anti-state'. Indeed, only a strong state can, for example, confront the movements of multinational capital, ensure the broad (intra-territorial) respect for principles of social justice, manage the impacts of increasing technological complexity, maintain inter-regional equity – and provide support for and protection of local, self-governing spaces. Nevertheless, the state as historically constructed and traditionally conceived is vastly inadequate to the ecological imperative, a situation that is particularly challenging for the state-centric Left. Retaining an attachment to bureaucratic management (as the primary political response to corporatist power), the Left largely eschews community-based alternatives, either economically or politically, and remains trapped in a grey incrementalism of state reform without state re-formation.

In comparison, an ecological 'network constitutionalism' would build on the foundational place of geographical localism in conjunction with a democratic transformation in the hierarchical character of the state. In place of the dominating hierarchy that has accompanied the rise of liberal democracies, ecological legitimacy attaches to the state to the extent that its power is democratically redirected to support, rather than erode, the 'preservation of the commons' (Esteva and Prakash, 1998, p. 158; Hempel, 1996). As well, this territorialism is inherently diverse calling for:

> a variety of different smaller-scale political territories, each with a specific range of governmental mandates. Many existing states would probably continue to function as one type of political territory in such a system, but they would coexist with political territories organized along ecological lines with competence over specific environmental matters; political territories organized along ethnocultural lines (for example, Basques or Tibetans) with competence over certain cultural, social, and educational issues; and political territories organized on the basis of socioeconomic patterns with competence over aspects of economic development and social welfare (Murphy, 1996, p. 111).

In contrast to this spatial rethinking, the failure of many liberal, and social democratic, environmental reforms reflects their partial character. For example, a whole generation of 'public participation' processes were merely intended to fine-tune economic development, not redirect it. Similarly, the success of the Right in seizing the initiative against 'big government' results, in great measure, from the inability of the Left to recognize, let alone address, the inefficiencies and narrow self-interest of bureaucratic centralism. Indeed, the Left positively resists giving active consideration to alternatives to bureaucratic control. In Canada, progressive state managers so oppose any constraints on 'Crown discretion' that the potential of many political innovations – direct local democracy, resource co-management, regional devolution – remains untapped. As a result, the role of the state as a facilitator and overseer of territorial governance is unappreciated, resulting in the squandering of both economic options and a vital future for progressive politics.[3]

Territorial Intelligence

Among the most subtle of the attributes of centrism is the particular, and exclusive, form of cultural knowledge that it embraces, and within which it is embedded. Again, an understanding of the tensions between centre and territory reveals a radical dialectic between competing ways of knowing, in particular, between the progressive social 'rationalization' that has underpinned Western growth, and the knowledge systems of myriad cultures that have resisted their colonization.

Despite the pervasive spread of 'Western' thinking, a growing recognition exists of the inherent limits of both the process and substance of Western science. The sources of this new awareness are many and varied. One of the foundational works is Kuhn's (1970) landmark explanation of the non-linear evolution and institutionally situated character of 'scientific' knowledge. More recently, the rise of systems thinking and chaos theory (in contrast to the reductionist techniques of the traditional sciences) has begun to shift attention from the futile pursuit of a final Cartesian certainty to learning instead how to live with the inevitability of a pervasive uncertainty (M'Gonigle, 1999b).

Meanwhile, in many social sciences (especially neoclassical economics), practitioners fail to reform their models when faced with foundational critiques (M'Gonigle, 1999a). At the same time, sociologists have demonstrated how scientific techniques (such as periodic testing regimes) produce a knowledge of the natural world that is necessarily based on spatially and temporally limited observations, and is thus 'anecdotal' in a manner that is often more limiting than the anecdotal local knowledge that science has long denigrated.

All these changes, of course, take place amid a growing awareness of the negative environmental and social costs associated with scientific and technological development itself. In light of the recognition of the embeddedness of 'truth' in one's historically constituted 'horizon' (Gadamer, 1994), centrist intelligence becomes highly problematic, a reflection of the preconceptions and situatedness of those asserting their positions. In this light, the necessity of moving to a 'multiperspectival polity' (Ruggie, 1993, p. 171; Tully, 1995) follows naturally.

Parallel with the postmodern understanding of the limits of scientific knowledge is the recognition that a broad territorial alternative exists to scientific thinking. This recognition is manifest in the growing literature on 'local' and 'traditional ecological' knowledge. At stake in these alternative knowledge systems is a very different social episteme – one that is rooted in the particularism of experience, the other in the universalism of technique; one that is oral and socially held, the other that is written down and gathered in (Esteva and Prakash, 1998). In contrast to the physically removed character of Western science, the insurgent forms of local knowledge spring from and reinforce directly productive relations with the immediate natural world (Wilson et al., 1994). Thus does a territorial structure of power imply, as Soya (1989) puts it, a 'spatialized ontology'.

CONCLUSION

Theory is never a matter of pure abstraction. Theoretical practice must be
constructed as a continuous dialectic between the militant particularism of lived
lives and a struggle to achieve sufficient critical distance and detachment to
formulate global ambitions (Harvey, 1996).

To the extent that we begin to identify the nature and limits of the centrist
forces in which we are enmeshed, the direction for change becomes clear.
Ours is a 'constitutional' crisis, in the largest sense of the word, and to begin
to resolve it we must invigorate (and, where we can, reinvigorate) territorial
forces at all levels. We can do so not with just a programme here and a policy
there, but by changing the evolutionary dynamics of our social institutions.
Creating the political space for this change is the imperative. After that, there
is no single path. Some innovations will involve market forces and state
regulation; others will involve cooperative alternatives and community
devolution. The strategies for fostering an ecological transition are many and
varied. Yet everywhere is there a common need, not to resolve but to
rebalance, the evolving dynamic between centre and territory.

NOTES

1. The current chapter builds on the arguments put forward by the author in his article
    'Ecological economics and political ecology: towards a necessary synthesis', tenth
    anniversary analysis article, *Ecological Economics* 28 (1999), 11–26.
2. The literature on the 'tragedy of the commons' has sought to legitimate this process as a
    natural one insofar as the absence of central authority was seen to be the cause of social
    conflict and environmental erosion. In reaction to this literature, 'common property
    theorists' harken back (and forward) to the importance of community institutions of
    collective, territorial management.
3. Two studies undertaken by the author's research teams point to concrete
    'ecoconstitutional' strategies. In one study (Burda et al., 1997), we explore the potential
    for landscape-level 'trust' arrangements for reforming forest production and management.
    In a second study (Walter et al., 1999), we develop the legal foundations for a regional
    network of community-based fisheries management systems.

2. Sabbaths, Shamans and Superquarrying on a Scottish Island: Religio-cultural Resistance to Development in a Contested Landscape

Michael S. Northcott

INTRODUCTION

The largely treeless Hebridean island of Harris, off the west coast of Scotland, has been the subject of a major environmental controversy because of the submission of a plan by Redland Aggregates, an English-based quarrying company, to locate a large quarry on the coast of Harris. Like other parts of the Western Isles, Harris has a distinctive religious and linguistic culture, elements of which, and in particular Sabbath observance, were mobilized in significant ways in local and national debates about the proposed quarry. This distinctive religious culture was also the occasion for the presentation of theological arguments by expert witnesses, including a Hebridean Quaker ecologist, a Free Church Professor of Theology, and a Canadian Native Indian Chief at the Public Inquiry held in 1995 to adjudicate the planning application.

Local evidence presented in opposition to the quarry focused on the potential damage the quarry would offer to local and traditional modes of production including crofting and fishing, and to tourism. Local support for the quarry, because of the potential benefit of local employment it offered, gradually turned into opposition as the community realized through the lengthy process of the public inquiry that industrial development on the scale of the superquarry would mean the end of forms of religious and community life that people have enjoyed on Harris for many hundreds of years.

The Harris superquarry controversy, the outcome of which is still indeterminate, demonstrates how local knowledge, traditions and ritual practices in pre-industrial communities of place may present resources for resistance to corporate and bureaucratic sponsors of the capitalistic transformation of natural goods into units of industrial production. It also illustrates how religious discourses and practices, particularly as these occur in traditional communities of place, challenge the differentiation of social life into distinct realms, a differentiation which legitimates the priority of economic considerations, such as the prospect of employment, over the maintenance and preservation of cultural and environmental resources. The case also illustrates the importance of local communities recovering power from the state in pursuance of the related projects of nature conservation and the quest for more sustainable lifestyles than those sponsored by the modern partnership between states and capitalist corporations.

THE LINGERABAY SUPERQUARRY: THE FINAL CLEARANCE?

The proposed superquarry was dubbed 'the final clearance' by a letter writer to *The Scotsman*, Scotland's Edinburgh-based newspaper of record (McIntosh, 1995). The 'Clearances' were a paradigmatic event in the history of the Scottish Highlands and Islands and appeals to their contested significance were to play an important role among resisters to the quarry. Mackenzie sees this appropriation of the symbol of the Clearances as part of the contested terrain of discourse and symbolism in the controversy surrounding the quarry (Mackenzie, 1998).

On the one hand, advocates of the quarry proposed that it would provide jobs for the local community, thus stemming continuing migration of people from Harris, and other Hebridean islands, in search of economic opportunities. Opponents of the quarry, on the other hand, argued that the quarry was itself another, if not the final, clearance. First, the people and their crops and domestic animals had been cleared from the land, and now even those rocks that they left behind were to be cleared also.

The first ground of controversy over the quarry, and the occasion of much of the evidence at the public inquiry, concerned the claim that the quarry would offer a major economic opportunity to the local community whose very existence was threatened by the spiral of depopulation and economic decline which the Clearances are said to have begun. Since the Clearances of the eighteenth and nineteenth centuries the remaining indigenous people of the Scottish Highlands and Islands have endured poor economic and environmental conditions and high unemployment.

The Clearances involved the conversion of local subsistence economies, many of which were viable, some of which were thriving, and some very poor, into a new commercial system of land ownership and control designed to maximize rents and income from animal grazing. In the process thousands of people were driven from their homes, the timbers of which were frequently burnt as they left to ensure that they could not return to rebuild in a land with few trees. Some were put onto ships to Canada and Australia, or forced into local exile in the burgeoning industrial slums of Glasgow and Edinburgh. Lands that had supported strip farming and cattle grazing were denuded of traditional crops such as barley, oats, turnips and potatoes and given over to sheep farming, and to the raising of animals for sport, including grouse and deer.

The breakup of self-subsistent Highland communities in the Clearances is represented variously by historians and in folk culture as an act of internal colonization, even genocide, by the emergent British state, or as the inevitable outcome of poor farming practices combined with a growing population which the overworked land could no longer sustain. The Clearances were preceded by the last Highland Rising, which was put down by the English at Culloden in 1746. Defeated chieftains had their lands confiscated and the 1747 Act of Proscription banned the carrying of arms, the wearing of Highland dress, the playing of pipes and many other distinctive cultural practices throughout the Highlands of Scotland (McIntosh et al., 1994).

Resistance to the Clearances was very limited because in the main the 'reforms' were prosecuted by Highland chiefs, rather than by English landowners as they had been in Ireland. Highland chieftains and landlords saw the rich potential of these lands for sheep grazing and as sheep displaced people income from land increased dramatically.

The depopulation of the Highlands and Islands has continued throughout the twentieth century as employment opportunities have shrunk further with the continuing demise of the traditional subsistence and barter economy, and as the land itself has become more sparse as a consequence of over-grazing and of deforestation. Much of the region has been characterized as 'wet desert' by biologists (Manning, 1996). Economic conditions on the Hebridean Islands have been particularly difficult and in the last 50 years the islands have been subject to a continuing process of depopulation wherein the children of islanders have migrated to the mainland of Scotland, and further afield, in search of economic opportunities.

This migration is characterized by a pattern of return in later life, however, and is offset to a certain extent also by the phenomenon of incomers who move to Harris, and other Hebridean Islands, from Scottish cities and from further afield precisely because of their remoteness from metropolitan life, and their distinctive cultural and communal traditions.

The response to the economic problems of the Highlands and Islands that has been fostered by lowland planners and economists has not challenged the concentrated pattern of land ownership established since the Clearances, wherein 80 per cent of the land of Scotland is owned by 0.08 per cent of the population (McIntosh, 1995). Neither has it challenged the predominant use of land for sheep, deer and grouse rearing with its dire impact both on the land and on the human ecology of Scotland. Instead government agencies, working in partnership with industrial corporations, have supported the establishment of large development projects such as hydroelectric generation, aluminium smelting, monocrop forestry and paper production. Large-scale quarrying is the most recent form of such industrial development in the Highlands and Islands and finds sponsorship by a combination of official government agencies, including the Scottish Office (SO), (1994) and the Department of the Environment (DoE), (1994), as well as quarrying companies.

In response to a claimed rising demand for aggregate in southern England and Wales, and a growing resistance to land-based quarrying in heavily populated England and Wales because of its deleterious environmental effects, superquarries are intended to capitalize on the increasingly exposed rocks of Scotland's eroded and underpopulated coastal regions whose minerals are shipped and traded as aggregate for highway construction in the south of England and for such engineering projects as the construction of the Channel Tunnel between England and France.

Coastal quarries allow a large scale of aggregate production while they are said to minimize disutilities to nearby communities as much of the detrimental impact of quarrying is defrayed by remote coastal locations, which limit sight and sound of quarrying activity to sparse local populations, reduce the impact of blasting and enable the use of ships rather than lorries for transportation on local roads. The ocean also provides a ready route for the importation of landfill, in the form of domestic, industrial and construction waste, which is typically used to refill quarrying sites.

Partly in recognition of government proposals on the provision of aggregate from coastal quarries in Scotland for construction projects in other parts of the United Kingdom, Ian Wilson, a businessman from Dunblane, purchased the mineral rights to a number of sites around Scotland, including Lingerabay on the Isle of Harris. In 1991, his company, Redland Aggregates, submitted a planning application for the removal of 600 million tonnes of rock from Lingerabay over 60 years at an annual rate of extraction of 10 million tonnes (Friends of the Earth, 1996). Daily blasting would involve the use of 3.5 tonnes of explosive and the blasting of 30 000 tonnes of rock.

The application also sought permission to expand an existing jetty, used for a small existing quarry, to permit the docking of bulk carriers of up to 120 000 tonnes capacity, for the hugely expanded scale of quarrying proposed. The proposed extraction would slice into the hillside of Roineabhal from 180 metres below sea level to 350 metres above, and would leave a giant hole in the ground some 2 kilometres long and 1 kilometre wide. The rocks at Lingerabay are pink anorthosite and of particularly high suitability for use as building and road aggregate and the application rested on the case for increased demand for such aggregate outlined above.

The planning application was submitted to the Western Isles Island Council and was given a mixed reception by the people of Harris. Initially the prospect of a large number of locally available jobs meant that it attracted a good deal of support from local people. The company at first claimed that the quarry would initially provide up to 30 local jobs and that up to 140 jobs would eventually be created for local people (Martin and Abercrombie,

1995). Against this would be set the despoliation of the side of a mountain that faces the sea, is more than 10 miles from the nearest substantial community on Harris and whose current inhabitants are sheep and sea birds.

This setting of jobs against environmental degradation is a common tactic in development discourse and in the case of Harris, as elsewhere, was designed to split the community (Mackenzie, 1998). In particular, on Harris, it was intended to split 'incomers' or locally born families from so-called 'white settlers', the pejorative language sometimes used to characterize Harris inhabitants who originate in Scottish lowlands or England and move to Harris for its distinctive culture and landscape (Warwick, 1995).

A referendum to gauge island opinion on the proposed quarry was organized by the Harris Council for Social Service in 1993. It revealed precisely the kind of split which the developers might have hoped for with 62 per cent of those voting in support of the quarry and 38 per cent against. In 1995, however, towards the end of the public inquiry, a second referendum was held and this time the position was reversed with only 32 per cent favouring the quarry and 68 per cent against. The turnout for the second referendum was also much higher than the first with 83 per cent of eligible islanders voting, 22 per cent more than on the previous occasion.

As a local councillor put it this considerable turn around in island opinion was clear evidence that 'the quarry is not wanted by the community, who have delivered a decisive "no" to the developer'. Another councillor saw it as a 'triumph for local democracy over municipal high-handedness, secrecy and manipulation' (An Tir, An Canan 'Sna Daoine, 1995). Shortly after the referendum, and before the final summative submissions at the public inquiry, the Western Isles Council debated the superquarry and resolved by 21 votes to 8 that 'the nature and scale of the proposed quarry is prejudicial to the integrity of the area and compromises other developments which depend on clean air and water' (Ross, 1995). The vote caused considerable controversy as the Council had strongly supported the proposed project, and spent £375 000 on making the case for the quarry, including instructing a barrister to put the Council's case, alongside Redland Aggregates, at the eight-month long public inquiry.

This dramatic change in opinion on the island appeared to be connected with the presentation and airing of evidence submitted to the public inquiry. Districts involved with fishing expressed the strongest opposition to the quarry after much evidence had been presented of the possible adverse effects on local fishing, for shellfish and other inshore fish, as a consequence of the deballasting of large supertankers before taking on the quarried aggregate. Environmentalists and marine pollution experts argued that ballast water from the tanks would contain contaminants from the aggregate and would also introduce foreign organisms into the seawater as it would have been taken on board from sea areas distant from Harris. Harris-originated shellfish fetch a market price premium because of their exceptional quality, which, in turn, rests upon the crystal clear and unpolluted waters of the seas around Harris.

The threat to this industry became a major concern as the inquiry proceeded. The possibility that jobs in the fishing industry might be threatened by the quarry became even more controversial when it emerged that, of the employment opportunities which the quarry would create, less than one quarter of these, around 30, would eventuate as long-term job opportunities for the inhabitants of Harris, the majority of jobs going to people elsewhere in the Hebrides and further afield. The other threat to jobs which the quarry was said to represent concerned the local tourist industry, which is currently the largest single source of employment on Harris.

The large scale of this industrial activity, with its associated noise and water pollution, would present a threat to the attraction of the unique environment of Harris to visitors. This threat would have a significant economic impact on local employment in tourism. Taken together these material threats to employment in fishing and tourism were significant factors in undermining the purely economic case for the quarry.

In the end the underlying material significance of the discourse of the Clearances asserted itself in the response of the local community to the evidence presented to the public inquiry. For the evidence indicated that far from the quarry bringing extensive economic benefits *into* the community, it would instead be an extractive experience whose material outcome would involve the extraction not only of a very large quantity of rock from the island, but the loss of other economic and production opportunities that are intricately tied up with the cultural distinctiveness, and unique natural heritage of Harris.

Advocates of the quarry had claimed, ironically, that the quarry offered an opportunity for 'sustainable development', a language that, as Mackenzie (1998) puts it was 'summoned as part of a modernist project of progress and growth: employment and prosperity would accompany the superquarry and ward off the spectre of a community portrayed on the verge of extinction'. The use of the language of sustainability was intended to subvert local environmental opposition by pointing to the prospect of new local jobs that would *sustain* the local economy. This polarization between economic and environmental sustainability is a common feature of the deployment of the term 'sustainable development' in bureaucratic and corporate circles.

Despite their deployment of the language of sustainability, the urban-based corporate and bureaucratic élite lost the argument about the material outcomes of the proposed quarry in this remote and culturally distinctive rural and island community. And it is clear that the argument over the economics of the quarry was not confined to economic criteria among the islanders, nor lost on these grounds alone, though they clearly played an important role.

As Mackenzie argues, suspicion about the underlying presuppositions, and even the framing of the evidence, by advocates of the quarry, began to emerge as the inquiry proceeded. This suspicion appears to have been related to the deeper cultural issues that were at stake in the controversy over the superquarry. During the long eight-month saga of the public inquiry, the islanders came to perceive the superquarry not just as a cost-benefit calculation of jobs lost and jobs gained, but as a threat to the distinctive character of their island community, and not just to the integrity of its natural environment, but to the integrity of its unique cultural and religious identity.

'I LIFT UP MINE EYES UNTO THE QUARRY': RELIGIOUS AND COMMUNAL CONSTRUCTIONS OF WORSHIP, NATURE AND COMMUNITY AT THE PUBLIC INQUIRY

When the Quaker ecologist and former Harris resident Alastair McIntosh declared in his oral and written theological testimony to the public inquiry that he opposed the quarry 'because it was not part of the movement of love', a Scottish journalist observed that Redland Aggregate's inquiry team found it difficult to keep a straight face (Allardyce, 1995). McIntosh's testimony was part of a half-day of presentations by himself, drawing on a distinctive combination of Celtic shamanism, Biblical exegesis and liberation theology, and by his two supporting witnesses, Donald MacLeod, a Free Church Professor of Theology, also hailing from Harris, and Chief Sulian Stone Eagle of the Mi'kmaq Nation in Nova Scotia, Canada. The occasion for this unique day of theological or spiritual testimony was McIntosh's argument before the Chief Reporter of the Inquiry in her precognitions in Edinburgh that the distinctive religious culture and community of Harris, under which the issue of Sunday working would be considered at the Inquiry, legitimated the presentation of related theological arguments on the matter.

Many of the people of Harris, like those of the other Outer Hebridean Islands, are devoted to a particular style of Scottish Presbyterianism whose adherents hold to a very strict moral code based upon close adherence to the Ten Commandments. Their ritual life is also patterned on the Commandments and on interpretations of elements of ancient Israelite culture in which the Commandments were first promulgated. Worship in Presbyterian churches on Harris is a unique cultural experience, involving a good deal of plain talk and long sermons, very infrequent celebrations of the Lord's Supper, and, instead of modern hymn singing, rhythmic and harmonic recitation of the Hebrew Psalter in Gaelic. The rituals of the Free Church resonate very strongly with two of the Old Testament Commandments, the first being the prohibition of idolatry – hence the plainness of the rituals and ritual spaces of Harris churches – and the second being the commandment to observe the Sabbath.

Life on Harris comes to a virtual standstill on Sundays. No work is to be performed on Sunday. All hotels and shops are closed and no newspapers are sold. Ferries run up to midnight on Saturday and from midnight on Sunday, but not at all in between. Harris householders save their washing up from the

Sunday meal for Monday morning, or else time their dishwashers to come on at midnight. Anyone who hangs out washing, or cleans their houses, or cuts peat for the fire on a Sunday is at risk of being ostracized by their neighbours.

Unlike the rest of Scotland, where on average only 10 per cent of Scots attend church on an ordinary Sunday, around 50 per cent of people on Harris and the other large Hebridean islands attend church at least once on a Sunday, many twice, and many attend a mid-week service as well. This distinctive religious culture is strongly at variance with mainland Scotland where Sabbath observance is mostly a distant memory and shops open seven days a week. It was the preservation of this culture that was of most concern to the islanders when they first encountered the quarry proposal from Redland Aggregates. The islanders were much less concerned about threats to the unique environment of Harris than they were about threats to the ritual time by which the Sabbath observance confers sacred significance on their lives.

Until the public inquiry, religious and cultural concerns about the superquarry had been primarily articulated on Harris in relation to the distinctive ritual and temporal concerns arising from the Sabbatarian traditions of the people. In response Redland Aggregates had drawn up a Sunday Agreement with the Island Council under which the company undertook that there would be no work on Sunday at the quarry barring an emergency (such as a flood or a storm) and 'essential maintenance' needed to enable the first shift to start work on time on Monday morning (Maltz, 1995). There would also be no regular loading or unloading of ships on Sunday, though again if they were delayed by bad weather they would be allowed to berth on a Sunday. The Sunday Agreement did not resolve the issue entirely, however, and there were concerns among the islanders both about the partial nature of these conditions and about the extent to which they actually bound the future operators of the quarry to abide by them.

Sabbath Observance was the principal religious issue that was raised at the Inquiry. John Reed, Queen's Counsel for the Western Isles Islands Council, raised the concern that the Sunday Agreement was not legally enforceable by the Council on the quarry operators, and that it would be even harder for the Council to enforce it against third parties such as shipping companies. The Reverend Kenneth MacLeod, a local minister, argued in his oral testimony that the Sabbath was a crucial local amenity, the keeping of which was a moral issue and fundamental to the ordered life of the people of Harris who are law-abiding and among whom there is no crime. He and other church witnesses were concerned that ultimately reverence for profits would take priority over reverence for the Lord's Day and that in a part of the world given to violent extremes of weather the quarry operators would seek to make up for lost time by working on the Sabbath (Maltz, 1995).

MacLeod and other church witnesses testified that they saw the quarry as a threat to the ordered and religiously rooted life of the community of Harris. They expressed the view that the superquarry's putative social and economic benefits might not be realized, while it could do lasting harm to the culture of the Western Isles if Sabbath Observance was undermined. Another church witness quoted the 121st Psalm, 'I to the hills will lift up mine eyes, from when doth come mine aid', and observed that 'I will lift up mine eyes to the quarry' did not have the same ring (Maltz, 1995).

Having argued that the Sabbath issue permitted a broader consideration of theological considerations, McIntosh led a half-day of theological testimony before the Inquiry that, while it may not figure greatly in the Reporter's final judgment (which has still to be released in full), nonetheless attracted much publicity on Harris and throughout Scotland, and further afield. McIntosh's opening argument referred to the anthropological premise of the Westminster Confession that the chief end of man is 'to glorify God and to enjoy him forever'. McIntosh argued that God is glorified or reverenced by humans and by nature, citing the Hebrew Prophet Isaiah as evidence: 'the mountains and hills will burst into song before you, and all the trees of the field will clap their hands' (Isaiah 55, 12). The providential and sustaining action of God is revealed in the non-human creation and this is why wild places such as the Outer Hebrides are places where people have traditionally experienced a 'composure of soul'. Against advocates of the quarry who argue that Harris is already like a moonscape, and that the quarry will not fundamentally alter an already desecrated landscape, McIntosh (1995) argued that the Lewisian Gneiss glaciated scenery of Harris, and other parts of 'the Celtic fringe on the Western edge of the continent of Europe' have inspired some of 'the greatest poetry, song and music of the European tradition'.

McIntosh's (ibid.) argument is essentially a theological aesthetic, arguing for the conservation of wild space as in such spaces people may experience evidence of the 'nature-conserving Creator who "sendeth forth" his spirit and "renewest the face of the earth . . . who laid the foundations of the earth"'. Against the economic value of aggregate, McIntosh argues that the undesecrated land of Harris has a spiritual value that requires that humans respect its 'integrity'. Reverence for nature is indicative of reverence for the creator God who sustains the creation and who gave Noah the sign of the rainbow as a sign that 'God will never again lay waste to the Earth', a symbol that is 'observed with frequency in the Western Isles' (ibid.).

Donald McLeod also opened his much more concise testimony by drawing on traditional Highland theology in the affirmation that 'God as creator has absolute sovereignty over the environment' and that 'we must use it only in accordance with his will'. Our use of nature will be part of God's judgement of our individual and collective lives at the Day of Judgement when 'we shall answer collectively, as well as individually, for all our decisions in this area' (ibid., 1995). Like McIntosh, MacLeod argued that 'the primary function of creation is to serve as a revelation of God' and that despoliation of the kind the superquarry represents 'disables' creation from performing this function. The people of Harris are, like all created people, intimately linked to the soil and have a responsibility to till the soil and to keep it, for the Bible 'designates man as the guardian and protector of the ground'. The conflict over the quarry is ultimately a conflict between capitalism, and a promise of jobs to sustain the economic viability of the island community, and the deepest instincts of the people of Harris which are to guard the land as their Christian calling.

MacLeod's testimony raised an issue which had begun to figure elsewhere in the debate over the quarry and this is the extent to which the proposed development would challenge the religio-cultural traditions of the people of Harris, and in particular the intimate connection between their religion and their traditional agrarian way of life, which derives livelihood from the keeping of the land. This potential threat to the community's cultural identity comes even more to the fore in the testimony of Sulian Stone Eagle Herney of Cape Breton Island, Nova Scotia.

Chief Stone Eagle argued that the people of Harris are an indigenous people like his own people, whose land is also the subject of a superquarry planning proposal, and whose way of life is threatened by 'the environmental destruction that is plaguing all of mankind'. He compares the threat from the quarry to the people of Harris to the longer-term threats to the cultural identity of his own Mi'kmaq people, threats which originate in 'the influence of non-natives to our territory' who 'became parasites of Mother Earth, thus destroying her natural bounty' (McIntosh, 1995).

The articulation by both a Free Church Professor of Theology and a Canadian First Nation Chief of the potential threat to the religious and cultural identity of the community that the superquarry represented was a significant moment in the wider publicity surrounding the public inquiry and the history of the superquarry proposal. During the inquiry, the people of Harris began to see themselves as an indigenous people whose distinctive and religiously guarded way of life was threatened by a non-native development whose economic outcomes, which were presented as a device to preserve the community, were, in fact, more likely to destroy its unique integrity and way of life. In the end environmentalist discourse about threats to wildlife, or the destruction of a mountain, did not count for much for the indigenous people of Harris. What did count was the realization of the fragility of their culture (Maltz, 1995). The presence of Stone Eagle was a powerful symbolic pointer, much imaged in the media, to the danger that the scale and intensity of the superquarry – by introducing the alien, non-native culture of industrialism –

would disrupt the ordered temporality of a Sabbath-observing community and that this alien culture would destroy the integrity of one of the last indigenous communities of Northern Europe.

PAROCHIAL ECOLOGY AND RELIGIO-CULTURAL RESISTANCE TO INDUSTRIALISM

The interaction between culture, religion, nature and power in the Harris superquarry inquiry and its aftermath may helpfully be interpreted in at least two different modes of discourse. It has significance for an understanding of the micropolitics of local communities as they struggle with large and increasingly global actors over the use of their own local space in the larger global economy. It also has significance for the differentiation between human cultural identity and natural space which modern capitalist culture increasingly sustains, and the related differentiation between religion and economic and political power.

In his fine ethnographic study of rice farming communities in the northern states of Kedah and Perlis in West Malaysia, Scott (1987) identifies a range of tactics of resistance that farmers and labourers used to defend themselves and their identity against the new urban landlords who have become the dominant power in the region as the costs of new hybridized seeds and expensive fertilizers have driven many subsistence and small farmers to bankruptcy. Scott found that the tactics of the weak involved the use of irony and wit, petty theft and forms of subversion which, while presenting no major threat to the economic power of the new landowners, nonetheless subverted their authority and enabled the local people to survive and to maintain some of their dignity.

The amused reaction of the corporately hired lawyers to McIntosh's reference to the 'movement of love', the realization that the people of Harris are an indigenous people and share the threat to their way of life experienced by indigenous peoples all over the world as modern industrial capitalism seeks new territory to transform into economic resources, and the ultimate irony that observance of the Sabbath came to count for more than the promise of corporately sponsored jobs, are all indicative of the kind of tactics of resistance of which Scott speaks. The resistance of the people of Harris to the proposed development of their island in the pursuit of the industrial transformation of the environment represents a local, micropolitical rejection of a global discourse, the utilitarian discourse of cost and benefit that sets the costs of ecological destruction to particular communities of place against benefits to the larger political community.

In this discourse, the people of Harris began to detect a hidden corporate strategy to incorporate the landscape of Harris into the global economy. Their suspicion was not, however, aroused primarily by the issue of ecological destruction, which was mostly raised by outside bodies such as Scottish Natural Heritage, and by outside witnesses such as McIntosh and McLeod, but by the perceived threat to what we may call the human ecology of the island, which was characterized by the different pace of life in which work is ordered by Sabbath.

Redland Aggregates had sought to divide the community using a traditional anti-environmentalist strategy, setting nature conservers against people and community preservers. But ultimately the strategy backfired for, as McIntosh confesses in his testimony, the people of Harris do not have an 'environmental theology' but what they do have, and what they came to realize during the Public Inquiry, is a religiously and culturally distinctive way of life, which is intimately connected with a particular place and landscape, and with the distance of its locale from the alien way of life of the metropolitan world.

Ironically, environmentalists and metropolitan capitalists frequently deploy discourses for their competing ends that share a nature-culture distinction. Both environmentalist and capitalist discourses frequently involve the oppositional representation of the conservation of wild nature and the material needs of people. Environmentalists and corporatists both mobilized this oppositional discourse in their testimonies before the public inquiry. This sharp distinction between people and nature is, of course, the legacy of Cartesian mechanistic cosmology and of Enlightenment rationalism in Western culture.

Environmental philosophers argue that only when Western culture resolves this fundamental tension between conceptions of human selfhood and self-interest and conceptions of 'wild' nature will modern societies begin to recover modes of economic and cultural production, which do not rely on the further fragmentation of ecosystems (Plumwood, 1995). This distinction is not, however, part of the world view of many indigenous groups and it is for this reason that environmentalists argue that Western culture may still have something to learn from indigenous communities such as the people of Harris.

The defence of their community, and its place, by the people of Harris, was represented by advocates of the quarry, and in some press comment, as an example of NIMBY-ism (Not in My Back Yard-ism). The argument went that the aggregate was needed for the transport infrastructure of the United Kingdom and that if it could not be quarried in this remote region of Scotland, then it would be necessary to quarry it in Norway or in some other community. By taking a stand against the quarry, the people of Harris could therefore be said to be displacing the environmental costs of development onto some other community. However, this accusation of NIMBY-ism is another classic feature of global corporatist discourse, though one which is frequently mobilized by political partners of corporate development in environmental controversies. This discourse relies on an underlying appeal to a utilitarian ethic, which sets particular communities and particular places that may be harmed by a certain economic development against the benefits which the larger political community may be said to derive from these localized costs (Sagoff, 1988). Thus, in the case of local pollution to fishing grounds as a consequence of aggregate quarrying on Harris, civil servants may set the reduced journey times of English motorists on widened sections of the London orbital motorway whose saved time can be quantified in monetary terms that far exceed the monetary losses to a small number of Hebridean fisherfolk.

Plumwood (1995) argues that this universalizing discourse of cost and benefit misconstrues the relationship between the flourishing of persons in particular communities and the natural spaces in which these communities are located, and that this misconstruction is related to the atomistic and rationalistic account of human selfhood which is derived from Enlightenment philosophy. She argues instead for a conception of self-in-relation, which conceives of the identity of the self as constructed in relation to significant others, where others are not only persons but also the particular natural spaces in which a person first discovers their embodied identity in the material world of nature.

This has important implications for ethics because instead of the exaltation of conceptions of impartiality and anonymity as guarantors of ethical propriety in Western ethics, such as those mobilized in Rawls (1983), this approach finds connectivity, relationality and care to be core components of ethical experience and discernment (Gilligan, 1981). Thus efforts of resistance towards environmental depredation of the local spaces that particular persons and communities actually inhabit are not to be understood as selfish NIMBY-ism but rather as expressions of the relational character of ethical consciousness. Such an approach involves an ethical validation of the attachments to place which are most characteristic of the spatially stable lives of primal communities, and least characteristic of the lives of metropolitan persons such as the author of this chapter whose attachment to place is continuously disrupted by the exigencies of a capitalist vocation (of knowledge production) (Northcott, 1996).

The attachment to place, which finally triumphed in the attitude of the people of Harris towards the proposed superquarry, is not primarily located in a distinctive attitude to 'nature' as distinct from persons. It is rather a feature of a larger constellation of symbols, pathways, life patterns and rituals, which together constitute the distinctive religious and cultural identity of the

Sabbath Observant people of Harris. In their experience of this constellation, indigenous communities such as that of the people of Harris, may be said to reject, or refuse to own, because they have never embraced it, the fundamental distinction between religion and social power that has become the reigning presupposition of modern political and religious theory and practice.

Scotland, like most of the United Kingdom and Northern Europe, is a society characterized by a considerable degree of secularization. The sociological theorization of secularization has laid emphasis on three related processes that characterize modern societies and accompany the process of secularization, and these are rationalization, differentiation and societalization. The public discussion of the Harris superquarry subjected elements of all three processes to critical scrutiny. As we have seen, the rationalization of a local pollution problem with reference to the larger benefits of society as a whole was rejected, as was the economic rationalization of jobs versus cultural and ecological disruption.

The people of Harris also rejected the modern differentiation of social life into different spheres such as education, economic activity, entertainment, domestic life and religion. On Harris, economic activity is controlled by religious time. Similarly, behaviour within the routines of domestic life is not a private affair but subject to public scrutiny and to the publicly affirmed moral codes of the dominant religious community. For the people of Harris, religion plays a central role in political decision making, hence the inclusion of religious rituals, beliefs and value systems in the evidence admitted to the public inquiry. Like most primal communities, Harris recognizes no separation of spheres of the kind obtaining in modern states between the religious and political, or between private (religious) life and public (political) life.

Resistance to the superquarry on Harris may be seen then as part of a principled religious rejection of key features of the secular culture of modern societies and, in particular, the splitting apart of religious rituals and codes of behaviour – such as the Ten Commandments – and the power relations which characterize state governance and economic production. The Hebridean islanders thus hold to a holistic approach to religion and culture which sustains the authority and social power of religion at all levels of social life, and rejects the fragmentation of modern social experience into 'religious' and 'secular'.

Casanova (1994) observes that the conventional sociological theorization of secularization has a hard time with this kind of public articulation of religious orientation, and its resistance to modern secular forms of social organization. He argues that such resistance is not necessarily to be read, however, as evidence of 'an antimodern fundamentalist reaction to inevitable processes of modern differentiation' but may better be understood as 'counterfactual normative critiques of dominant historical trends, in many respects similar to the classical, republican, and feminist critiques'.

Giddens (1991) calls this kind of resistance to dominant trends in modernity 'life politics' and suggests that the articulation of religious traditions with this kind of resistance is one of the possible consequences of the hegemonizing tendencies of the putatively progressive modern project. Ecological life politics involves the rejection of the universalizing power procedures of modern nation-states. These procedures subvert the capacity of local communities to order their own natural places in favour of a larger project of governance that hands control over to bureaucrats and democratic representatives who are predominantly representatives of a metropolitan culture in which corporate capitalism is the dominant productive and cultural force.

The impersonal procedures of modern production systems generate a disarticulation between people and place that is one of the principal features of societalization, the third social process which has contributed to secularization. Societalization involves the transformation of human exchange relations from ones which rely on face-to-face relationships between persons who are known to one another into rational and impersonal systems in which most transactions take place between persons who are unknown to each other and that therefore depend on varying degrees of trust and increasingly of risk and electronic or legal surveillance. Once again, in rejecting their incorporation into this larger anonymous economy of risk and surveillance, the people of Harris are effectively affirming a cornerstone of the distinctive religious culture of their island – face-to-face community – while at the same time rejecting one of the key social processes which generate secularisation.

In conclusion, it may be judged that the religio-cultural character of resistance to the superquarry on the Isle of Harris points to a larger set of phenomena in the emergent life politics of late modern societies in which the progressive discourses of modern development, even of 'sustainable' development, are sometimes countered by the ironic articulation of seemingly weak and powerless symbols and rituals such as Sabbath observance in small indigenous communities that are on the frontiers of the territorial expansion of metropolitan capitalist culture. As Mackenzie (1998) says, through these symbols opponents of the quarry in the community created 'an alternative framework of meaning which implicitly challenged the claims to truth of RAL's (Redland Aggregate Limited) discourse of sustainable development'.

The entry of religious rituals and cultural symbols into the public world of economic development and legal judgment at the Superquarry Public Inquiry may also be said to represent a challenge to the political arrangements under which nation-states partner and champion the corporate industrial assault on nature, for in indigenous communities there is no separation between place and community, persons and nature, religion and politics, or ultimately public and private. The prominent role of religious functionaries, rituals and symbols is an emergent feature of environmental resistance in places as diverse as Rajasthan, Borneo, Zimbabwe and Thailand (Gottlieb, 1996).

Oelschlaeger (1994) argues that the secular discourses of scientist progress and economic welfare lack the motive power to change the direction of modern civilization whereas by contrast religious traditions present a significant resource in the expression of ecological dissent to the utilitarian framing of human-nature relations. Analogously, Callicott (1994) argues that the different world religions present a shared discourse of responsibility for the Earth that modern humans urgently need as their sheer numbers as a species have enhanced so dramatically their physical dominance over, and hence responsibility for, the planet.

For many modern political theorists, the claim that relatively small geographically isolated communities of place, which are also religious in character, may represent sources of environmental resistance, is a highly ambiguous one. In conventional Western political theory, religion is represented as a source of war and conflict, ethnic intolerance and gender oppression (Cavanaugh, 1995).

It is also a common assumption in modern political discourse that small communities of place characterized by face-to-face relationships are intrinsically more intolerant of diversity and more patriarchal than large, anonymous, metropolitan and multicultural communities. But ironically these kinds of universalist claims about religions, and about small communities, are strongly related to the kinds of imperialist discourses of progress and 'civilization', even of sustainable development, which have undergirded and continue to legitimate the forcible wresting of land and natural resource access from indigenous peoples.

The claim that traditional First Nation communities were and are less hospitable to the outsider than the suburban communities of modern Canadian cities is one which visitors to such communities – including the early European colonists who ultimately stole their lands, but not without first enjoying their at times life-saving hospitality – have reason to dispute. Similarly, few visitors to the Hebridean Islands complain of a lack of hospitality. Analogously, the claim that communities in which religious traditions, such as the Sabbath, are respected are necessarily more gender repressive than modern industrialized and consumerist societies is by no means indisputable.

In the case of Harris's sabbatarianism, rest from work on Sundays is not confined to men's work. It was also noted by those who observed the superquarry saga that women on the island were prominent in the mobilization of the community around the issue. Even though Free Church Presbyterianism preserves a gendered approach to worship leadership, this did not preclude a significant mobilization of both genders in the micropolitics of the superquarry controversy.

Communities of place have an ambiguous status in modern political theory precisely because their existence challenges the progressive and rationalist discourses – of the nation-state, of economic development, of moral progress – that have legitimated so many features of the modern assault on the environment, and especially on the environments of premodern and precolonial peoples. The Harris superquarry story indicates the potential role that the political and religious traditions of such peoples can play as a vehicle for the expression of a political ecology which, unlike the abstract and universalising discourses of modern Western political theory, sees the welfare of place and people as intricately connected.

It is evidence of what I have elsewhere called 'parochial ecology', in which communities of place recover from the universalizing hegemony of state and corporate actors a collective sense of responsibility for their own locale, including the birds, grasses, shrubs, trees, waterways and airways which delineate the pathways and rituals of local community life (Northcott, 1996). This parochial ecology does not sustain, nor is it sustained by, a dualistic sense of the sacrality of nature, as opposed to ordinary (secular) human life such as is commonly found among modern Western and mostly urbanized environmentalists. Rather, it demonstrates a consciousness of the commonality of createdness that both persons and nature share, and the relationality of the human quest for transcendence to the spaces that nature affords for that quest to find ritual and communal expression.

3. 'Community' and Natural Resource Conservation

Arun Agrawal

This chapter focuses on and examines the recent emergence of 'community' as a critical actor in renewable natural resource management. Externalities associated with environmental resources, especially renewable resources such as forests, pastures and fisheries, had prompted many governments to pursue exclusionary policies to ensure conservation. But several decades of the pursuit of intrusive resource management strategies in the post-Second World War era has forced policy makers, funding agencies and scholars to confront the fact that such strategies often failed in accomplishing their conservation goals. Intrusive conservationist strategies that sought to protect resources by excluding human populations have had singularly unappealing distributive effects. Based as these policies were on implicit assumptions about the public good nature of environmental resources, backwardness and traditional nature of local communities, and the necessity for centralized management, their net effect was the exclusion of local populations from resources, especially land- and water-based renewable common resources. They tended to marginalize and disempower precisely those poor populations who depended most on resources deemed worthy of protection efforts.

The motivation for the focus on community and its advocacy can be located in the dissatisfaction with the adverse effects of exclusionary protection on marginal populations. Most scholars, policy analysts, donors and activists who argue on behalf of a central role for community in conservation are impelled by the belief that such arguments can help improve the lives and life chances of poor rural peoples. Their arguments mesh well with more widespread claims for community in other arenas of social organization, among them development, ethnic cooperation and democratization (Bhattacharya, 1995; Etzioni, 1996). The cumulative pressure exerted for community has resulted in significant policy changes. More than 50 countries, according to a recent survey by the Food and Agriculture Organization (FAO,1999), claim to be pursuing policies that will facilitate partnerships with local communities and distribute the benefits of environmental management more widely among their populations.

Despite its popularity, the concept of community as it is deployed in most contemporary writings on conservation remains deeply problematic and difficult. It has only recently begun to receive the attention and analysis it needs from those concerned with resource use and management (Li, 1996; Zerner, 1994). Yet, a continuing preoccupation with certain features of a 'mythical community' characterizes general beliefs about community.

This chapter examines recent conservationist writings by looking at how they conceptualize community in conservation and resource management.[1] I begin by exploring the origins of community in writings on resource use. The ensuing analysis reveals that three aspects of community are most important to those who advocate a positive role for communities in resource management – community as a small spatial unit, as a homogenous social structure and as shared norms.

Suggesting a more political and institutional approach, I argue that analytical and policy efforts in favour of community need to focus more explicitly on: (a) the multiple interests and actors within groups that are termed community; (b) the relationships of these actors with actors and institutions supposed to be outside the community; and (c) how the nature of community is and always has been shaped in interactions with what is seen to be outside the community. A focus on multiplicity of actors and interests, institutions and processes, and the production of community can lead to more careful representations of communities. It is also likely to have more enduring and fruitful results for those interested in community-based natural resource management.

The chapter concludes by suggesting that research and policy on community-based conservation should move away from universalist claims either for or against community. Instead, community-based conservation initiatives need to develop more careful images of community, recognizing their internal differences and processes, their relations with external actors, and the institutions that affect both.

COMMUNITY AND CONSERVATION

The history of community in conservation is a history of revisionism. Images of pristine ecosystems and innocent primitives yielded over time to views of despoiling communities out of balance with nature, mostly due to the double-pronged intrusion of the state and market. A recuperative project on behalf of the indigenous and the local (community) has attempted to rescue community. But the rescue project has itself come under attack by new anthropological and historical research that suggests communities may not necessarily be as friendly to the environment. The practical and policy implications that accompany these changing images are immense.

The basic elements of earlier policy and scholarly writings about local communities and their residents are familiar. 'People' were an obstacle to efficient and 'rational' organization of resource use owing to their traditional ways and the inability to act collectively.[2] Population growth and increasing marketization meant that even if people had successfully managed resources in some harmonious past, that past was long gone. Instead, the way to effective conservation was through the heavy hand of the state or through the equally heavy, if less visible, hand of the market and private property rights. Such schematic arguments, popularized by Garrett Hardin and bolstered by several theoretical metaphors that served to (mis)guide policy, provided a persuasive explanation of how resource degradation and depletion took place.[3]

While many of these beliefs persist,[4] other ideas about community's role in conservation have changed radically: communities are now the locus of conservationist thinking.[5] International agencies such as the World Bank, IDRC, SIDA, CIDA, the Worldwide Fund for Nature, Conservation International, The Nature Conservancy, The Ford Foundation, The MacArthur Foundation and USAID have all 'found' community. A flood of scholarly papers and policy-centric reports feature community-based management (for example, Arnold, 1990; Clugston and Rogers, 1995; Dei, 1992; Douglass, 1992; Perry and Dixon, 1986; Raju et al., 1993; Robinson, 1995).

Exemplifying the swing toward community, a recent collection of essays on community-based conservation tells us, 'Communities down the millennia have developed elaborate rituals and practices to limit off take levels, restrict access to critical resources, and distribute harvests' (Western and Wright, 1994, p. 1).[6] The introduction to another set of essays on community-based conservation argues:

> local traditional communities have often recognised this: the widespread practices of leaving alone entire habitat stretches ('sacred groves') and species alone; the myriad myths and folklore representing animals and plants as ancestors and totems; lifestyles which were incredibly fine-tuned to the rhythms and limits of their natural surrounds (Kothari et al., 1996, p. 19).

In such arguments, a historical idealization of communities becomes the basis for championing communities in the contemporary period. At the same time, the posited characteristics of idealized historical communities become the ones toward which resource management strategies should strive.

A host of factors have aided advocates of community-based conservation. The past several decades of planned development and top-down conservation practices have made one fact amply clear: the capacity of states to coerce their citizens into unpopular development and conservation programmes is limited. These limits are seen starkly when state actors attempt to discipline resource users. Faulty design, inefficient implementation, fiscal limits and corrupt organizations have played an important role in the poor outcomes associated with state-centred policies. In their review of 23 conservation and development programmes, Wells and Brandon (1992) argue that weaknesses of state-centric policy means few options other than community-based conservation exist.[7]

Other contextual factors that have helped to bring community to the fore include the spread of democratic political structures, the attention to participation, the increasing prominence of indigenous and ethnic claims about the stewardship role of native populations in relation to nature (Clay, 1988; Redford and Mansour, 1996), and the important role of non-governmental organizations (NGOs) in amplifying the voices of local and indigenous groups (Borda, 1985; Borghese, 1987).

The recognition of the limits of the state and the emphasis on popular participation have come roughly at the same time as new revisionist ecological research. Historical ecologists emphasize that environments have histories from which humans cannot be excluded (Posey, 1984, 1985).[8] Denevan (1992) argues that most forests are, in fact, anthropogenic. An increasing number of scholars have marshalled evidence about how humans manipulate biodiversity and influence the species composition and structure of forests around them (Alcorn, 1981; Bailey and Headland, 1991; Balee, 1992, 1994; Brookfield and Padoch, 1994; McDade, 1993; Roosevelt, 1989).

Such studies undermine arguments that portray communities only as despoilers of natural resources. In addition to the above empirical and historical works that have helped resurrect community and local participation, a choice-theoretic foundation for the role of community in conservation has become available as well. Research from scholars of common property has shown communities to be successful and sustainable alternatives to state and private management of resources (McCay and Acheson, 1987; McKean, 1992; Ostrom, 1990; Peters, 1994).

In light of the significant symbolic, theoretical and intellectual resources available to advocates of community, it is somewhat surprising that claims on behalf of community-based conservation often retain a rather simple quality. One form such claims assume is that 'communities' have a long-term need for the renewable resources near which they live, and they possess more knowledge about these resources than other potential actors. They are, therefore, the best managers of resources.[9]

Some refinements to this view can be found: if communities are not involved in the active management of their natural resources, they will use resources destructively (Sponsel et al., 1996; Western and Wright, 1994). In its prescriptive form, this thesis of community-based conservation and resource management uses new beliefs about the suitability of communities to suggest policy recommendations. The implicit assumption behind these recommendations is that communities have incentives to use resources unsustainably when they are not involved in resource management. If communities are involved in conservation, the benefits they receive will create incentives for them to become good stewards of resources (if only the state and the market would get out of the way).[10]

This vision of community – as the centrepiece of conservation and resource management – is attractive. It permits the easy contestation of dominant narratives that favour state control or privatization of resources and their management. Positive, generalized representations of community make available 'points of leverage in ongoing processes of negotiation' (Li, 1996, pp. 505, 509).[11] However, such representations of community ignore the critical interests and processes within communities, and between communities and other social actors. Ultimately, they can undermine their advocates' long-term goal of increasing the role of community in natural resource management.

UNDERSTANDING COMMUNITY

The vision of small, integrated communities using locally evolved norms and rules to manage resources sustainably and equitably is powerful. But because it views community as a unified, organic whole, attached to a particular place, this vision fails to attend to differences within communities, and ignores how these differences affect resource management outcomes, local politics and strategic interactions within communities, as well as the possibility of layered alliances that can span multiple levels of politics. Attention to these details is critical if policy changes on behalf of community are to lead to outcomes that are sustainable and equitable.

Although current writings on community-based conservation assert that community is central to renewable resource management, they seldom devote much attention to analysing the concept of community, or explaining precisely how community affects outcomes.[12] Some authors refuse to elaborate on what it might mean, preferring to let readers infer its contours in the descriptions of specific cases (for example, Western and Wright, 1994). However, most studies in the conservation field refer to a bundle of concepts related to space, size, composition, interactions, interests and objectives.

Much of this literature sees community in three ways: as a spatial unit, as a social structure and as a set of shared norms. It is on the basis of one or a combination of these three ideas that most of the advocacy for community rests. They offer, however, a weak foundation on which to base policy.

Community as a Small Spatial Unit

Small size and territorial affiliation have been proxies for community since the very beginning of writings on the subject. These two aspects of community – smallness (of both area and numbers of individuals) and territorial attachment – also mark many current writings on community in conservation. Many scholars see community as a village, or at least as a rural settlement.[13] The point is not whether existing communities are small or large. Surely there is significant variation in the size of communities. But much of the writing on community-based conservation takes size, rather uncritically, as a basic fact defining communities, instead of examining and drawing out the possible connections of shared space and small size with the political processes of local conservation. Further, studies of community in conservation tend to assume a link between the territorial conception of community and successful resource management.[14]

For example, Wells and Brandon (1993, p. 162) provide testimony about how conservation professionals think of communities as small when after examining 23 protected area projects around the world, they say that often these projects attempt to promote wide ranging programmes in 'numerous small communities spread over large areas'. There are other instances of how writings on community-based conservation conceptualize community implicitly as a small entity. Poffenberger (1996, pp. 28–29), in a description of community-based conservation in Ghana, speaks of small forests (less than 200 hectares) and communities (fewer than four thousand people) as being the actors to whom forest management is being devolved.

In the same vein, many scholars of community-based conservation, when they speak of community, see it as coincident with small villages or rural settlements (Durbin and Ralambo, 1994; Gadgil, 1992; Parry and Campbell, 1992; Shackley, 1998). In a study of more than 20 cases from all around the world, the Biodiversity Conservation Network funded by the US Agency for International Development (USAID) reports on scarcely any case that is not one of small, place-based groups working for conservation (BCN, 1999).

The popularity of this view of community can be traced, at least in part, to the fact that the renewable resources that communities use, manage and sometimes protect, are themselves usually located near territorially fixed homes and settlements. If top-down programmes to protect resources failed because of the inability of governments to exercise authority at a distance, the reasoning goes, then decentralization of authority to those social formations that are located near the resource might work better. There may be other contributing factors at work. Members of small groups sharing the same geographical space are likely to interact with each other more often. Such regular, more frequent interactions can lower the costs of making collective decisions.

These two aspects of community – fewer individuals and shared small spaces[15] – may also contribute to group distinctiveness. Because of continuing interactions among members over time, territorially circumscribed communities might also be able to develop specific ways of managing the resources near which they are located. These advantages have led some policy makers and analysts to define strictly the size of 'communities' that should be participating in community-based resource programmes.[16]

But because many small, territorially contained groups do not protect or manage resources well, and because some mobile, transitional groups manage them efficiently, important processes are at work that are not captured by spatial location alone (Agrawal, 1999). Indeed, the territorial attachment of small groups may make them *inappropriate* managers for particular resources because the geographical spread of the resource (large watersheds, forests, lakes and so forth) could be larger than a small community could ever hope to control. Consequently, it becomes important to consider the negotiations and politics to which common spatial location and small size might contribute.

The bounded and stationary character of terrestrial resources such as forests and pastures does not imply a consequent ease in their allocation to particular spatial communities, for example, a piece of forest or pasture for every community. Because more than one community (in the spatial sense) may be located near a given patch of forest or pasture, and because the members of each would have an interest in the resources nominally belonging to the other community, spatial bases for allocating resource management rights can prove untenable. For fugitive resources such as wildlife and fish, an added dimension of complexity might be introduced (Naughton-Treves and Sanderson, 1995).

The literature on community-based conservation also often elides the thorny question of densities: does the success of a conservation practice depend on the density of individuals per hectare of land, per hectare of productive land or per hectare of a certain natural resource (Matzke and Nabane, 1996)? Focusing on a community's shared space and small numbers alone, therefore, is necessarily incomplete and possibly misleading in analysing local level management of resources.

Community as a Homogeneous Social Structure

The uncritical acceptance of the idea that communities should be small fits well with the additional presumption that small groups are less likely to be highly differentiated or marred by political conflicts among their members. Much of the rhetorical weight of community exists by the papering over of differences. Typically, many conservationists assume communities to be (small) groups of similarly endowed (in terms of assets and incomes), relatively homogeneous households who possess common characteristics in relation to ethnicity, religion, caste or language. Such homogeneity is assumed to further cooperative solutions, reduce hierarchical and conflictual interactions and promote better resource management. Outside the community conflicts prevail; within, reigns harmony.[17]

Assumptions about homogeneity of communities are often highly implicit and for that very reason extremely difficult to address. Even when some believers in local community management confess to diversity in interests and attributes of group members, they often claim that benefits from conservation must flow to all members of a community, or to 'the community as a whole' (Owen-Smith and Jacobson, cited in Brown and Wyckoff-Baird, 1992, p. 9). In another example, government officials in a community-based wildlife conservation programme in Botswana, when talking about who benefits from their programmes, argue, 'the community will be entitled to the benefit, the entire community' (Twyman, 1998, p. 761).

The notion that a community is homogeneous meshes well with beliefs about its spatial boundaries. In the rural areas of poorer countries (the sites where most advocates of community-based resource management locate their analyses and projects), people living within the same location may indeed hold similar occupations, depend on the same resources, use the same language and belong to the same ethnic or religious group. These similarities may facilitate regular interactions among group members.

Even if members of a group are similar in several respects, however, it is not clear at what point the label 'homogeneous' can be applied, nor is it clear that these shared characteristics are critical to conservation. Because all human groups are stratified to some extent or the other, it becomes important to analyse the degree of homogeneity and those dimensions of it that are important to resource conservation. Few studies, however, wrestle with the difficulty of operationalizing social homogeneity.[18] Most studies, when they do focus on the social composition of a community rather than assume it to be homogeneous, indicate intentionally or unintentionally that within the same group (for example, Masai, or pastoralist, or women), multiple axes of differentiation exist.[19]

Recent studies of resource use at the local level have recognized the salience of intra-community conflicts (Agrawal, 1994; Gibson and Marks, 1995; Ilahaine, 1995; Moore, 1996). Yet, even highly differentiated communities may be able to take steps to use local resources sustainably (Agrawal, 1994). These studies show that there is no easy correspondence between social homogeneity and sustainable resource use.

Community as Common Interests and Shared Norms

The concept of community as shared norms and common interests depends strongly on the perceptions of its members; in this sense all communities are imagined communities. This imagined sense of community attracts scholars of conservation to community. It is this notion of community that is supposed to grow out of common location, small size, homogeneous composition and/or shared characteristics. As Ascher (1995, p. 83) states, community exists among individuals who share '*common* interests and *common* identification . . . growing out of shared characteristics'. Common and shared rather than individual and selfish is what makes successful resource management more likely.

In a community, 'individuals give up some of their individuality to behave as a single entity to accomplish goals' (Kiss, 1990, p. 9). A number of other scholars argue that the norms and values of communities lead them to conserve resources so that renewability is ensured over future generations (Brownrigg, 1985; Norton, 1989). Raval (1994, p. 305) suggests, for example, that residents near the Gir National Park protect its resources because of their 'inherent love for the land and their religious attitudes'.

Internalized norms of behaviour among members of communities can guide resource management outcomes in desired directions. Community as shared norms is itself an outcome of interactions and processes that take place within communities, often in relation to those perceived as outsiders. But community as shared norms also has an independent positive effect on resource use and conservation.

Shared community-level norms can promote conservation in two different ways. First, norms may specifically prohibit some actions. In many villages in semi-arid western Rajasthan, for example, existing norms impede villagers from cutting *khejri* trees (*Prosopis cineraria*), especially when these trees are present in the local *oran*, a common area set aside for grazing, and often dedicated to a religious deity.[20] In the same region, the *Bishnois* have strong norms against the killing of wild animal species such as deer.

Cook (1996, pp. 279–82) details how the Amung-me in Irian Jaya protect certain groves of trees as sacred, and a marsupial (*amat*) that plays a role in the propagation of the Pandanus trees. Mishra (1994) explains that women belonging to *Juang* and *Saora* tribal communities in Orissa follow strong norms about the timing and season for collecting non-timber forest products. Other examples of 'conservationist' norms also exist.[21]

Second, it is possible that the existence of communal norms will promote cooperative decision making within the community. If members of a community believe in shared identities and common experiences, they also may be willing to cooperate over more formal decisions to manage and conserve resources. The presence of community-level norms can facilitate resource management by preventing certain behaviours, or encouraging others. But although community as shared norms, especially when such norms are about the management of resources or conservation, may be the hope of conservationists, the extent to which norms aid conservation needs to be questioned.[22]

At a minimum, current research indicates that conservationist norms cannot be equated with particular identities such as 'woman', or 'the indigenous'.[23] Norms, in fact, may be a significant part of the problem to a conservationist if a norm promotes exploitation (posing an enormous obstacle for those interested in community-based conservation).[24] For example, as a result of land laws in the early colonial periods of many countries in Latin America, there is a strong norm that land is only useful when cleared of trees and used for agriculture.[25]

In many parts of Africa, wildlife is considered a threat to crops and human lives, not a resource to be conserved (Marks, 1984; Naughton-Treves, 1997). Further, norms cannot be taken as a set of beliefs that communities hold, never to give up. They come into being in relation to particular contextual factors, and even when codified and written do not remain static.[26] Just because some small social groups hold conservationist norms today, they will not necessarily hold them in the future.

Those who conceptualize community as shared norms may fail to recognize the difficulties this position poses for conservation. Unlike the factors of community size, composition, and links to a specific territorial space which can be directly influenced through external intervention, community as shared understandings is probably the least amenable to such manipulation. Conservationist norms cannot be easily introduced into a community by external actors (although the current emphasis on participation and conservation by state actors means that at least the attempt is being made in many locations). Indeed, we hardly know which strategies successfully alter the norms people hold about conservation, especially when the resources in question are a critical part of the family income.

ACTORS, INTERACTIONS AND INSTITUTIONS

To summarize, advocates of community-based conservation forward a conceptualization of communities as territorially fixed, small and homogeneous. These characteristics supposedly foster those interactions among members that promote desirable collective decisions. However, although certain types and levels of these characteristics might facilitate collective action, few studies demonstrate that this collective action is necessarily connected with positive conservation outcomes. In fact, some characteristics considered important to collective action may actually thwart conservation efforts. Small-sized groups may be unable to defend their resources in the face of strong external threats, or manage resources that are spread over large areas. Strongly held norms may support exploitative behaviour, or be resistant to outside attempts at modification.

To be more accurate in our efforts to depict local populations and their relationship with their natural resources, greater attention is necessary to three critical aspects of their settlements and existence: multiplicity of actors and interests, the processes through which these actors interrelate and, especially, the institutional arrangements that structure their interactions. These three proposed foci for the study of community-based conservation allow for a better understanding of the factors critical to the success or failure of efforts related to local level actors.

Multiple Interests and Actors

A growing number of studies that explore natural resource management at the local level do not find that residents and settlements comprise just one group of individuals who possess similar endowments or goals. Instead, they find many subgroups; and within subgroups they find individuals with varying preferences for resource use and distribution. These authors bring to light the politics of the local. There may be conflicts within any group conceptualized as community, or a unit of the community: economic and religious élite, women and men, and those who are politically marginalized or dominant.

Different axes of identification and interests cleave all presumed groups. Recognizing and working with the multiplicity of actors and interests is crucial for those advocating community-based programmes. Such recognition indicates that empowering local actors to use and manage their natural resources is more than the decentralization of authority over natural resources from the central government to 'a' community. The far more challenging task is to understand patterns of difference within groups and facilitate negotiations despite the presence of these differences.

Recognizing that multiple actors exist at the local level is a useful step forward because it forces researchers to consider different and dynamic interests. A more acute understanding of community in conservation can be founded only by understanding that all actors seek their own interests in conservation programmes, and that these interests may change as new opportunities emerge.

Local Level Processes

Individuals negotiate the use, management and conservation of resources. They attempt to implement the agreed-upon rules resulting from their negotiations, and they try to resolve disputes that arise over the interpretation of rules. These three types of local interaction are irreducibly influenced by the existing distribution of power and the structure of incentives within a given social group.[27] Because the exercise of power and incentive-oriented behaviour are variable over time and space, and because all groups have members who can be strategic in their behaviour, planned conservation efforts can never address all contingencies completely.

Analyses of only local level phenomena are insufficient to explain interactions at the local level. All local interactions take place within the context of larger social forces. Attempts by governments to implement community-based conservation and specific projects of non-government organizations that seek to involve local populations are examples of directed influence. Such initiatives bring into the local context those larger political forces that generated the programmes. Other pressures – changes in prices of different resources, development assistance, demographic shifts, technological innovations and institutional arrangements at different levels – also impinge on local interactions.[28]

Local interactions may also prompt responses from macro-level actors. Local reactions to conservation programmes can lead to modifications in the shape of these programmes. Thus, although it is convenient to talk about the community and the state, or about the local and the external, they are linked together in ways that it might be difficult to identify the precise line where local conservation begins and the external (that helps construct the local) ends.

Institutional Arrangements

Institutions can be seen as sets of formal and informal rules and norms that shape interactions of humans with others and nature. They constrain some activities and facilitate others; without them, social interactions would be impossible (Bates, 1989; North, 1990). Institutions promote stability of expectations *ex ante*, and consistency in actions, *ex post*. They contrast with uncertain political interactions among unequally placed actors, and unpredictable processes where performances of social actors do not follow any necessary script. Strategic actors may attempt to bypass the constraints of existing institutions, and create new institutions that match their interests. But institutions remain the primary mechanisms available to mediate, soften, attenuate, structure, mould, accentuate and facilitate particular outcomes and actions (Alston et al., 1996; Gibson, 1999). This holds whether change is radical, moderate or incremental.

When actors do not share goals for conserving resources and are unequally powerful, as is likely the case in most empirical situations, institutions are significant for two reasons. On the one hand, they denote some of the power relations (Foucault, 1983, pp. 222, 224) that define the interactions among actors who created the institutions; on the other hand, they also help to structure the interactions that take place around resources. Once formed, institutions exercise effects that are independent of the forces that constituted them. Institutions can change because of constant challenges to their form by the actions of individuals whose behaviour they are supposed to influence. No actual behaviour conforms precisely to a given institutional arrangement. Everyday performances of individuals around conservation goals possess the potential to reshape formal and informal institutions.

Institutions can also change when explicitly renegotiated by actors. Institutions should be understood, therefore, as provisional agreements on how to accomplish tasks. Rather than setting the terms of interactions among parties with varying objectives, they help the behaviour of actors congeal along particular courses.

Authority to manage resources effectively at the local level requires control by local actors over three critical domains mentioned previously: (a) making rules about the use, management and conservation of resources; (b) implementation of the rules that are created; and (c) resolution of disputes that arise during the interpretation and application of rules.[29]

The authority to make rules defines who has the rights to access, use and conserve resources and exclude others from carrying out these activities. It also includes the determination of the ability to transfer these rights. The authority to implement implies the rights and the abilities to meter and monitor the use of the resource, and specify sanctions against those who violate existing rules. The authority to resolve disputes includes the rights and capacities to ensure that sanctions are followed, and adjudicate in the case of disputes.

The problem of analysing community-based conservation, thus, requires exploring a three-step process of institutional formation. At each step, two issues must be addressed: who will exercise the authority to make the rules?

And, what will be the content of the rules? Typically, community-based conservation programmes devolve to local actors only the authority to implement rules created elsewhere. Government agencies generally reserve for themselves the right to create rules and to arbitrate disputes.

INSTITUTIONS AS SOLUTIONS

A focus on institutions, conceptualized as sets of rules describing and prescribing human actions in three related domains, leads to a substantially different focus for locally oriented conservation policies in comparison to policies that result from an acceptance of the 'mythic' community. Rather than assume the primacy of size, space or norms, an institutional approach focuses on the ability of communities to create and to enforce rules. Institutional analysis requires identifying the possibly multiple and overlapping rules, the groups and individuals affected by such rules and the processes by which particular sets of rules change in a given situation.

In some cases, the homogeneity of a settlement's members or the norms they hold may be crucial to explaining the rules that people follow and the outcomes that their behaviour engenders. In other cases, formal and informal rules may have little to do with the conventional view of community and an institutional analysis instead notices overlapping, multi-level and differentiated sets of rules that help explain resource outcomes.

There are substantial arguments in favour of recognizing that actors in the local space may be the more appropriate source of rule making for a significant range of problems because of their specialized information about the local context and resources. Government agencies and bureaucracies are unlikely to be familiar with the specifics of local resource systems. Community actors and their representatives may possess far greater knowledge, as a raft of literature on 'indigenous knowledge' has begun to indicate.[30] But it is also important to ensure that local level institutions for making rules about resource use have representatives from the multiple groups that are affected by the rules in question. Members of these groups should also have opportunities to exercise a right to remove their representatives if the performance of the representatives is unsatisfactory as deemed by those affected by rules (Ribot, 1996).

Further, vesting the authority to arbitrate disputes in distant government agencies can only increase the costs of dispute resolution. Arrangements to decide local disputes within local groups by their representatives can be far more cost effective. Appeals against these decisions and disputes involving individuals from multiple groups could be settled in meetings attended by government officials and representatives from concerned local groups in a far more cost-effective manner. What is critical in the settlement of disputes is the easy availability of institutional locations where parties to a dispute can hope for decisions that are not systematically biased in favour of one set of social or political actors.

This does not eliminate the need for national or regional government involvement. Local actors often do not possess the material or political clout to fend off invasive actions by outsiders. Indeed, conflicts among them may need the arbitration or enforcement efforts of formal government agencies. And there is almost always room for non-exploitative technical assistance from extension agents regarding management techniques.

To say that local actors, with assistance from state actors, should possess the authority to make rules, implement them and resolve disputes, already specifies some of what the content of these rules should be: it should be what specific peoples and their representatives decide. Such an answer to the question, one might argue, leaves very real concerns unresolved. What if these local groups are dominated by élites? What if they have scant interest in conservation?

To such concerns, one response may be that specifying the concrete content of rules at different stages goes against the very notion of community-based management. A second response is more realistic and more pointed. It is precisely because of the deficiencies of centralized, exclusionary policies ('communities should protect wildlife, stop cutting trees, stop overgrazing, leave protected areas and so forth') that community-based management of resources has come to the fore. A focus on institutions does not necessarily lead to better outcomes (more biodiversity, more biomass, sustainable stock levels and so on) but it does offer the tools for understanding local-level processes and outcomes better. It also offers more concrete points of intervention and design than a general reliance on community.

It is important to recognize that not all local institutions can be changed in desired directions through an external intervention. Especially difficult to change would be deep-seated informal norms. Especially impotent in bringing about change would be policies that do not allow resources and authority to users for management, enforcement and dispute resolution.

This study's focus on institutions and organizations rather than on general beliefs about homogeneity of community members and norms in communities should not be taken to imply the imposition of an external value on local actors. Indeed, part of the burden of this discussion is to undermine precisely such arguments about communities being self-contained entities, independent of external pressures and values. All communities always have been impacted by factors beyond their control. The values and social structures that prevail within any group are the result of its interactions with actors and factors that are presumed to be external. To this extent, the only choice that exists is about the nature of external pressures for which it is possible to advocate. To believe in the existence of community values, as if they arise spontaneously from within and are therefore necessarily superior to values espoused by outsiders is naivety at (its) best.

The plea to establish partnerships between state actors and those within local contexts comes with two crucial qualifications. First, we must recognize that state officials and local representatives are located within asymmetric organizational structures. They enjoy access to very different levels of resources and power. We are all familiar with contexts where state officials use their superior powers violently to impose non-negotiated solutions. It may be in such contexts, where state officials are willing to use power coercively, that community as a symbolic figure for mobilization may make sense. But even here, advocating for community may be self-defeating without attention to how multiple local groups and peoples can come together in organizations/federations that can collectively oppose coercive solutions.

Even where state actors are willing to establish partnerships, many-to-one relationships between local and state actors may only advantage the structurally more powerful state actors. For local users and actors to possess leverage in their dealings with state officials, it is imperative that they organize themselves into larger collectives or federations that can span the gap between the local and the national. To advocate for community-based conservation without simultaneously considering how resource users in multiple locations can organize to offset state power is to advocate structures that can be overwhelmed by state actors at will.

A second qualification also flows from the recognition of asymmetric power relations between state actors and those dependent on resources and without access to formal power structures. But it also accepts that local actors have the ability to alter introduced institutions in unanticipated ways. External forces, such as new state policies in relation to community-based conservation, can drastically change the shape of existing local institutions (Agrawal and Yadama, 1997; Peluso, 1996). But introduced changes will be contested in the local context, their limits tested and their meanings transformed by the communities whose actions they are supposed to alter.

In light of the above discussion of multiple actors and interests, political processes and institutional arrangements around conservation, a different conceptualization of the relationship between different aspects of local groups, their representatives and resource management outcomes is possible. Such a conceptualization would highlight differences within groups, attend to institutional arrangements and processes that recognize these differences and promote negotiated settlements about how resources are to be used and managed. It would also focus on the means through which those groups at the local level can come together and produce platforms for negotiating with powerful government actors. Characteristics related to size, composition, levels of dependence on the resource, prevailing norms and types of technology would have an impact on resource management.

But rather than assuming that these kinds of characteristics will lead to similar impacts always, it will be necessary to see how they affect interactions of different actors around conservation. Interactions will be shaped by and would simultaneously shape prevailing institutions. Viewed at any one point in time, institutions may be seen as constraints on political processes and the actions of individuals. Over time, however, they are under constant contestation and (re)formation through the performances and negotiations of actors.

CONCLUSION

The focus of this study is community, and how communities have found a place in recent discussions of conservation. This focus is motivated by the belief that ultimately environmental outcomes unfold at micro levels and therefore it is necessary to understand how local social structures influence, shape and subvert larger processes. Much literature that seeks to understand the effects of environmental change devotes attention to international agreements and negotiations, global processes and international or national level political structures. But the belief that such phenomena are the most important in understanding environmental politics, or that by attending to these macro-structures and processes it is possible to know environmental dynamics is precisely what my focus on local action and its role in conservation seeks to undermine.

In examining the role of community in recent writings on conservation, this study suggests that to understand the impact of environmental changes, it is also critical to gain an understanding of a cascade of institutional and social structures and processes. Although it is important to understand processes that occur at levels far removed from that of the everyday lives of humans, the real import of such processes can be assessed better by analysing more locally situated phenomena. As Breckenridge (1992, p. 736) observes, 'grassroots empowerment has become a centerpiece of the environmental agenda' and 'the articulation of international environmental requirements is accompanied, strikingly, by a new recognition of local communities' roles in protecting biological diversity and ecosystem viability'.

To analyse community-based conservation, this study begins by casting a critical historical eye at the notion of community. Although in agreement that the celebration of community is a move in the right direction, I argued that the form of community with which conservationists are often preoccupied is limiting, and inattentive to political and social differences. Much of the existing literature on community-based conservation reveals a widespread preoccupation with what might be called 'the mythic community': small, integrated groups using locally evolved norms to manage resources sustainably and equitably.

Such characteristics describe few, if any, existing communities. The vision of 'the mythic community' fails to attend to differences within local populations whom conservationists seek to empower. By casting communities as unified actors, the vision of the mythic community ignores how social stratification and institutional processes affect conservation goals, the differential access of the multiple actors within local populations to channels of influence, and the possibility of 'layered alliances' spanning levels of politics.

Small, territorially attached and relatively homogeneous groups of local peoples, where they exist, may find it easy to make decisions collectively. But there is little reason to believe that such groups will necessarily meet conservationist expectations. In any case, such groups will find it difficult to withstand external threats (even from other groups competing for access to the same resources), or manage resources that have a wide geographical spread. A focus on the shared norms of local groups is also incomplete because norms may not prevent over-exploitation of resources, and they are scarcely amenable to change through external interventions.

This chapter, although sympathetic to the advocacy of community, suggests that it is necessary to move the emphasis away from some usual assumptions: small size, territorial fixity, group homogeneity and shared understandings and identities. Instead, it is necessary to focus on the divergent interests of multiple actors within groups, the political interactions in which these interests emerge, and the institutions that influence the outcomes of political processes. This changed focus is especially apposite in a globalizing world if those against the tyranny of the market and the state are to find 'points of leverage'. Rather than seeing globalization as a behemoth intent on erasing heterogeneity and forcing similarity on the world in the image of the West, it is necessary to move away from traditional visions of what makes community and instead examine how alliances spanning place and place-based identities may be possible and necessary.

Seeing globalization simply as the juggernaut that is to be opposed by resistance based in communities conforming to traditional forms will be a mistake both in terms of apprehending the variability of the forms that globalization assumes, and understanding the variability in potential points of engagement. The forces and strategies that combine to produce the effect called globalization cannot be contested simply by adhering to outdated assumptions about community, identity and belonging. Believers in community must recognize and deploy new forms of and opportunities for communication, interactions and alliances.

This chapter advocates for a changed emphasis for those who believe in locally oriented management of resources and a move away from states and markets. Greater autonomy to local groups means that external actors would have to relinquish control over the rules and the outcomes of community-based conservation. Additionally, the directions in which institutional outcomes in local spaces will unfold cannot be plotted precisely; they can only be roughly assessed. Demands for greater certainty suffer from the same utopian longings that identify community-as-shared-norms as the solution to problems of conservation.

NOTES

1. Throughout the chapter, I use the terms conservation, resource use and resource management interchangeably: renewable resources such as forests, pastures, wildlife and fish have been, are being, and will always be used by people; those who wish to conserve must incorporate use and management in their strategies (Robinson and Redford, 1991, p. 3).
2. See, for example, Eckholm (1976). Ives and Messerli (1989) present a discussion of some of the literature, especially in the Himalayan context.
3. See Ostrom (1990) for a discussion of how the metaphors of the 'Prisoner's Dilemma' and the 'Logic of Collective Action' have been important in shaping understandings about the (im)possibility of cooperation.
4. Although new beliefs have entered the picture, not all who think about the role of community in resource use have begun to subscribe to new views. The result is a complex mosaic of notions about how villages or other non-urban groups may be connected to the resources upon which they depend. The ensuing lines on community in conservation attempt to pick on the most important beliefs that depart from earlier themes.
5. An enormous outpouring of literature bears witness. See Bhatt (1990), Ghai (1993) and Gurung (1992). See also Wisner (1990) for a review.
6. Scholars in developed countries have also argued for the importance of community in resource management. See Huntsinger and McCaffrey (1995) for a study of the state against the Yurok in the United States, and Hoban and Cook (1988) for a critique of the conservation provision of the US Farm Bill of 1985 for its inadequate involvement of local communities.
7. Ecologists have also underscored the limits of the state in protecting resources. Even if states had the power to enforce perfectly, some ecologists argue that protected areas are often too small to maintain valued biological diversity (Newmark, 1996).
8. Anderson and Posey (1989) present a later work on the same group of Indians. For a strong critique of Posey's work, see Parker (1993).

9. For two examples of this view, see Lynch and Talbott (1995) and Poffenberger (1990). Often the last part of the claim is probabilistically modified, 'Communities are likely to prove the best managers'.
10. See the various chapters in Western and Wright (1994) for an elaboration of this perspective, and Gibson and Marks (1995) for a critique.
11. Zerner's essay on *sasi* (1994), a highly variable body of practices linked to religious beliefs and cultural beliefs about nature in Indonesia's Maluku islands, also makes the same point. Current images of *sasi* depict it as a body of customary environmental law promoting sustainable development. *Sasi* has, thus, emerged as a site and a resource for social activists to contest an oppressive, extractive political economy. In *sasi*, the rhetoric of local environmental management can be united with culturally distinctive communities. The result is an unusually potent political metaphor. See also Baines (1991) for a similar argument in relation to assertions on the basis of traditional rights in the Solomon Islands.
12. One exception can be found in Singleton and Taylor (1992, p. 315). They conceive of community as implying a set of people with some shared beliefs, stable membership, who expect to interact in the future, and whose relations are direct (unmediated), and over multiple issues. Significantly, they do not include shared space, size or social composition, a concern of many other writers, in their discussion.
13. For a review of some of this literature, see Bhattacharya (1995).
14. See, for example, Donovan (1994), Hill and Press (1994) and Poffenberger (1994). The point is not that links between group size and the emergence of community are non-existent. It is, rather, that such links, if present, require substantial attention and institutionalization if they are to become a foundation for community-based conservation.
15. Indeed, the place-attachment of community is evident not just in conservation-related studies. Three recent books on community in the United States also focus on place and localism, social solidarity and the grounding of daily life as issues of community (Heskin, 1991; Powers, 1991; Rouner, 1991).
16. For example, Murphree (1993) refers to the 'optimal' size for communities (around 90 families) for revenue sharing schemes incorporated within the CAMPFIRE wildlife programme in Zimbabwe. See also Agrawal and Goyal (2000) for a game theoretic argument about the relationship between group size and successful collective action in the context of resource management by village residents.
17. See Twyman (1998, p. 763) who provides evidence about how the wildlife conservation programme in Botswana, based on community participation, conceptualized the community as a cohesive and homogeneous actor.
18. Taylor (1982) uses anthropological and historical sources to provide an extensive survey of hierarchy and stratification within even supposedly egalitarian communities.
19. See Western (1994) whose study of the Amboseli National Reserve shows, even though this is not a focus of the study, the differences within the putative community of 'Masai'. Agrawal (1999) and Robbins (1996) point to stratification within Raika pastoralist groups who see themselves as distinct from landowners within their villages.
20. For similar proscriptions on cutting particular tree species, see Dorm-Adzobu and Veit (1991).
21. See, for example, Nikijuluw (1994) for a discussion of *sasi* and *Petuanang*, which influence harvests of fish; and Rajasekaran and Warren (1994) for a discussion of sacred forests among the *Malaiyala Gounder* in the *Kolli* hills in India.
22. Michael Dove demonstrates how developers, planners, academics and bureaucrats working with the *Kantu* of *Kalimantan* incorporated their own desires, hopes and fears into the construction of a local 'community' (Dove, 1982).
23. The history of massive deforestation that occurred even prior to industrialization, and recent empirical literature that shows wasteful practices among indigenous groups, shows that 'the indigenous' cannot be identified with a conservation ethic. See Abrams et al. (1996) for a review of evidence in the case of the early Mayans and Fairservis (1976) for the Harappan civilization.

24. Western and Wright broach this idea in their first chapter (1994). See also the discussion in Wells and Brandon (1992) who point out that sometimes communities may not be as effective as state officials in protecting resources or ensuring conservation.
25. Tully (1994) presents a clear argument about how Western theories of property, which provided the justification for taking over lands from native Americans, were founded on land being used for agricultural purposes.
26. For insightful discussions of how tradition may often be only recently created but change through politicized memory into a timeless, unchanging tradition, see Hobsbawm and Ranger (1983). Related work on how the past may be constituted in the present, or exert a strong influence to shape contemporary regimes of conservation, see Saberwal (1996) and Sivaramakrishnan (1995). In various forms these points are also being made in several recent writings on community, but rarely together. For some representative works, see Anderson and Grove (1989), Baviskar (1995) and Sivaramakrishnan (1996).
27. The reverse also holds true. Power is visible only when it is put in action – its workings cannot be imagined or understood outside of the trace it leaves on processes. See Foucault (1983, pp. 219–20).
28. Indeed, the list of the possible political-economic factors that impact upon processes at the local level can be increased several times without redundancy. See Sanderson (1994) and the other essays in Meyer and Turner (1994) that examine land use and cover change more generally.
29. For this conceptualization of the different domains, we have drawn upon a number of different works, even if the manner in which we state them might differ from the works we have consulted. See especially Agrawal (1996), Dahlman (1980), Ostrom (1990), Ostrom and Schlager (1995) and Schlager and Ostrom (1992).
30. The local knowledge of different members of a community, also often called time- and place-information (Hayek, 1937; Ostrom et al., 1993), may be invaluable to the success of conservation projects. The entire corpus of writings on indigenous knowledge is based precisely on this premise (Chambers, 1979; Richards, 1985). For the significance of such information and the need to incorporate local expertise, see also Jagannathan (1987) and Tendler (1975).

PART TWO

Ecological Political Economy and Critical
Theory

4. Democracy, Ecology, Political Economy: Reflections on Starting Points

Laurie Adkin

BEGINNINGS

The editors of this book have asked us to think about the elements of an 'integrated ecological political economy' that might provide 'a theoretical framework that leads to practical proposals to restructure social practices in the interests of the environment and the people who depend on it'. While I share their holistic bent, I confess that the ambition underlying this formulation strikes fear into my heart – a fear that goes by the name of hubris! It has been difficult to grasp a thread on this infinite web, not because I see none, but because there are so many! Like Haraway (1990, p. 193) I am 'wary of holism, but needy for connection'. I feel somewhat reassured by the 'practical' qualification of this endeavour.

If I think of this grand project from the perspective of a *practitioner*, or partisan, in the various struggles that we might herd into the corral of 'ecological political economy', or 'political ecology', then my focus becomes the starting points for action, for mobilization, for discursive interventions. And as it becomes clearer to me that, as a practitioner, I can only begin from my own tenuous belonging to (and partial knowledge of) networks, communities and places, I also become aware of how my sense of *what needs to be done* has already been shaped by an extensive body of political and ecological thought.

I place 'political ecology' in quotation marks in these reflections since, having struggled for some years with my yearning for something to replace the kind of coherent world view that was provided by socialism, I have come to see the search for this kind of identity, or label for 'the' new social project, as putting the cart before the horse (Adkin, 2000). As Haraway (1990, p. 197) puts it: '*affinity* is the name of the game, not "identity"'. The task I see before me, therefore, is to identify the grounds for 'affinity' among our

59

many subject positions[1] (and to be attuned to the ways in which these are continually being reconstructed).

What kind of political-philosophical discourse can 'craft a poetic/political unity without relying on a logic of appropriation, incorporation, and taxonomic identification' (ibid., p. 198)? The projects we are seeking to construct will, of course, eventually name themselves (according to the ways in which they articulate culturally and historically specific struggles). But no 'political science' can foretell their names. On this matter, I adopt a Baptist stance![2]

Ecological perspectives are slowly penetrating many areas of social, economic and political (as well as scientific) theory; they are also contributing to concrete proposals for reforms and to strategic debates at multiple 'territorial' levels of collective action: local, regional, national and international. This impressive, multidisciplinary body of work sets out for us important guiding principles for programmes of reform. Increasingly, we do have a general *ecological* framework for understanding what kinds of change are necessary and possible.

However, the problem of how to intervene, or how to construct collective action for political-ecological reforms immediately requires that we identify the philosophical underpinnings and the historically and culturally specific contexts of such projects. Thus my contribution to this discussion takes the form not of an inventory of the elements of a grand theoretical framework ('ecological political economy'), or a blueprint of its structural architecture, but rather, some reflections on the relationships of such a project to democratic struggles[3] and their underlying assumptions about the good life, as well as on the problem of how to construct collective action for a *democratizing* political ecology.

ECOLOGICAL THINKING ABOUT ALTERNATIVES

In the 1970s, ecologists introduced evidence of natural 'limits' to the exploitation of resources, dumping of wastes, industrial growth and pollution underpinning the Fordist era of 'development' (entailing fossil-fuelled mass production for mass markets in the industrialized societies). These limits referred to the absorptive capacities of the earth and its atmosphere, to the finiteness of its resources, to the irreversibility of certain forms of destruction (of wilderness, biodiversity, poisoning of soils and water systems by, for example, radioactive contamination), to such concepts as bioaccumulation, ecosystem and the limits of technological hubris, and raised questions about scarcity and human population growth.

The first photographs of the 'blue planet' – seamless, fragile, finite and 'whole' – contributed to a shift in popular consciousness towards a 'global' framing of environmental and other issues. This framing neatly obscures, of course, the very real *political* boundaries which organize the planet's human population. While there may be finite limits to growth imposed by nature (even taking into account technological innovations), the question of who gets what share of the resources available is not a scientific or 'environmental' question *per se*, but a political one – one having to do with relationships of power.

Ecological arguments challenge neoclassical economics in profound ways. To provide a few examples: the cyclical processes of nature have been contrasted to the environmentally unsustainable linear processes of capitalist-productivist economies. Natural rhythms of life and regeneration (including climatic) are said to be threatened by the incessant acceleration of economic processes driven by technological innovations and growth imperatives (Sachs et al., 1997). Ecosystem sustainability as a foundation for local and regional economies has been proposed as an alternative to the currently centralized economies that are gobbling up the ecological 'carrying capacities of distant elsewheres' and contributing to global inequality (M'Gonigle, 1998b; Rees, 1992; Wackernagel and Rees, 1996). Instead, we are called upon to exercise the principles of restraint, prudence, reciprocity and respect.

Many general directions for a transition to an ecologically sustainable economy were summarized in the Wuppertal Institute's study, *Greening the North: A Post-Industrial Blueprint for Ecology and Equity* (Sachs et al., 1998), which I have summarized in Table 4.1 below. The ecological reforms proposed by European Green parties fly in the face of neo-liberal orthodoxy. Ecological objectives have been linked to the reduction of work time to reduce unemployment, and such a strategy is now being implemented in France (Gorz, 1989; Lipietz, 1993, 1996).[4]

Structural adjustment policies which compel Third World countries to pillage and export every available natural resource in order to repay debts are shown to be ecocidal not only for future development prospects in the South, but also for the populations of the North (as a consequence, for example, of accelerated global warming) (George, 1992). The developmentalist ideology and policies of international financial institutions and development agencies have also been challenged by the emergence of 'sustainable development' perspectives in the wake of the World Commission on Environment and Development Report (the Brundtland Commission, WCED, 1987) and the United Nations Conference on the Environment and Development (UNCED) (1992), not to mention the spectacular *débâcles* of various World Bank-funded 'development' projects. To some extent new concerns – such as the relationship between ecological sustainability and gender equality – have penetrated development thinking and policies in the 1990s (Agarwal, 1998; Kettel, 1998; Mies and Shiva, 1998; Shiva, 1989).

Table 4.1   Greening the North

Directions for a transition to an ecologically sustainable economy

- shifting from linear to cyclical production processes;
- orienting technological innovation towards the maximization of the productivity of resources, rather than towards the maximization of the productivity of labour;
- shifting taxation bases from the taxation of labour to the taxation of resource use;
- promoting 'sufficiency' as a good life, rather than consumerism;
- deceleration rather than acceleration of economic processes and transportation norms;
- reducing the distances over which economic inputs and goods are transported;
- shifting from a fossil fuel-based economy to alternatives (solar, biomass and conservation).

Source: compiled from Sachs et al. (1998)

ECOLOGY AS POLITICS: A HIGHLY CONTINGENT DISCOURSE

A thermodynamic definition of 'sustainability' (Daly, 1991a) may help us to understand why fossil-fuelled economies must be converted to a 'solar strategy', and may entail many consequences for existing economic arrangements (investment strategies, markets and so forth). Yet, whether or not 'sustainability' is articulated to a democratic project of social transformation, and what philosophy of human needs informs its political and social agenda, are questions which will only be resolved (and never decisively) by the discursive struggles of a multitude of different actors.

As many authors have pointed out, the Brundtland Commission's definition of 'sustainable development' – development which 'meets the needs of the present without compromising the ability of future generations to meet their own needs' (WCED, 1987, p. 8) – has been highly susceptible to such interpretations as the World Bank's: 'Sustainable development is development that lasts' (Sachs, 1993, p. 10), or to being equated with environmental management.

Big business had no difficulty endorsing *Our Common Future*'s reaffirmation of faith in the inventive potential of capitalism, science and technology, as well as the market, to solve environmental problems (Tokar, 1997; Welford and Starkey, 1996). One Canadian Chief Executive Officer (CEO) of a major mining corporation (Roy Aitken of INCO) thanked the commission for 'creating an intellectual climate within which industry could move' (quoted in Adkin, 1992, p. 137). The World Business Council for Sustainable Development, formed in 1990, was a key player in the subsequent UNCED meeting, and processes leading up to it (Elliott, 1997, pp. 126–7). The Business Council represents about 130 of the world's largest corporations, including 3M, Du Pont, Shell, Mitsubishi, ALCOA and British Petroleum (Dryzek, 1997, p. 128).

The interpretation of 'sustainable development' (SD) which has become predominant in international institutions, government and business circles emphasizes technological modernization and downplays equity issues. The content of 'development' itself has been largely preserved from critical examination. Dryzek (1997, p. 132) describes SD as 'a rhetoric of reassurance': 'We can have it all: economic growth, environmental conservation, social justice; and not just for the moment, but in perpetuity. No painful changes are necessary.'

The strategy of environmental modernization preferred by large corporations and their associations includes:[5]

- voluntary agreements rather than legislated regulation and monitoring by state agencies;
- renegotiation of permits and compliance deadlines (subject to ministerial discretion) rather than judicial enforcement of environmental regulations;
- close (and, if possible, closed-door) industry-government collaboration in the development of the regulatory framework; limitation of public involvement in consultation and decision-making processes;
- deregulation or reform of existing legislation to weaken environmental 'barriers' to investment and resource exploitation;[6]
- notwithstanding 'free market' ideology, corporations seek government subsidies or tax incentives for reduction of industrial emissions and clean-ups;
- externalization of the long-term environmental costs of production;

- continuation of tax and pricing regimes which maximize returns from resource extraction and export, while excluding proposals such as energy or environmental taxes; companies oppose taxes or energy price increases aimed at reducing emissions or energy throughputs.

At the end of this century, neo-liberal discourse has largely succeeded in defusing the threat to liberal productivism posed by the environmental movements of the 1970s and 1980s. This has been achieved in a number of ways that are too complex to describe in detail in this study. Market discipline has eroded the opportunity structures both for social movement activism and for alliances among labour movements and other social movements, and perhaps most of all – ecologists. Many environmentalists have been persuaded that market mechanisms offer the only achievable gains for environmental objectives. There has been a trend towards professionalization of environmental organizations, and the adoption of an environmental management approach linked to technological modernization, productivity improvements and technical expertise, and divorced from transformative social projects (Adkin, 1992; Sachs, 1989). This does not mean that environmental 'issues' are not being discussed in the media, university seminars, conferences and other venues.[7] As Sandilands (1998, p. 87) points out:

> The environment may be omnipresent as a topic of concern, but its political potential is under threat because of how the issues are approached and acted upon. Although issues continue to be raised (not insignificantly, through natural science), once raised they are passed over to panels of experts – planners, waste managers, engineers – with expediency taking absolute precedence over public discussion, over the light of scrutiny. Part of this desire for expediency resides in crisis-talk ('the planet must be saved in the fastest way possible'), and part of it resides in the expert and professional relations generated by environmentalism.

In this post-Brundtland environment, Canadian environmentalists, at least, appear to have made a number of adaptations that reinforce the discourse of environmental management. We might refer, for example, to:

- the concern among movement organizations to allocate scarce resources to institutional viability, and to the maintenance of core constituencies, leading them to focus on fewer 'target' issues;
- the growing specialization of labour among environmental organizations, which may create the perception that they are focusing on (and fund-raising in support of) 'single' issues, even if their *analyses* of these conflicts may be complex;

- the sense of urgency to prevent decisions and actions that will have irreversible outcomes, entailing the necessity to act in the absence of coalitions with other actors which require long-term investment and commitment (court actions to delay or prevent environmentally destructive projects). Such situations are presented more frequently as the regulatory framework created in the 1980s is eroded and governments abdicate monitoring and enforcement functions (Adkin, 1998a).

The manner of the integration of many environmentalists into government-corporate consultation processes, and their professionalization/separation from a grassroots social movement,[8] appears to have reinforced the predominant popular perception of 'environmentalism' (to which ecology is reduced) as a blinkered concern with wilderness conservation on the part of a (fanatical) band of ascetics.[9] There is thus a significant disjuncture, in Canada, between 'social' or 'political' ecology (which may be predominantly academic discourses) and the public representations of environmentalists by the media, and, arguably, by themselves. Despite such pedagogical efforts as David Suzuki's television series, *The Nature of Things*, there is little association of ecology with a complex analysis of social conflict or with an alternative 'blueprint' for societal development.[10]

As one veteran of Canadian Green politics states: '"Ecology" keeps being degraded or narrowed into "environmentalism"' (Timmerman, 1998, p. 332). The construction of numerous conflicts as having 'environmental' stakes which are opposed to 'economic' or 'livelihood' stakes seems to have become as self-replicating as the coded term 'political correctness' (Smith, 1995).[11] In both cases, figuring out why and how this replication proceeds sheds light on hegemonic interests and agency, and merits more attention.[12]

Possible explanations include: shrinking sources of public funding and other resources for mobilizing; a failure on the part of environmental activists and organizations to appreciate the importance of articulating environmental objectives to a broader societal project, or their belief that the conditions for such a project do not exist. Alternatively, environmental activists may *lack* the kind of societal discourse associated with 'social' ecology; they may view their activities in any number of other ways (including anti-humanist or conservative world views). Attempts to build coalitions with other social actors (for example, the labour movement) may have failed, leading to a sense of hopelessness or antagonism.

To explain public perceptions of environmentalists, we also need to examine media representations of 'events' or 'issues' involving environmentalists. Arguably, these: (a) emphasize conflict with other social interests or actors (especially workers and livelihood issues); (b) provide little contextualization of these conflicts; and (c) do not explore alternatives to the status quo framing of these conflicts and the available solutions. A further concern is the marginalization, or disappearance of, environmental issues in the agendas of political parties and government discourse.[13] Lastly, the political insignificance of provincial and federal Canadian Green parties relative to their counterparts in Western Europe is part of the explanation for the weak politicization of ecological critiques and alternatives, and calls for more comparative analysis (Sandilands, 1992; Timmerman, 1998).

Although the sketch provided here of some of the existing signposts for an 'ecological political economy' is incomplete, it suggests that we do already have many insights regarding what needs to be done, in order to shift our societies towards a new, ecologically sustainable future. However, it is equally evident that the transformative potential of this knowledge is by no means assured. Whether ecological knowledge will substantially subvert and redirect the hegemonic model of development – in any part of the globe – will be determined by the discursive struggles of social actors. It is here that we confront very difficult questions regarding the possibilities for, or ways of conceptualizing, collective action from various starting points (including the 'territorial' ones: local, regional, national and international).

COLLECTIVE ACTION; OR, SHE GOT ON HER HORSE AND RODE OFF IN ALL DIRECTIONS

In thinking about collective action as a political sociologist, trained in comparative methodology, I tend not to think in purely metaphysical terms, or in terms of international state systems, but in terms of comparisons among spatially and temporally delimited local, regional, or national 'cases'.[14] I find it quite impossible to conceptualize collective action (for an 'integrated ecological political economy' or any other project) at a universal level of abstraction and have instead sought to ground my responses in specific contexts. For example, we could discuss collective action in relation to proposals to reform the international trade and financial, as well as environmental regulatory regimes, aimed at instituting new rules that will permit more ecologically sustainable and equitable development choices. In the following section I outline in very broad terms some of the emerging possibilities for a global discourse of 'ecological political economy' – its agenda of reforms, the actors likely to advance this agenda and their possible collective identities. Yet this is only one of the directions in which our question rides off. My own work has focused on the Canadian and European contexts of these problems, and it is to these regional, national and local contexts that I will subsequently turn.

Global Political Ecology: Universal Citizenship or Global Apartheid?

This is without doubt the most complex and difficult level at which to mobilize collective action or to construct new (global) identities, given the existing political organization of the world's population by nation-states and these states' various international associations and commitments. Yet there is evidence that consensus may eventually be constructed in support of reforms aimed at countering the neo-liberal, patriarchal and racist-imperialist orthodoxies that have deepened both social inequalities and the ecological crisis. For example, calls have been growing for the democratization of the structures of international financial institutions (the World Bank and the International Monetary Fund (IMF)) and a restructuring of their functions and mandates. Some have characterized the environmental or 'environment and development' conferences and accords of the last two decades as an emerging framework of international environmental regulation (its considerable inadequacies notwithstanding). Altvater (1998, p. 35) observes:

> As a result of global communications and global networks, nation states and the diplomats representing national governments are losing their monopoly in shaping international relations. 'Civil society' is in the process of becoming internationalized and transnationalized . . . The threat to the natural environment has led, on the one hand, to 'new concerns' . . . and, on the other hand, to international networks which are growing into organisational forms. In the meantime, NGOs have taken on important tasks in the negotiation of international agreements, particularly in the realm of environment and development.

Important actors in this regard, as Altvater argues, are the international NGOs, linked to coalitions and social movements in countries around the world, and working in such areas as environmental protection, human rights, Third World development and gender equality. Not only do the international conventions in these areas have regulatory effects, but the campaigns leading up to their establishment alter the terrain of discursive struggles, for example, regarding the legitimacy of decisions made by local governments and other actors (for example, corporations, development agencies, unions).

As the 'blue planet' suggests, ecology, like humanism, is evocative of universal identities (global citizenship, humankind) which supersede nationalist identities and constructions of human conflicts. Some observers have argued, for example, that a universal conception of citizenship, based on the discourse of human rights, is increasingly being invoked in struggles around the territorial authority of nation-states over their citizens (Soysal, 1994).[15] The international campaign against the Multilateral Agreement on Investment (MAI) has been led by a diverse network of organizations, in which environmental NGOs have figured prominently. In this case, governments are being called upon not to cede to multinational corporations their sovereign powers to regulate the terms of investment within their territories.

While this campaign therefore constructs nation-states as necessary bulwarks against the predations of highly mobile global finance capital and the interests of multinational corporations, it also seeks to identify grounds for solidarity among 'peoples' around the world – to construct, perhaps, an international (citizens') common front against the (global) imperialist ambitions of international capital.

However, as we know, international environmental campaigns, and various forms of environmentalism (most notably, neo-Malthusian), may also link environmental concerns to societal discourses which are neither solidaristic nor democratic. They may construct understandings of human nature which differ little from that of Hobbes, and, indeed, the view that 'human nature is fatally flawed' by incapacity for foresight, by greed, or uncontrollable drives, is often expressed in environmentalists' explanations of environmental destruction and Third World poverty, and may be articulated to racist, Eurocentric and authoritarian discourses.

'Environmentalism' may also turn a blind eye to the global inequities of resource exploitation, seeking to 'green' capitalist economies in the North while the highly polluting basic industries are relocated to the South. This is precisely the danger signalled by Sachs (1992), who argues that environmentalism in the North may ultimately opt for a strategy of 'containment', in which 'the negative consequences of the over-exploitation of resources and sinks in the "South"' are confined in order 'to perpetuate the accumulation model, mode of regulation, and cherished lifestyle of the privileged industrialized countries in the North'. That is, 'affluent societies try to secure their access to resources and sinks, but must ensure that others make the necessary sacrifices to stay within the recognised limits of global ecosystems' (Altvater, 1998, pp. 32–3). Altvater warns against an emerging 'global apartheid'.

> The principle of equality of needs, wants and rights for all human beings in the world is being replaced with another one: the principle of rationing limited resources of highly utilized and partly overburdened ecosystems (resources and sinks). One part of humanity is assigned a large ration while another part gets only a small ration. In the 'new' world order, the rationing effects of the price mechanism (citizens of G7 countries with an annual income of $20 000 can claim larger shares than citizens of G77 countries with an annual per capita income of $500) is being perfected by economic, political and military means (ibid., p. 33).

Thus, in the discourse of international institutions and actors, ecology may help to construct an egalitarian conception of universal citizenship, or it may contribute to the institutionalization of a new form of global apartheid. The lesson we should draw from this is the determining importance of the discursive struggles that seek to articulate ecological knowledge to other elements of political discourse.

WE ARE ALWAYS THINKING AND ACTING LOCALLY AND GLOBALLY SIMULTANEOUSLY

It is often said that in building coalitions for a project of social change, we need to start from where we are – from a knowledge of a place, its social configuration, political economy, cultural characteristics, its natural 'resources', and so on. If we reflect on our daily practice as critical intellectuals, this is what we do when we intervene in 'local', 'provincial' or 'national' debates. In this sense there is a tremendous fluidity in the territorial crossings of our interventions. Many of the actors in these conflicts (unions, environmental organizations, corporations) exist organizationally and function at multiple levels (local, provincial, national, international). At issue is not whether certain conflicts are 'local' and others are 'global' (or national and so on), but how we cast our net when trying to interpret the meanings of these conflicts, and alternatives for their resolution. I have difficulty conceiving of any 'local' conflict involving environmentalists that is not enmeshed in a complex web of political, economic and juridical relationships, which will be referred to in explanations of the conflict, called upon as resources by the antagonists in the conflict, and which will play a role in determining the possible outcomes of the conflict.

Almost any ongoing conflict involving environmentalists, workers, communities, corporations and governments would serve as an example here. A handful that comes to mind within Alberta alone includes multinational companies' logging, pulp and paper operations in the northern boreal forest, the expansion of oil extraction from the tar sands, the provincial government's Special Places policy and Natural Heritage Act (introduced in 1999),[16] oil and gas well drilling and exploitation in provincial parks, and the proposed coal mine on the border of Jasper National Park (see Appendix 1). None of these conflicts or the webs of actors involved in them are in any way purely 'local', although intervention in them does, of course, call for local *knowledge* – and for 'situated' knowledge – about experiences of inequality, exclusion, deprivation and dis-ease.

The problem of collective action for radical social change, therefore, lies not in what has been represented as the 'fragmentation' of the 'central' social conflict (which established a hierarchy of priorities) into a multitude of 'single-issue' struggles or identities. Nor does it consist of the disintegration of a national (political) project into localized struggles or identities. The problem of collective action lies in transforming the *meanings* of social conflicts in such a way that the commonalities, or affinities, among different subordinate subject positions become evident to their participants. This simultaneously means demonstrating the links among conflicts with different spatial locations – thus, showing how what is going on in one place is connected to what is going on in another place.

The territorial problem of collective action (should coalition-building efforts be focused locally (urban-based), regionally or provincially, nationally or globally?) is a problem mainly in regard to a particular understanding of politics and of power, and this perspective's territorial and reductionist framing of the 'central' political struggle as one opposing nation-states to global capital. Within some Canadian left circles, at least, the restoration of national (state) sovereignty *vis-à-vis* global capital has been seen to depend on a renaissance of nationalist identity. This identity is mobilized largely in opposition to a 'globalization agenda' (or something similar) which is frequently, in Canada, conflated by left-nationalists with 'Americanism' or 'Americanization' (Laxer, 2000). There is, in any case, some 'other' identity or values which are said to be antithetical/threatening to 'Canadian' values, traditions or interests.

Why is this strategy of collective action problematic for a project of democratic political ecology? First, the construction of nationalist (Canadian) identity (as the collective identity of a broad-based social movement) necessarily rests upon a binary opposition (us/them) that is both hierarchical ('our' values are better than 'their' values) and falsely homogenizing (obscures important internal differences on axes of class, race, gender, region, political orientation and so on). These criticisms mesh with the problems of nation-state framing examined in more detail by Conca in Chapter 8. Second, the left-nationalist discourse attributes the central agency role to the state, or to the élites which direct state policy, whose performance is judged in relation to how well or poorly they are seen to be defending the 'national interests'.[17] All kinds of consequences flow from the conceptualization of power as, ultimately, the capacity of corporations and states to determine economic outcomes, and hence as a zero-sum game in which more 'power' for one means less 'power' for the other. This conception of politics implicitly privileges the institutional competition for control of the nation-state and makes such control the primary objective of mobilization.

Apart from the limitations of such understandings of power and politics, there is certainly a danger that the national/global or inside/outside oppositions of left-nationalist discourse may obscure and subordinate such axes of analysis as ecology, race and gender, along with their criticisms of the hegemonic modern conceptions of economic and social progress (which have been shared by liberals, social democrats, dependency theorists and Marxists). Let us therefore try to take seriously the conception of our project not as 'a logic of appropriation, incorporation and taxonomic identification' (nationalist or otherwise), but as the crafting of a 'poetic/political unity'.

The rejection of nationalist identity (as a mobilizing discourse) is not equivalent to rejecting the importance of states' regulatory roles (either with regard to domestic regulation or to international regulatory regimes). Oppositional struggles for a 'liveable' world need, however, to be interpreted as *democratic struggles*, in order to build *the most inclusive solidarities possible*. We can talk about democratizing political institutions to enhance participatory citizenship, meaningful decision making for communities, or solidarity with groups/communities elsewhere, without laying claim to particular values or orientations as 'national' ones that set us apart from 'less civilized' nations elsewhere. We can defend particular visions of the good life without claiming that these are what define 'us as a nation', and differentiate us from other nations.

DEMOCRATIC STRUGGLE, IN ALL DIRECTIONS

My conceptualization of collective action as a gradual and expansive form of counter-hegemonic struggle that seeks to link together (and thereby to radicalize and transform) diverse forms of struggle against inequality, oppression, deprivation and dis-ease by means of democratic discourse, does not imply a 'working out' from a logic which is rooted in ecological knowledge, or a picture in which ecology is 'at the centre' of a web. It is not *ecology per se*, which provides the meaning of all of the other struggles to which we wish to connect ecology, but the way in which ecology is articulated to these other struggles (for example, for 'social justice', or gender equality, or anti-racism). Likewise, the political meaning (or 'identity') of ecology is transformed by its innumerable and shifting articulations to other such 'elements' of discourse.

What it means to be an 'ecologist' (or, for that matter, a feminist) is determined by the connections established between a view of appropriate and desirable human-nature relationships, and an underlying philosophy of human needs and of justice. This 'philosophy' is necessarily a partial perspective, rooted in a situated knowledge (Haraway, 1991).[18] We need to draw on this knowledge (though not exclusively) in order to grasp the possibilities for articulating ecological goals to an agenda of social, economic and political reforms *in particular contexts*.[19]

In my work on the problem of political ecology and collective action in the Canadian context, I have argued that ecologists need to articulate their struggles to those of other subjects in ways that construct shared understandings of a 'good' life (its essential conditions), and that it is only *through the examination of their relationships* that the meaning of various struggles are transformed, radicalized, and their commonalities discovered. Such initiatives will not lead far in the absence of interlocutors, of course. Movement-building is a long-term commitment that may need to begin with deconstructing stereotypes, or putting aside historical grievances, and this process can only succeed when there is a willingness to acknowledge the relationships of power and privilege which have too often been represented as mere 'differences', or as 'natural', or as having origins outside the relationship itself.

Clearly, for those who enjoy privileged subject positions, there must be incentives (negative or positive) to engage in such disarming. Likewise, for those who occupy subordinate positions in these relationships, there must be grounds for trust. In my experience, it is through the work of coalition-building itself that such transformations – such discursive shifts – become possible (which is not to say that they always happen). It is when the old categories constructing (opposing or different) interests give way to new constructions of conflict that new solutions or alternatives also become thinkable.

These are the stakes of attempts by ecologists to propose feasible economic alternatives to workers and communities whose livelihoods are dependent on resource exploitation, or chemicals and automobile manufacturing, or other economic activities. In the absence of such efforts, not only will ecologists repeatedly be opposed in such struggles by alliances of corporations and their workforces, but they will lack the *knowledges* of these workers which are essential to the *creation* of alternatives.

On the other hand, workers' organizations bear a responsibility to critically re-examine old commitments to a model of economic growth and distribution of wealth which offers less and less in the way of sustainable livelihoods, or a good life for the majority, and which confronts finite limits. The shrinking room for employed workers to manoeuvre (to protect particular interests) within the changing parameters of this model has encouraged some workers' organizations to enter into dialogues with environmentalists around the possible alternatives of 'sustainable development' (Adkin, 1998a).[20]

Such engagements between workers and environmentalists constitute only one point of intersection in a very complex web of such intersections, in the construction of collective action for a common agenda of social, political and economic reforms. Others that seem particularly important in the Organisation for Economic Co-operation and Development (OECD) countries today include: ecology/movements of the unemployed; ecology/gender equality; ecology/anti-racism; and ecology/inter-generational needs (such as child care and care/integration of the elderly).

In the 1970s and early 1980s the most prominent social movements in Western Europe and North America were the environmental, peace, Third World solidarity and women's movements (and the black civil rights and Native American movements in the case of the United States). Today, it is anti-poverty organizations and movements of the unemployed that are moving to centre stage. Since the mid-1980s new populist parties of the right, many espousing xenophobic, anti-immigrant views, have shifted the terms of political discourse and attached significant sectors of electorates in many countries. Ethnic nationalisms have taken hold in many of the regions undergoing extreme social and economic dislocation following the collapse of the communist states.

What do these conflicts mean for ecologists? What do they mean for an 'ecological political economy'? What positions should political ecologists in France, for example, take towards the *Front National*, or government expulsions of the *sans papiers*? What positions should Canadian ecologists take on racism towards immigrants from Asian countries? Is there a specific *ecological* perspective on such issues? I would argue that there is not – that what we need to link such issues is a democratic discourse, and a philosophy of human needs.[21]

These examples demonstrate, again, that it is not ecology *per se* (as a set of perspectives about the necessary and desirable relationship between humans and nature) that provides the meaning of every other social struggle, but rather, ecology becomes linked to these struggles in particular ways through the discursive practices adopted by ecologists.

Let us focus for a moment on some possible linkages between ecological goals, unemployment, gender inequalities and other social conditions widely characteristic of North American and Western European societies today. In these societies, I would argue, substantial majorities are experiencing – though from different subject positions – deprivations and dis-ease which are linked to the changing conditions of work (including acceleration and intensification effects, the 'just-in-time' workforce), insecurity of subsistence and the consumption and lifestyle patterns that these conditions reproduce and reinforce.[22]

Given this reading of how and why people are suffering (and its underlying 'philosophy' of the good life), I find many useful, practical answers to the above questions in the debates and programmes of the European green movements, which have had to develop responses to all of these developments. In the programme of the French Greens, for example, a very persuasive case is made for reforms which advance the principles of egalitarianism, or solidarity, individual freedom and ecology (*Les Verts,* 1994, 1995, 1999; Lipietz, 1989, 1993, 1996, 1999).

The proposal to reduce work time and to increase 'free' (or leisure, or 'self-directed') time is put forward as, simultaneously, a (partial) solution to unemployment, an improvement in the quality of life for those employed, an egalitarian way of redistributing gains in productivity and wealth production, a condition for redressing the unequal sexual division of domestic labour, and a condition for changing consumption norms that underpin excessive resource exploitation and waste production. I would add to this list the possible implications for the social opportunity structures for involved and participatory citizenship: people who have more free time and greater security of subsistence are more likely to participate in a whole range of social, cultural and political activities.

More free time would create, at least, the *potential* for individuals to substitute their own labour power for purchased services and goods (for example, house repairs, gardening, cooking); it would allow more involvement in activities (playing with children, visiting elderly parents, exercise, recreation, socializing with friends, learning, and so on) which *require* time; it would reduce the necessity of reliance on high-speed and private modes of transportation. More free time thus makes more possible the de-linking of our ways of living from commodity, transportation and communication circuits (everything from fast food, to how we get to work, to things we buy as substitutes for giving time) which consume energy throughputs. This is not to say that some of the activities we choose to pursue with our free time will not also entail the purchase of goods or services, or that the reduction of work time alone will be sufficient to reorient consumer choices in 'ecological' directions.

This dimension of the argument needs to be understood in conjunction with other aspects of the agenda of economic and social reforms being proposed (for example, the concomitant reduction in income for the highest earning groups, some form of minimum guaranteed universal income, the creation of a 'third sector' of socially and environmentally useful labour) and with other elements of the ecological agenda (for example, transition from fossil fuel and nuclear forms of energy to conservation and other alternatives; redesign of cities) in order to appreciate the complexity of the possible outcomes of increasing free time. This agenda of economic and social reforms provides, at least, a framework for achieving the kind of 'sufficiency' revolution that Sachs and others have argued is necessary not only for greening the 'North', but for reducing global inequalities in resource consumption.

The expansion of economic blocs whose mode of regulation is oriented towards an egalitarian growth of free time and security of subsistence (through increased employment and minimum universal income) also has important implications for the global regime of capitalist accumulation. The neo-liberal model promotes export-led growth and competition for markets based (in large part) on the reduction of labour costs. Lipietz refers to the possible reduction in domestic demand for imported goods, which will function as a kind of 'quiet protectionism' (market-determined rather than state-regulated).

In ecological and global justice terms, reduced consumption (of imports) in the OECD economies will correspond to a reduced drawing on the 'carrying capacities of distant elsewheres', and reduce the demand which is fuelling the pillage of Third World countries' resources by multinational corporations. How and whether such changes 'translate' into opportunities for a reorientation of production within Third World countries towards meeting the needs of the majorities and the goal of gender equality, towards ecologically sustainable forms of economic activity and so on, will of course be determined by struggles within those countries, as well as by the struggles to reform the priorities and the representative structures of international economic and political institutions.

This is, of course, a very incomplete picture of the kinds of proposals that have been made by Lipietz and others, and there is no space here to enter into a discussion of their claims, or even the assumptions about conceptions of happiness and well-being which underpin them. Clearly, these proposals do stem from a particular interpretation of the ways in which the majorities in the OECD countries are experiencing (more precisely – suffering) many aspects of their living conditions. (This interpretation draws not only on various kinds of statistical documentation (medical, sociological and so on), which provides evidence for particular characterizations of these experiences, but also on simply 'listening' to the ways in which many individuals are experiencing their lives, and reflecting on our own 'life worlds'.)

This interpretation therefore also expresses (more or less explicitly depending on the author and the approach) a 'philosophy' of the 'good' life – of our needs and desires as members of these societies, differently situated in important ways, but interconnected insofar as we are all implicated in certain social relationships, institutions and regulatory frameworks which discipline, circumscribe and direct our options and choices.

This underlying philosophy of the good life, and the agenda of reforms which derives from it, leads us to certain conclusions regarding the agency for such a social project. In identifying those 'social subjects' who have the greatest stakes in the realization of such an agenda, we are at once struck by their heterogeneous subject positions, and hence by the different ways in which these subjects may be persuaded to support such an egalitarian, ecological agenda of reforms. This is a question about which I cannot say more here, although elsewhere (Adkin, 1998b) I have made some tentative attempts to explore the agency of democratic political ecology in the Canadian context.

Theorizing collective action, or the agency and discursive strategy for the kind of 'poetic/political unity' sketched in the above discussion, is clearly an undertaking beyond the scope of a paper, a conference or a single researcher. Hopefully this discussion has suggested some of the potential 'linkages to be made among diverse subject positions and ecological alternatives. One conclusion which emerges from it, I believe, is that ecological knowledge must not only be articulated to a political and social discourse (instead of submerged within an anti-political 'environmentalism'), but must be articulated to a *democratic* political discourse. Democratic discourse is the key to creating a non-reductionist, non-essentializing 'poetic/political unity', in which ecological knowledge will help to create the conditions (and the poetry) for a good life.

APPENDIX 1.   SUMMARY OF THE CHEVIOT MINE CONFLICT IN ALBERTA

On 9 April 1999, the Federal Court revoked the federal government's approval of the Cheviot Mine (open pit coal mine) project on the border of Jasper National Park; the approval had been based on the findings of a federal-provincial panel appointed to conduct an environmental review of the project. The appeal of the approval had been filed by a coalition of environmental organizations (Alberta Wilderness Association, Canadian Parks and Wilderness Society, Canadian Nature Federation, Pembina Institute for Appropriate Development, and Jasper Environmental Association) represented by the Sierra Legal Defence Fund. The Federal Court ruled that the panel had failed to conduct a proper review of the project as required by federal law (that is, the terms of the Canadian Environmental Assessment Act (CEA Act)). The panel had not considered the cumulative effects of the mine and other projects in the area (specifically, forestry and other mines), as required by the CEA Act. Nor had it considered 'in any meaningful way' alternatives such as underground mining. Further, there was substantial evidence that the dumping of mine rock into streams would destroy bird habitat, which is protected by the Migratory Bird Conventions Act.

Expressing the frustration of the mining company with the hurdles presented by such review processes, the President of Luscar described the CEA Act as a 'very flawed' piece of legislation. He warned, '*There must be something wrong with it for us to end up in this position*' (quoted in Hryciuk and Howell, 1999: A1, italics added). He noted that the Act would be up for review at the end of 1999, and stated, 'It would be our intent to present to the federal government, along with other companies, the deficiencies that we have identified' (Hryciuk and Howell, 1999).

The Federal Court decision has implications for similar appeals being filed by environmental organizations against environmental approval for other resource exploitation projects. The manager of crude oil and fiscal policies for the Canadian Association of Petroleum Producers (CAPP) expressed the view that 'oilsands, heavy oil and diamond mine developers could all face greater frustration and delay if the environmental battleground moves *from regulatory channels to the courts*' (Avery, 1999, italics added). (Evidently 'regulatory' hurdles are no longer considered to be the threats to corporate interests that they were depicted as being in the 1980s. See Adkin, 1998a.)

In the Cheviot Mine case, it is also important to note the solid support of both the United Mineworkers of America as well as the residents and municipal officials of the town of Hinton (near the mine site) for Luscar's mine project, who characterize their environmentalist opponents as 'non-residents' (Hall, 1999; Hryciuk and Howell, 1999).

The local economy has been based mainly on logging, the Weldwood pulp and sawmill in Hinton, and the (Luscar) Cardinal River coal mine, which employs 450 workers, and is now exhausting its coal supply. The new mine site on the eastern outskirts of Jasper National Park has been represented as a crucial employment alternative for the men who will lose their jobs when the Cardinal River mine closes. Notwithstanding the low prices for both pulp and coal (construction of the Cheviot mine had in fact been delayed by Luscar by one year due to low coal prices), and the 'finite' employment possibilities offered by these economic activities (not to mention that they offer, directly, only jobs for men), the (employment) potential of ecotourism and recreation activities has hardly been considered. The environmentalists who oppose the coal mine project have, however, proposed that the Hinton area should develop ecotourism, pointing to the example of Canmore, a town which has become an important retirement centre and tourist accommodation base for Banff National Park.

NOTES

1. 'Subject position' refers here to a collective identity (political, social or cultural) with which an individual identifies (or which may be ascribed to an individual); it follows that any given individual may occupy more than one subject position, and that an individual's primary identification may shift depending on changing contexts and positioning within social relationships. For example, a woman is simultaneously a raced and gendered subject; in some situations, she may identify primarily with a racial group; in other situations she may be more aware of a subordinate status stemming from gender oppression. The meanings of subject positions are not 'fixed', but determined by ongoing discursive practices and their outcomes. They are, at the same time, inter-determining, as, for example, different constructions of femininity are determined by racial, ethnic, religious, class and other discourses. Subject positions are politicized when they are seen to be embedded in (antagonistic) relationships of domination/subordination, rather than merely 'descriptors' of a taken-for-granted status or nature. Thus, for example, to be a woman is a subject position, but does not in itself imply that one is a feminist. (Feminism is a theory, or a set of theories, about what it means to be a woman.) Likewise, to be a worker is a subject position (in which recognition of differences (workers/non-workers) is implied), but does not necessarily coincide with a socialist world view. 'Worker' is, in this sense, a subject position; socialism is a political identity/ideology. It has been argued that certain subject positions (for example, sex, race, sexuality) should be differentiated from political-ideological identities, insofar as the former are not (for different reasons) social constructs which can be donned or shed at will by individuals. For example, while race is a socially constructed category (criteria of, for example, 'blackness' 'whiteness' – and the very existence of such concepts – vary historically and culturally), individuals are born into societies which ascribe races to them. Thus a 'black woman' cannot simply decide on a Tuesday to no longer identify herself as black, in the same way that a 'liberal' might decide to join the conservative party. Alternatively, the extent to which gender and sexual differences may be attributed to biological, as opposed to purely sociological determinants, is the subject of much debate among feminist and queer theorists. The above discussion focuses mainly on the social positioning aspects of 'subject position'. It should be noted, as well, that 'subject' has the connotations of 'subject to' (social structures or relations) and 'subject of' (action, movement, history).
2. Baptist as defined in my old Oxford English dictionary: 'one of those Christians who object to infant baptism and believe that baptism should be by immersion and at an age when a person is old enough to understand the meaning of the ceremony' (Hornby, 1974, p. 62).
3. I refer here to struggles for equality, understood as freedom from unwarranted discrimination; for autonomy, understood as respect for difference (or freedom from unwarranted assumptions of sameness in relation to some pseudo-universal norm); and for deepened and broadened participation by individuals and groups in decisions about the direction of society (*vis-à-vis* states, élites, corporations and other institutional actors).
4. The *Loi* Aubry, named for the Socialist Minister for Employment and Solidarity, Martine Aubry, passed in 1998, establishes a statutory 35-hour work week to take effect between 1 January 2000 and 1 January 2002, depending on the type of establishment. The law allows for flexibility in the methods negotiated in each workplace to reach this target, and offers certain financial incentives to employers to effect reductions in work time, while increasing employment. The full text of the law (Loi no 98–461 du 13 juin 1998 d'orientation et d'incitation relative à la réduction du temps de travail), as well as updates on its implementation, may be obtained from the French Ministry of Employment and Solidarity, at the website <www.35h.travail.gouv.fr/textes/loi/texte.htm>. The reduction of

working time, as well as the creation of a 'third sector of ecologically and socially useful employment' are central elements of the economic programme of *Les Verts français*, and their leading economic theorist, Alain Lipietz (1989, 1999). (See also France, 1993.) The reduction of work time was part of the electoral accord agreed upon between the Socialists and *Les Verts* prior to the last legislative elections. Similar reforms have been called for in Canada. See Adkin (1998b), Hayden (1999) and Willis (1998).

5. The Business Charter for Sustainable Development, published by the International Chamber of Commerce in 1990, and Business Council for Sustainable Development, advocate (corporate) self-regulation (as an alternative to government regulation), and argue that global market liberalization will be the 'cornerstone of sustainable development' (Schmidheiny, 1992, p.14). See Elliott (1997, pp. 123–9).

6. Amendment of the Canadian Environmental Assessment Act, for example, was called for by the President of Luscar in the conflict involving the Cheviot Coal mine project, as described in the appended case study.

7. Arguably, the environmental management approach has now largely 'displaced' more radical ecological perspectives in university-based interdisciplinary programmes and institutes. I place 'displaced' in quotation marks here because it is questionable whether the critical approaches to environmentalism were ever predominant in these institutional milieux. Although there are some notable exceptions (for example, York's Faculty of Environmental Studies), there appears to be a trend towards the association of 'environmental studies' with schools of business, biology or engineering, rather than with the social sciences and humanities, and for researchers in these areas to draw on corporate sources to fund research. The Environmental Research and Studies Centre at the University of Alberta, for example, is based in (and directed by a professor from) the Business School, and is now funded by an energy corporation, TransAlta.

8. Some evidence of this tendency, in the Canadian context, is provided by Carroll and Ratner's (1996, p. 605) study of social movement activists drawn from eight movements and coalitions in the Greater Vancouver area. Categorizing the social movement activists in their sample of 212 as 'locals' (active in a single social movement organization (SMO)), 'intermediate' (active in multiple SMOs in one movement), or 'cosmopolitans' (active in multiple SMOs in multiple movements), the authors found that among the least 'cosmopolitan' were environmentalists.

9. Ascetic: 'adj. – self-denying; austere; leading a life of severe self-discipline. n. person who (often for religious reasons) leads a severely simple life without ordinary pleasures' (Hornby, 1974, p. 44). I can offer some anecdotal evidence for this characterization of popular perceptions, based on my teaching of a section on 'ecological perspectives' as part of a second-year university course. Every year I encounter students' associations of 'environmentalists' with the desire to return modern industrial societies (like Canada's) to the age of hunters and gatherers, or, as one of my students put it: 'picking berries'. Another perception is also linked to the ideas of deprivation or scarcity. They seem to come to the class already familiar with the 'limits to growth' discourse, and convinced that the underlying cause of the scarcity problem is overpopulation in (guess where) Third World countries. At the same time, they express great confidence in the capacity of technological advances to overcome resource scarcity in the North. Together, these views suggest their anticipation of the very global apartheid of which Altvater (1998) writes.

10. On the basis of a thematic discourse analysis of 140 episodes of *The Nature of Things*, from 1960 to 1994, sociologist Glenda Wall points to the ways in which this series has also reinforced 'greening capitalism' arguments as opposed to more radical ecological alternatives, and has advanced a 'human nature' explanation of environmental destruction, or a deified view of nature. She concludes that even the later episodes, which depicted nature as 'wise and deserving of respect', 'while seemingly consistent with a more radical critique of dominant economic practices and anthropocentric views, are in some ways just as conducive to a system of industrial growth that depends on nature as a storehouse of resources, and amenable to economic concepts such as production, consumption, and efficiency, as was the earlier discourse' (Wall, 1999, pp. 5–7).

11. Smith (1995, pp. 26–7) sees 'political correctness' as an 'ideological code': 'My model is the genetic code and the replicating capacity of a DNA molecule, which produces copies identical to itself, passing on its genetic information and its ability to replicate . . . Reproduction occurs, of course, as people "pick up" its organization from reading it or about it or hearing it used, and using it themselves, hence passing it on to readers or hearers'.

12. This outcome should not, of course, be understood as the result of some process wholly external to environmental actors. Some have argued – especially in the context of environmentalism in the United States – that many environmentalists have, in an instrumental fashion, adopted various anti-social, even politically reactionary, discourses. On the linkage of environmental problems to militarism and US 'security' concerns, see Conca (1998b) and Foster (1999).

13. In the 1999 provincial budget speech in Alberta, not a single mention was made of the environment as an area of expenditure, or of policy concern. This is a reflection of the virtual monopoly of the Conservative government over the definition of the political agenda, given the comparative weakness of the opposition parties, labour movement and other opposition elements within the province. Bill 15 (the Natural Heritage Act), recently introduced in the provincial legislature, has been described by this author as a disguised industrial development policy (Adkin, 1999). Sandilands (1998, p. 76) observes a similar 'disappearance' of environmental issues in the discourse of the neo-liberal Conservative party in Ontario. 'An observer of the [1995 provincial election] campaign,' she says, 'would have concluded that there is no environment about which to be concerned.'

14. Elsewhere, I have explored the problem of collective action in relation to post-Marxist social movement theory and postmodernism, basing my arguments on historical analyses of developments in Canada, France and Western Europe more generally (Adkin, 2000). I have also examined the limitations of Canadian political economy with regard to ecology and social movement building (Adkin, 1994).

15. This is, indeed, one of the interpretations of the NATO-led war against the Milosevic regime in Yugoslavia.

16. A critical review of Bill 15, the 'Natural Heritage Act' of Alberta, may be found on the website of the Environmental Law Centre, at: www.elc.ab.ca.

17. Both neo-liberals and socil democrats have advanced their strategies for 'economic competitiveness' in the name of 'national interest'. 'Success', in this game, is measured by macro-economic criteria such as rates of GNP, investment or exports. They render invisible women's unpaid domestic and other labour, disregard ecological sustainability concerns and reinforce a world (nation-state?) view which pits workers in one country against workers in other countries.

18. Elsewhere (Adkin, 1998b), I have argued that a philosophy of justice and human needs does underlie all prescriptive theories of social change, although it is often merely implicit. Post-structuralist criticisms of theories which posit essentialist categories (for example, a universal woman), binary oppositions (for example, women/men) or falsely universal categories (for example, mankind) draw our attention to the pitfalls of ethnocentrism, phallocentrism, anthropocentrism, ahistoricism and so on. On the subject of human nature or human needs, much has been said about the questionable claims and assumptions of sociobiological theories, and the pendulum has swung – in social theory, at least – in the direction of social-constructivist explanations of behavioural norms. There may, however, be limits to the 'de/reconstructibility' of the conditions for human well-being, or humans' perceptions of their well-being. Where these limits lie is, of course, difficult to ascertain, but we are provided with many markers in the forms of data on health/sickness and their relationships to environmental and lifestyle factors, psychological suffering, crime and suicide statistics, and countless cultural expressions of loneliness, grief and the search for 'meaning' in existence. Much social theory suffers from somatophobia, refusing to recognize the knowledge about our social condition and needs that is to be gained from paying attention to bodily and emotional experience. For this reason, I am unwilling to reject all 'foundational' (universal) arguments about human needs. Moreover, the so-called

'progressive' political ideologies invariably appeal to such conceptions of needs and happiness. (How else, for example, do we know what 'oppression' is, and why it is to be resisted?) However, we do not need to agree on a universal philosophy of human nature or the good life in order to make some claims about the necessary conditions for meeting basic human needs and for realizing a diversity of conceptions of happiness. In so doing, however, we need to acknowledge that we begin from situated knowledges, and that the name of the game is to identify affinities with others.

19. In terms more familiar to a comparativist, the objective is to develop 'middle range' theories of counter-hegemonic political ecology and its potential agency, rather than a universal theory of social agency or stages of societal development.

20. A bridging discourse in such conflicts has been 'sustainable development', but as I suggested above, this is very problematic in a number of respects. It may mean 'environmental management to permit a continuation of the existing framework of the economy and society', in which equity issues – among others – are not on the table. Hence the importance of linking such discursive elements to democratic struggles.

21. Such a discourse has guided the positions of *Les Verts* in domestic and European politics (see *Les Verts* 1994, 1995, 1999), as it has guided *Die Grünen*.

22. The philosophy of the good life pertains not only to social relationships, but to human/nature relationships. Aboriginal cultures offer very important insights into the relationships that are 'appropriate' or 'natural' between humans and the earth, including all of its species. In my work on Canada, I have tried to draw attention to the importance of articulations among indigenous peoples' struggles (recognizing how these, too, are intersected by gender, generational, class and other axes), ecological knowledge and visions of 'sustainable development'. There are many potential outcomes of such articulations, as revealed by the (Saskatchewan) Dene views of deep burial of radioactive waste on their land, the interventions of First Nations representatives during the hearings on uranium mine expansion, the involvement of First Nations in struggles around Clayoquot Sound, or the understandings of the natural order of things which underpins the Hopi concept 'Koyaanisquatsi' (life out of balance) – discussed by M'Gonigle (1996) – and many other cases.

5. An Ecological Historical Materialism

Ted Benton

INTRODUCTION

This chapter attempts to set out in a very condensed form a general approach to understanding, *within the same conceptual framework*, both the material dimensions of human social 'metabolism' with nature and the various ways in which groups of social actors understand and respond to the problems it poses. This is to make an attempt at the sort of large-scale social theorizing that is widely disapproved of, especially by people influenced by postmodern thought. Also, trying to set out a whole approach, rather than giving a more narrowly focused study means that I will have to depart from some scholarly conventions that under normal circumstances I strongly support.

It also means that I run a serious risk of being radically misunderstood, so where possible I have referenced other publications of my own (and sometimes by other people), which present some of the arguments in a more qualified and thoroughly referenced way. Finally, I want to emphasize the very tentative and provisional character of this study. It is already significantly revised in the light of very telling comments made at the workshop for which it was written, and by the editors of this book.

The theoretical heritage of the 'mainstream' traditions in the social sciences, and especially in sociology, presents serious obstacles in the way of understanding the interrelationships, or 'metabolism' between social life and its non-human conditions and contexts ('nature') (Benton, 1991; Catton and Dunlap, 1978). The most promising alternative is historical materialism. In its classic formulations this puts at the centre of historical understanding the relationship between the forms of human social life and their mode of appropriation of nature. This makes it a promising resource for those who acknowledge the importance of reworking social theory in such a way as to comprehend these material dimensions of social existence. However, this legacy, promising though it is, still presents some deep problems. It needs to be reworked, both as an explanatory theory, and (still more) as a source of normative orientations, political strategies and visions of possible futures.

My main focus in this study will be on developing conceptual resources for *explanatory theory*, with only a few asides on questions of value commitment, strategies and 'feasible utopias'. To guard against some reasonable misunderstandings, I should make it clear that I make a distinction between 'Marxism' and 'historical materialism'. Marx and Engels were certainly the key 'founding figures' of historical materialism as an explanatory theory, and their work remains an indispensable source of insights. However, subsequent thinkers and researchers have developed their legacy in ways they might not have predicted (and would probably not have endorsed).

The legacy of historical materialism that we are able to draw on at the turn of the twenty-first century has been enriched by the cultural thought associated with Western Marxism and Critical Theory, by the work of black and Third World Marxists, and, especially in the last two decades, by materialist feminist and ecological critical revisions of the heritage.

Since Marxism is also commonly understood to imply not just commitment to a broad explanatory theory, but also to a set of normative and strategic orientations, and to a state-centralist vision of socialism, I should make it clear that none of this is implied in my endorsement of a reworked historical materialism. The importance of sources of unhappiness, oppression and exclusion which are not reducible to class relations has been emphasized by feminist and black activists, especially, and this entails a much more complex and contingent approach to oppositional coalition building than the Marxist classics could grasp. The experience of the state-centralist regimes of Asia and Eastern Europe, especially, has exposed the inadequacy of that version of 'socialism' with respect to human rights and justice, and its relation to nature: again, green political thought, feminism, the utopian traditions and the practices of non-Western peoples are among the resources for new thinking about alternative futures.

The work of 'rethinking Marxism' in these respects is being carried through in many countries, so that we now have a large and growing dialogue among 'ecological', or 'green', Marxists and socialists, and between them and other traditions of radical ecological thought and practice, such as deep ecologists, social ecologists and ecological feminists. This is not the place to review all of this work, but the journal *Capitalism, Nature, Socialism*, and its associated book series contains much that is of value in this dialogue. What I propose to do in this study is to outline some themes and arguments which indicate the explanatory potential of a reworked historical materialism (where possible, in comparison with 'constructionist' approaches to understanding 'environmentalism' and 'nature', and with the influential alternative tradition whose central concept is 'reflexive modernization').

REWORKING HISTORICAL MATERIALISM

The Centrality of the Mode of Production

The key concept to be retained is that of 'mode of production', and the connected concepts of social relations of production, forces of production, means, agents and conditions of production and raw materials. The importance of these ideas is that they pose the question of our relationships to nature in terms of *specific, historically and geographically variable* forms of social organization. This undercuts the tendency in both technocratic and some deep green approaches to see the question as one of 'man', or 'exponential growth', or 'population' versus 'nature' in the abstract. The concept mode of production and its cognates allow us to investigate *specific dynamics* of socio-economic articulations with specific materials, places, natural mechanisms, ecosystems, non-human species and so forth.

Implicit in this claim is a 'critical realist' approach to epistemology (Archer et al., 1998; Collier, 1994). This recognizes that knowledge (including social scientific knowledge) is an always provisional outcome of a social practice, but at the same time insists that the knowledge so constructed has an object which exists independently of our thought about it. Against radical social constructionist approaches, this allows us to include within the analysis of socio-ecological processes the causal powers (and what some call the 'agency' – Latour, 1987) of such materials, natural mechanisms, ecosystems and so forth. This, in turn, makes it possible to investigate the contribution of non-human living and non-living beings and processes to the shaping of social life and to the genesis of what come to be recognized as ecological 'problems'.

A second benefit offered by the idea of mode of production is the way it allows theorization of the internal tensions and potential contradictions arising between its elements. Marx and Engels were centrally concerned with the contradiction in class-divided modes of production between the agents of production (the 'direct producers') and the class of owners of the means of production who also appropriate the surplus product. For them, analysing the structure of the prevailing mode of production was the way into understanding the principal sources of social division in that society: both in terms of the dominant pattern of power relations and characteristic relations of distribution of the social product (pattern of distributive inequality).

However, Marx and Engels were clear that each class-divided mode of production is at one and the same time both a form of social organization through which nature is worked upon to provide means of subsistence, and a power relation through which a dominant class appropriates a surplus product. Partly because they tended to take for granted certain widespread nineteenth-century assumptions about the development of technology and growing mastery of nature, Marx and Engels paid relatively little attention to developing a critical understanding of the modes of production as forms of appropriation of nature. In this respect, they tended to take over the assumptions of the classical political economists, while criticizing them in their characterization of the capital/labour relationship.

Elsewhere, I have argued (Benton, 1989, 1992, 1996; see also Grundmann's criticisms, 1991) that, as a result, the theory of the capitalist mode of production which Marx developed is under-theorized with regard to the 'metabolism' between this socio-economic form and its non-human conditions, contexts and media ('nature'). I offered some ideas about how this defect could be corrected, most especially through the notion of 'intentional structure'. My argument was that different labour processes (I focused on primary appropriation, ecoregulation and 'production') and, indeed, practices in general, involve different kinds of combination between human social action and its material conditions, means, objects and outcomes.

As against the classic historical materialist (and generally 'technological optimist', 'nature-mastery', 'productivist') view of the 'development of the forces of production' as an ever-expanding transformative power, I wanted to draw attention to 'productive' practices that were better characterized through concepts such as extracting, tending, nurturing, nourishing, renewing, harvesting, educating, preparing, protecting, sowing, regulating, training, explaining, curing and so on.

The intentional structures of these practices involve relations between human agency and its material conditions that are resistant to the dynamics of 'mastery' as conceptualized in terms of means/ends transformative action. They are resistant because of their relative space/time dependency, and because in such practices as these human agency is conditioned in its deployment by (absolutely or relatively) non-manipulable forces, mechanisms and processes (seasons, genetic constitution, developmental rhythms, psychological dispositions and abilities, and so on of living organisms, including humans, geographical distribution of mineral resources, high diversity ecosystems and so on), and also because these practices tend to have distinctive emotional and normative features not reducible to the means/ends schema.

The main point here is not, of course, that these practices are somehow absolutely impervious to the imposition of means/ends rationality, or, indeed of capitalist commodification (as a particular type of that rationality). Rather, the point is that the obstacles to it posed by their distinctive intentional structures and normative character affect the *pace* and *form* taken by such impositions, and often provoke forms of active resistance, as well as generating a variety of other unintended consequences.

Some commentators (Burkett, 1998; Vlachou, 1994) have read my work as an attempt to shift the focus of the analysis of capitalism towards these features of its relation to nature, and away from the analysis of class and other forms of power relation and social division. But this is not the case. My argument has been that developing the account of capitalism as a distinct type of social relation to nature is necessary in order to understand aspects of class division not fully recognized by Marx (though better grasped by Engels), but also in order to understand the sources of relatively new forms of social division and political agenda that are now framed as 'environmental' or 'ecological'.

The outcome here is an understanding of class struggles as, in part, environmental struggles, and an understanding of ecological issues, as social issues. I will return to outline a little more of how this might work. In the meantime, it will be necessary to indicate some of the ways in which the historical materialist tradition, as it has commonly been understood, needs to be revised, as distinct from further developed, if these tasks are to be addressed adequately.

Revisions to Historical Materialism

In most formulations of historical materialism, the concept 'mode of production' is taken to characterize the form taken by the 'economic structure', or 'base' of a society, or 'social formation'. But clearly the structured practices referred to through this concept are not (fully) self-sufficient. Their constitution and relative permanence through time require more or less systematic and continuous 'metabolism' with other practices. The most significant among these are those practices through which human individuals are themselves 'produced', socialized and allocated to social positions (including those involved in production itself).

Engels was inclined to include these practices alongside 'production' in the narrow sense in his concept of the economic base or 'foundation' of the social formation. On that interpretation of the materialist approach, the 'economic foundation' includes both production and 'reproduction'. Subsequent feminist reworking of the tradition has tended to endorse that theoretical move, in that it renders more explicit the gendered character of the division of social labour (Hartsock, 1983; Mellor, 1992; Salleh, 1995).

In the case of specifically capitalist societies this provides a sound theoretical basis for a feminist critique of the much narrower notion of the 'economic', which remains in common use in these societies and in 'unreconstructed' Marxist discourse. Both notions serve to conceal the unpaid labour conducted in the domestic sphere, predominantly (though not exclusively) by women. In addition to the 'foundation' provided by the practices of production and reproduction, social formations also include more or less institutionalized 'superstructures' – institutional forms which define property relations, enforce contracts, adjudicate disputes and so on, maintain order within territorial boundaries and defend those boundaries (legal-political system of nation-states through most of the history of modern capitalism), codify and promulgate the dominant cultural forms (church, education system, media and so on). These non-economic institutions and the practices they sustain were theorized in the classics by way of the metaphor of 'foundation' and 'superstructure' but, especially in the thought of Gramsci, Althusser and Poulantzas among twentieth-century Marxist writers, there are now more analytically sophisticated ways of theorizing them.

This is not the place to enter into the theoretical issues posed by this immense literature. For our purposes it will be enough to draw attention to a small number of relevant themes and arguments. First, the risk of falling into an 'economic determinist', or 'reductionist' version of historical materialism can be countered by the insistence in these writers on the *complexity* of social formations, in the sense that each institutional nexus/social practice has its own specificity and irreducible causal efficacy as a 'moment' within the overall metabolism and continuity of the social formation through time.

It was not a coincidence that the above account specifies the 'superstructures' in terms of the functional requirements of economic practices, but it would have been no less possible to represent economic practices as fulfilling functional requirements of, say, the nation-state, the church or the educational system. The fact that each practice has its own necessary conditions of existence and its own inner dynamics (including tensions and contradictions) makes the 'reductionist' view untenable.

Second, however, the smooth functionality implicit in the above model is a consequence of its one-sided abstraction. At the core of each (antagonistic) mode of production is a power relation between social classes, and these power relations also pervade, shape and transform the other social practices and their forms of interrelationship. With regard to specifically modern capitalist societies, Marx and Engels themselves tended to emphasize the role of direct physical coercion on the part of the legal-political system in suppressing the resistance offered by the working class to its subordination. However, twentieth-century Western Marxists have attempted to theorize the role of institutional practices sustained by the family, educational system, church, voluntary associations, unions, political parties and communications media ('civil society') in securing the active consent of individuals in the processes of subject constitution and allocation to their 'places' in society. Gramsci's concept of 'hegemony' has been central here.

But it is important to see that this is not just a matter of 'ideological mystification'. Those capitalist regimes that have achieved relative stability and social integration over prolonged stretches of time have done so through significant material concessions to the demands of organized labour and other social movements. Welfare/security states have extended citizenship rights from political to include social and economic conditions of life. This has involved significant extensions of the state's power to intervene and regulate employment practices and labour processes, as well as direct state provision of resources and services to compensate for or ameliorate 'market failure'. The participation of labour and other social movements in building these integrative structures has been crucial to their relative success in securing active consent to continuing capitalist social and economic domination. However, this should not be understood as mere 'co-option'.

The post-Second World War settlement which was established through much of the advanced capitalist world won a very real amelioration of the conditions of life and enhanced opportunities for the great mass of working people. However, its status as a provisional outcome of struggle means that it remains highly vulnerable to shifts in the balance of social forces, and, as everyone knows, is now particularly at risk as a result of capitalist globalization and deregulation.

So, historically contingent and always provisional 'settlements' between capital and organized oppositional movements are one important source of the 'relative autonomy' of the social and political order of a society in relation to its 'basic' economic relations. However, the modern Marxist emphasis on the role of discursive processes in securing consent to social domination opens up another set of questions that have tended to be pursued *outside* the frame of the Marxist tradition. Foucault's 'genealogical' approach to the relation between discursive forms and power relations in the prison, factory, asylum, hospital and so on can be drawn upon as a contribution to theorizing specifically modern capitalist forms of social subjection through 'subjectification'.

However, Foucault's anti-humanist discourse-determinism renders resistance to power untheorizable, so that the 'necessity' of resistance becomes a near mystical adjunct to his analyses, associated with the body as a marginal 'exterior' to the domain of power/discourse. This can be avoided by drawing (again, critically and selectively) from Habermas's key idea: that of an 'ideal speech situation'. Implicit in any practice of coordination of human social activity through linguistic communication is the possibility of dialogue: that knowledge claims, commands, normative judgements made by authoritative speakers and so on will be called into question by those to whom they are addressed.

To the extent that powerful actors resort to linguistic discourse to persuade as distinct from the use or threat of force to compel, they are committed to deploying the resources of linguistic persuasion to overcome or reach accommodation with articulate resistance. For this reason, hegemonic, discourse-dependent forms of social domination can provide more deeply rooted and broadly based legitimacy, but are at the same time perpetually open to the constitution of oppositional social movements which resist at least in part, through the deployment of counter-discourses that demand discursive, rather than merely repressive, responses.

In broadly liberal democratic capitalist social formations, then, *cultural* struggles over the discursive representation of power relations, policy issues, normative orientations, political identities and so on play an indispensable and irreducible part in the conduct of social and political struggles. This is another source of the autonomy of legal-political institutions and their practices from the 'functional' requirements of the economic system and the material interests of the organized representatives of capital. This relatively open and fluid domain of discursive/cultural practices in civil society constitutes the space within which diverse social movements may form, constitute particular collective identities, establish alliances, fuse, disintegrate, create new meanings and values, transform pre-existing ones and so on.

The openness, fluidity and internal complexity of this domain makes any simple class reductionist model of social cleavages and political interests in liberal democratic capitalism inappropriate. Nevertheless, the pervasiveness of ruling class power and its hegemonic discourses, together with its effects on the material conditions of life of those who occupy subordinate positions in the social division of labour, is such that no social movement is likely to remain unaffected by class relations. While many social movements (women's, peace, ethnic, nationalist and, indeed, environmental movements) are not accurately theorized as parts or aspects of class division, they are always riven through and shaped by the *consequences* of class division.

Societies as 'Open Systems'

Marx and Engels have often (and plausibly) been read as being committed to what Althusser called 'historicism': some notion of cumulative directionality in the historical process. For many of their followers, this gave rise to expectations that the development of capitalism was leading inexorably towards its own transcendence in the shape of a future socialist society of abundance, conviviality and fulfilment of human potential. Loosely, the revolutionary tradition tended to see this as something to be realized through the revolutionary action of a unified and transnationally organized working class movement. The revisionist/reformist wing of the Marxist movement came to see the transition to socialism as an outcome of the evolution of capitalist society itself, consolidated by growing participation of organized workers in liberal democratic political systems. In the early works of Marx, history is understood in terms of a philosophical theory that represents its *telos* as the overcoming of human self-alienation in the future communist society.

In the later works, human self-realization comes to be seen as presupposing the drastic reduction of 'necessary labour' brought about by the development of the forces of production in previous phases of history, but most especially by the dynamic revolutionizing of the means of production wrought by capitalism.

These images of history as directional, cumulative and as passing through definite developmental stages inherit much of influential Enlightenment conceptions of 'progress'. Classical Marxism tended to share this view of historical progress not only with most nineteenth-century views of history, but also with the great weight of twentieth-century social evolutionism, 'development' and 'modernization' theory and practice, though, of course, with varying normative content and emphases. Althusser challenged this reading of Marx, and inaugurated a non-historicist version of historical materialism that gave *due weight to the contingency, complexity and open-endedness* of social and historical change.

If we follow this line of argument, then some important consequences flow from it. One obvious consequence is that it throws open all pre-existing settlements of questions about collective agency for historical change, the socio-economic, cultural, political, psychological and, now, ecological conditions for historical transformation. Once the underlying theme of progressive mastery of nature through technological innovation as the key presupposition of human emancipation is called into question, then it becomes possible to think in quite different ways about the possibility of qualitatively different pathways of scientific and technical innovation, shaped by different sorts of embedding in human social relations and value commitments. It becomes possible to think of post-capitalist 'realizable utopias' centred on qualitatively different relations between human social life and the rest of nature, and mediated by forms of understanding and technologies 'appropriate' to those transformed relations.

However, to give 'contingency' in history its due weight is not to retreat into an empiricist view of history as 'one damn thing after another'. The epistemological grounding for the view offered here is drawn, again, from critical realism. On this view, societies are 'open systems' in the sense that they exist as complex combinations of structures, each with its own specific 'causal weight', and dynamic tendencies. On the account suggested above, this must also include non-human living and non-living 'components' in human social life. The resultants of the complex interactions between the processes governed by these structures are certainly technically (if not in principle) unpredictable, and in this sense historical outcomes must be seen as 'open'. On the other hand, this does not rule out the disaggregation and analysis of key causal dynamics, and assigning relative causal weightings to them.

The causal weight of capitalist economic relations and the effects of the dynamic tendencies of capital accumulation are rightly emphasized in the historical materialist legacy. These dynamics, and related forms of national and transnational state power, can be understood as abstract tendencies which are variably and incompletely realized in concrete local situations, depending on the ways in which other structures and practices intervene as obstacles or modifiers. One of the key differences between this sort of approach and the more influential 'reflexive modernization' alternative (Beck, 1992; Giddens, 1994; for a fuller development of this argument, see Benton in O'Brien et al., 1999) is that the term 'modernity' favoured by that tradition is both sociologically empty (or illegitimately ethnocentric) and indifferent to the specific causal dynamics of capital accumulation. Both Beck and Giddens, despite the many insights in their work, share with other 'modernization' approaches, and with much environmentalist literature, a surprisingly un-social concept of 'industrialism'. For them, this concept, and an associated notion of technological innovation as an autonomous dynamic, serve to ground their analyses of the ecological problems of 'modernity'.

To some extent, the explanatory purchase of these different forms of conceptualization is open to empirical testing. Very broadly, quantitative work on materials and resource flows (Fischer-Kowalski and Haberl, 1993; Fischer-Kowalski et al., 1994; Fischer-Kowalski and Haberl, 1997; Wernick and Ausubel, 1995) as between different social types certainly does show that hunting and gathering, agricultural and 'industrial' societies make radically different per-capita demands on environmental materials and energy sources. If we were concerned solely with the interface between 'society' and 'nature' it would seem that the concept of 'industrialism' would have a good deal of explanatory purchase. However, an adequate socio-ecological theory faces a rather different challenge.

It has to include in the analysis not just material flows (the 'metabolism') between 'society' (black box) and nature, but also the patterns of flow within specific social forms, and also the power relations and forms of calculation which shape, regulate and transform those patterns. This entails, among other things, being able to assess the capacities of different types of system to adapt to ecological contingencies, including ones generated by their own dynamic tendencies. My claim (not fully defended here) is that a revised historical materialist concept of capitalism has better prospects of doing this than the concepts of 'modernity', 'industrialism' and 'technological development'.

Value Commitments

These reworkings of the explanatory theory both necessitate rethinking of the value perspective of classical socialisms, and also open up possibilities for new kinds of normative vision infused by the cultural creativity of the green, feminist and other radical social movements. The central socialist value commitment expressed in the formula 'to each according to need, from each according to ability' acquires a new urgency, but it needs to be supplemented by new forms of normative reflection on the relation between justice in the relations between humans, and the proper conduct of humans towards non-human nature (Dobson, 1998, 1999; Benton in Hayward and O'Neill, 1997). The early works of Marx contain a profound but ultimately flawed response to this question (Benton, 1988, 1993), while the later writings tend towards a narrowly anthropocentric commitment to instrumental mastery of nature (Eckersley, 1992).

THEORIZING CAPITALISM'S RELATION TO NATURE

There is a very strong case for critical analysis of the environmental record of the 'formerly actually existing' state-centralist regimes, and it is clearly an important challenge for any reworked historical materialism to develop such an analysis. A serious study of the environmental record of those regimes would have to take into account their late and extremely rapid in-dustrialization, and lack of access to colonial resources and markets, compared with the earlier industrializing nations. There is now evidence that in the early years after the Russian revolution great progress was made in the scientific study of ecology, and its application to Soviet agriculture (Gare, 1993; Weiner, 1988). It is also true that very large areas were set aside as natural reserves, both in the Soviet Union and in their 'satellite' states in Eastern Europe. However, the record on industrial pollution and health and safety was poor – most tragically expressed in the Chernobyl catastrophe. It seems likely that the closure of civil society with the Bolshevik monopolization of power, intensified by Stalinist rule, was a significant factor in this. In the absence of autonomous labour and environmental movements, central planners were under no pressure to modify or abandon the mainly 'productivist' priorities they adopted in competition with Western technical and military challenges.

However, since the overwhelming mass of human social metabolism with nature is now conducted through capitalist relations of production, circulation and consumption, it is the theoretical analysis of these forms that demands the most urgent attention. The key concept here, again, is capitalism as a mode of production, qualified by the revisions suggested above. The US writer, J. O'Connor, has developed a systematic theoretical revision (O'Connor, 1988, 1998), which postulates a contradiction between the forces and *conditions* of production as endemic to capitalism (he terms this the 'second contradiction', the first being the contradiction between forces and *relations* which is the basis of class division). To oversimplify considerably, O'Connor argues that capitalist industrial development tends to undermine its own conditions, through pollution, waste, over-exploitation of labour, overuse and degradation of infrastructures, ecological damage and so on.

This downside of industrial development thus becomes an obstacle to further capital accumulation and requires public intervention in the shape of state action to restore and regulate use of environmental and human conditions of production. This necessity of wider social intervention to save capitalism from its own environmental destructiveness parallels the wider social action prompted by the labour movement to ameliorate the social destructiveness of capital. The environmental movement can thus be seen as an alternative possible agency for socialist transformation, acting in alliance with the labour movement.

This is an imaginative and powerful theory, and is in many respects compatible with the revision of the concept of mode of production indicated above. However, instead of working with the idea of a general contradiction to characterize the relation between capitalist forces and relations, on the one hand, and their material and human 'conditions', on the other, I propose to analyse the complex consequences of the superimposition of 'logics' of capital accumulation upon diverse 'concrete' labour processes, each with their distinctive 'intentional structures'.

In the case of industrial 'factory' production, this superimposition was the outcome of a long and complex historical process through which independent skilled artisan labour was first brought together under a single authority in the manufacturing workshop, then subjected to increasing specialization, de-skilling and division of labour as a condition for the replacement of human labour by machinery. The technologies deployed in these labour processes (smelting, moulding, dyeing, spinning, weaving, pressing, printing and so on) have overwhelmingly been applications of physical and chemical mechanisms (steam pressure, electrical energy, chemical synthesis, distillation, kinetic energy, electronic circuitry and so on).

The imposition of a capitalist value-maximizing, means/ends rationality, or 'intentional structure' upon these labour processes involved both the application of scientific knowledge in the design of reliable, predictable physical replacements for human (and animal) labour, and long-running class struggles to overcome resistance to the forms of labour regulation necessary to introduce them. Social historians and social scientists generally tend to put the emphasis on the social dimensions of these struggles, but it is one consequence of the approach I am advocating that these struggles should be seen as inseparably bound up with the material and technical dimensions of the emergence and consolidation of 'machinofacture'.

In general, the kind of predictability, and manipulability that the introduction of machinery offered was premised on the relative ease with which physical and chemical processes can be regulated given the provision of standardized conditions of operation. Enclosure within the physical space of the factory building has provided both the required standardized operating conditions, and an arena within which labour could be subjected to whatever discipline was not already provided by the rhythms of the machine. Moreover, the factory provides an enclosed space within which optimal conditions for operation can be provided in a way that is open-endedly replicable. These processes do not share the space-time dependencies associated with climate, season, soil condition, landforms, ecological embedding and so on which characterize farming, horticulture, forestry, fishing, hunting and gathering, extractive processes and so on.

However, staying with the material dimensions of industrial production, factories do occupy physical space and so exclude other uses of that space. They require to be integrated within a wider material infrastructure, including transport connections for the supply of raw materials and means of production, and for the physical distribution of the product. They will usually need to be linked into physical communication systems, power supply lines and have some means of disposing of waste products of various sorts. They also require a regular supply of workers, appropriately equipped with physical strength, skills, dispositions and so on. All of this presupposes, in terms of social structure and organization, some form of family life, educational institutions, transport system, residential neighbourhoods and related services, procedures for allocating decision-making powers regarding allocations and flows of the elements making up these interrelated processes and practices and so on. Under capitalism, property relations and markets play the dominant role in these respects, but they are in turn to a greater or lesser degree constituted, enforced and regulated by legal-political institutions at local, nation-state and (increasingly) supranational levels.

Now, the 'concrete' consequences of the emergence of factory production in reshaping class and other social struggles, including those associated with transformations in the relation between social practices and their material conditions and means, cannot be specified *a priori*. They depend on the complex and localized articulation of cultural resources, normative and political traditions, balances of power between rival social forces, the wider national and international context, but also, and importantly, on the specific technologies, labour processes, social relations of production and distribution, physical siting of plant in relation to other adjacent land uses and so on.

Engels's *Condition of the Working Class in England*, his classic study of English industrial cities in the middle of the last century, is an example of the sort of analysis suggested here (see Benton and Dennehy in Arthur, 1996). He links together the exploitation of labour 'at the point of production' with a wider analysis of the residential segregation of the social classes, the environmental and moral degradation of the working class districts, the pollution of air and water, the adulteration of food and so on. Much of this analysis remains pertinent in our own time, and not just in so-called 'Third World' cities.

Although the causal connections are immensely complex and subject to a great deal of local and historical variation, it is possible to specify, at a more abstract level, key causal mechanisms that tend to generate broadly comparable 'complexes' across many different localities (note my earlier reference to the critical realist epistemology that informs this approach). The causal mechanism I want to emphasize here is the superimposition of specifically capitalist 'logics', or 'forms of calculation' upon the materially embedded 'intentional structures' and material flows of industrial labour processes. The forms of calculation in question are ones which presuppose (a) the quantitative equivalence of qualitatively different skills, operations, materials, needs, wants, artifacts, services, tools and so on; and (b) the disaggregation of these items into measurable units for purposes of regular exchange.

Given these assumptions, together with the institutionalization of property rights and market exchange, forms of calculation emerge in which the accumulation of wealth can become the purpose of productive activity, in abstraction from the material means of its production, the material character of its current 'embodiment', or the needs or uses to which it is put. *The resulting 'logic' of means/ends value maximization is abstract, but this is not simply a 'mental' or 'cultural' distortion which fails to acknowledge qualitative difference, but it is also a social reality: its outcomes distribute the material factors of production, including the human agents involved, set them in motion, regulate their operation and set the terms of their disposal or destruction. The 'abstraction' is thus not simply a discursive, but also a substantive 'moment' in social life, with causal powers whose exercise shapes and reshapes the material conditions of social life, and determines human life chances.*

Now, the abstract quantities which figure in these calculations are the values-in-exchange of the elements which have to be purchased for production to take place (costs), and those of the saleable commodities produced, the difference between the two constituting the basis for (abstract) wealth accumulation. The logic is to drive costs down, and to increase the value of the product. I have already indicated some of the historical trends induced by the imposition of this logic on industrial labour processes: specialization and division of labour, de-skilling, replacement of labour by machinery and so on.

But this imposition encounters resistances, and not solely or even primarily ones expressed in the form of articulate discourse (though, of course, such discourse will often play a significant part). There will also be, intertwined with the articulate resistances, ones which derive from the 'inertia' of pre-existing habits, skills, divisions of labour, forms of cooperation, rhythms of working and relationships between work and non-work, but also from the material, spatially ordered, substances, materials, tools, machines, buildings, infrastructures and so on. These resistances are a consequence of the mismatches between the items which figure in the value-maximizing forms of calculation and the *much larger class* of causally significant things, attributes, flows and so on which play a part in or are materially affected by, the production process.

To put this more directly, a piece of machinery, or a raw material may be used because it serves a particular purpose (it speeds up production, it is more easily moulded into a required shape than a previously used alternative and so on, and these properties contribute to profitability), but it will also have other properties which appear irrelevant to the process of value maximization, and do not figure in value calculations. However, these other properties may well have *unforeseen* consequences which under some conditions may come to have effects which *are* relevant to value creation, or to other social practices. Again, depending on the circumstances, these may turn out to be resistances, or obstacles to capital accumulation.

An example might be the introduction of the conveyor belt as a means of effectively coordinating and regulating the labour of many workers engaged in a single industrial process. However, once workers get the hang of jamming the machinery, transposing or omitting operations and so on, the technology turns out to render the whole production process vulnerable to sabotage by individuals or small groups of discontented workers. The way human activity is combined with definite material conditions and means, and subjected to specific sorts of economic calculation, can, as this illustrates, play a significant role in the genesis and development of class struggles at the 'point of production'.

But this sort of analysis can be taken much further. The value-maximizing form of calculation takes no account of necessary conditions for the production process which do not present themselves as commodities which have to be paid for. These include infrastructures of various kinds, ecological 'life support systems', the reproductive and domestic labour involved in the day-to-day and generation-by-generation reappearance of the labour force and so on. In some cases these conditions are to a limited extent covertly reflected in the prices paid for raw materials, the wage bill and so on, but to a very considerable extent they are treated as 'free goods'. The value-maximizing form of calculation also takes no account of the materially mediated unintended consequences which flow from the production process, but which do not enter into the value-in-exchange of the product. These will include contamination of water, land and air by gaseous, chemical, thermal and other 'waste' emissions (what economists term 'externalities').

ENVIRONMENTAL SOCIAL MOVEMENTS

These unacknowledged conditions and materially mediated unintended consequences may become relevant to further capital accumulation in two broad ways. First, they may allow for an over-exploitation of necessary free goods ('pollution sinks', transport networks, workers' health, women's unpaid labour) to the point that production itself is threatened, or reduced in scale or profitability (loosely, the sort of analysis offered by Gorz, 1980 and O'Connor, 1994). Second, they may come to be recognized as 'threats' to health, family life, 'the environment', amenity use of local rivers or open spaces, to property values and so on, and, through the formation of social movements and campaigns, constitute a source of civil opposition to the industrial plant. In the first sort of case, the impact on capital accumulation may occur independently of whether an oppositional social movement is formed. A recent example is the public concern voiced by the Institute of Directors in the United Kingdom about the costs to industry of rising levels of stress-related illnesses among employees.

The second sort of case is more readily dealt with by 'constructionist' approaches to the sociology of social movements. As this literature insists, there is no necessary or one-to-one correlation between the existence of an 'objective' change in the environment, and the formation of a social movement that assigns a negative value to it and seeks a policy response. Whether or not this happens is indeed a contingent outcome of the availability of cultural and financial resources, local value systems, traditions, social networks and the like, as well as the nature and accessibility of the wider policy-formation process and political system.

However, to say that the materially produced changes in people's conditions and contexts of life are not *sufficient* to explain the formation of social movements is not to concede that they play *no part at all*: they are, after all, what those movements are *about*. Indeed, the very concept of an environmental conflict presupposes that no matter how disparate rival discursive constructions of issues may be, they have common, or overlapping, material referents. For example, there would be no conflict between anti-road activists and construction companies if it were not for the fact that their rival discourses made *materially incompatible* claims to the cultural meaning, aesthetic or amenity value or economic utility of *the same* physical stretches of countryside.

The target of my criticism here is the tradition of social movement analysis which as a matter of *methodological principle* rules out reference to the 'objective conditions' which figure in the 'social problem claims' of social movements, and proceeds to analyse them in abstraction from the object of their concern. On this view, a social problem exists only insofar as there exists a social movement making claims about it. A clear example is the 'constructionist' approach pioneered by Kitsuse and Spector, and endorsed by Steven Yearley:

> The existence of social problems depends on the continued existence of groups or agencies that define some condition as a problem and attempt to do something about it. To ask what are the effective causes of social problems, or what keeps social problems activities going, is to ask what keeps these various groups going (Kitsuse and Spector, 1981, quoted in Yearley, 1991).

Of course, since what gives movements their identity is precisely their concern about such 'objective conditions', it is quite impossible to write coherently about social movements without breaching this methodological rule. So, in practice, 'constructionist' work in its treatment of actual case studies tends to oscillate unreflectively between constructionist rhetoric and common-sense realism.

The approach advocated here is one that tries to link an analysis of the dynamic tendencies of institutional structures together with their impact on the life experiences and valued social practices of social groups. Whether or not social movements arise in response to such impacts, whether or not those movements turn out to be sustainable and effective, the cultural resources they are able to draw on in framing the issues for a wider 'attentive' public and so on all deserve sociological analysis. There can be no question of 'reading off' from an analysis at the levels of material or structural dynamics' predictions about what affected social groups will do. Equally, however, any adequate analysis of social movement activity, manifestly so in the case of environmental movements, needs to combine a socio-cultural and political analysis of the formation and activity of movement organizations *together with* an analysis of the genesis of the conditions and experiences to which they are a response.

So, to return to the case of the relation between the ecological consequences of industrial production and the formation of social movements. As we saw, the imposition of value calculation on industrial labour processes is liable to set in motion unintended or unforeseen ecological consequences which either *directly* depress production, or *indirectly* have impacts of a highly mediated kind on other social practices. These may or may not, depending on socio-cultural and other variables, contribute to the formation of oppositional forces in the wider civil society. In the first sort of case, capital itself may appeal to the state for publicly financed repair, infrastructural provision, or regulation in the general interest of capital (or organized fractions of the class, industrial lobbies and coalitions and so on). In the second sort of case, environmental social movements may demand state action to control, ban or regulate, or impose costs of repair or compensation on offending companies. Alternatively, they may take direct action against the companies concerned or their operations.

However, although I have spoken of these as two distinct sorts of case, they are better thought of as 'ideal typical' theoretical constructs. Both sources may contribute in some measure to the formation and shaping of actual social movements, and to sources of pressure for environmental reform. But the point of conducting the analysis in this way is to provide a rather different 'take' on the environmental movement to that offered by those who see it, as in O'Connor's classic statements, as primarily an oppositional movement in relation to capital. Rather, the above analysis suggests that the broad spectrum of what have come to be recognized as 'environmental' issues and movements should be understood as an internally *heterogeneous and potentially contradictory constellation* within civil society.

Significant sections of organized capital are active within this constellation advocating environmental change, while others are mounting a 'backlash' against it (Rowell, 1996). At the same time, popular environmental movements campaign against specific direct and mediated consequences of (unregulated) capitalist development, and particularly against identifiable and manifest abuses. Some forms of state intervention and regulation are welcomed, even positively demanded, by capitalist interests. Others are resisted, but, depending on the strength of environmental mobilizations, their penetration of the policy process, and the structural relations between different industrial lobbies and the state, provisional compromises may be reached which are significantly suboptimal with regard to the economic interest of capital.

A very recent example is the much publicized 'climbdown' by US biotechnology transnational Monsanto over its intent to purchase and deploy the notorious 'terminator' gene. This does represent a significant victory for green and farmers' organizations, which successfully mobilized public opinion in Europe and some 'Third World' countries. However, while the institutional power relations and regulatory regimes remain unchanged, such 'victories' are always limited and provisional. The wider programme of subordinating the global food system to the control of the biotech transnationals remains intact.

'SUSTAINABLE DEVELOMENT' AND ITS PROSPECTS

The discursive representation of these processes is quite crucial for the wider legitimacy of their outcomes. The emergence of the discourse of 'sustainable development' in the mid-1980s has played a very important part in this process of legitimation, and in integrating diverse strands of the popular environmental movement into a policy agenda largely shaped by capital and technocratic interests in the state. The key innovation effected by this discourse has been to overcome the anti-capitalist potential of earlier environmental discourses, which counterposed environmental protection to the growth-dynamic of contemporary society. The discourse of sustainable development postulates a link between poverty and environmental degradation, and advocates a growth strategy to ameliorate both. Economic growth is thus represented as not only compatible with, but required by, the twin aims of poverty-alleviation and environmental protection in favour of future generations. The semantic openness of this discourse has enabled it to 'capture' and transform a huge diversity of movement organizations and interests, to the extent that environmental political disputes are now almost wholly conducted in terms of rival articulations of its key concepts.

A consequence of this has been that forms of environmental policy and regulation favourable to enhanced capital accumulation can be represented as concessions to the campaigning of environmental social movement organizations. One example of this is the widespread policy shift in favour of reduced car usage and greater public transport investment. Strongly canvassed on grounds of nature conservation, environmental health, social justice and restraint of CO_2 emissions, this shift has also been powerfully canvassed by industrial, and commercial capital and the road transport lobby itself, on grounds of escalating costs of transporting goods on a road system clogged by private cars. Another example of growing importance is the linkage between biodiversity conservation and the biotechnology industries, though here the demand from the industries is for transnational forms of regulation which underwrite their access to predominantly tropical and 'Third World' wild and domesticated biodiversity.

To the extent that discursive constructions of sustainable development favourable to capitalist interests and technocratic élites prevail in policy communities and state institutions, the policies which are generated tend to reduce the requirement of 'sustainability' to the much narrower objective of securing the conditions for future capital accumulation. On the other hand, to the extent that versions more favourable to popular environmental organiza- tions gain wider public legitimacy and a foothold in policy communities, public policy may deviate significantly from the perceived requirements of narrowly economic interests, and may even point in the direction of a qualitatively different material and social order.

We are now in a position to say a little about the conditions under which this latter possibility might be realized (a fuller version of the following argument is presented by Benton in Dobson, 1999). First, the conditions have to be present in civil society for the formation and mobilization of energetic, creative and widely supported oppositional social movements campaigning on environmental issues. This will generally require not only well-entrenched civil liberties, but also a diverse and independent press and media, as well as freedom of information.

Policy communities and the relevant state institutions need to be accessible to such movements. Legal-political institutions need to have established a high level of independence of organized economic interest groups. There has to be both political will and an effective inspection and monitoring apparatus for enforcement of environmental compliance. In short, there have to be conditions favourable to the formation of an independent popular will, a state apparatus sufficiently democratically accountable to be affected by that popular will, and sufficiently authoritative to enforce policies shaped by it.

This provides a framework for thinking about the prospects of the reformist environmentalism currently mobilized around influencing powerful economic and state institutions in the direction of 'sustainable development'. First, the very abstract specification I gave of the relation between capitalist calculation and 'concrete' manufacturing labour processes can be elaborated by bringing into the analysis other labour processes (such as agriculture, mineral extraction, forestry, fisheries and so on) and other social practices (childbearing and rearing, education, socialized health care provision, many forms of leisure activity and so forth), which have *so far* not been *fully* subordinated to capitalist forms of calculation (commodification), and associated dynamics of capital accumulation. Forms of resistance that may be provoked by the continued extensive and intensive commodification of these domains may provide important sources of popular support for oppositional politics.

Second, we can move from the abstract specification of characteristically capitalist logics, or forms of economic calculation, to more concrete levels of analysis of current forms of organization of capital. There are five (interconnected) features of contemporary institutionalizations of capitalist relations which are likely on balance to intensify the socio-ecological destructiveness of continued capital accumulation. These are:

- the increasing ratio of internationally traded to domestically traded goods, and greater international mobility of capital;
- the dominance of financial over industrial and commercial capital;
- the increasing economic and political power of large transnational corporations;
- the forms of regulation of international trade and investment (that is, the WTO, World Bank, IMF);
- the massive shift of scientific research and technological innovation from the public sector to research and development (R&D) departments of large companies.

The last-mentioned shift is particularly threatening in the field of molecular biological research, with the associated patenting of 'created' life forms and the elements of the human genome itself.

In their different ways, these shifts in the institutionalization of capitalist relations all tend to intensify processes of socio-ecological degradation and risk-generation. The first four features serve to render the key dynamics driving patterns of capital accumulation more free than before of material constraints imposed by local conditions, and to insulate them from social and ecological resistances. Finance capital can move freely from one branch of production to another, big logging companies can shift operations from one country to another as forestry resources are over-exploited, the big package tour companies avoid fixed investment in the resort destinations to enable them to focus operations elsewhere when local environments deteriorate, or fashions change: the contemporary equivalent of 'slash and burn'.

The increasing subordination of scientific and technical innovation to commercial priorities, together with enforcement of knowledge as private property, makes likely an unprecedented commodification of life itself, bringing increasingly large sectors of global food production and distribution under the control of a small number of giant agribusiness and food processing transnationals.

So, while there are strong reasons for thinking the new order of globalizing capitalism poses ever more stark threats to both humans and their ecological conditions of life, changes have been occurring at the level of relations between capital, the nation-state and civil society which simultaneously remove the conditions for effective regulation of capital in the service of a democratic popular will.

The literature on 'globalization' disputes whether, and if so to what extent, forces of globalization have undermined the powers of the nation-state. In fact, it can be argued that globalization itself is a term which misleadingly confuses together a diverse array of quite different processes (see Benton in O'Brien et al., 1999). However, to the extent that recent decades have seen the establishment of international regimes and technologies, which have favoured historically high rates of mobility of capital, the powers of nation-states have been reshaped. In general terms, nation-states have been *empowered* both by the ideology of globalization, and by the fact of increased mobility of capital, in their capacity to suppress independent labour and social movement struggles, deregulate labour markets and employment conditions, weaken environmental legislation and generally to align state policy more closely with the interests of domestic and transnational capital.

Correspondingly, national regimes with residual commitments to imposing societal interests on both domestic and transnational capital are *dis-empowered* by these features of the international economy. Even in large trading blocs such as the European Union's, in a period with majority social democratic governments, the pressures to import and allow commercial production of genetically modified food, end trade preferences for poor Third World producers, deregulate labour markets and so on seem near irresistible.

This line of analysis yields rather pessimistic prospects for the approach that currently predominates in Western environmentalism. The pessimism is confirmed by the lack of real advances even in terms of the agenda set out at the Rio conference in the seven years since that major event. However, there are signs of the emergence of alternative approaches. The significant practical success and wide popular support won in the United Kingdom by direct action methods, particularly against live animal exports and road building, resistance by 'Third World' farmers to the new agricultural technologies, and the development of alternative 'green' agricultural projects in Cuba and parts of South America, are examples of grass roots activity which cut against the current tendency to rely on influencing the rich and powerful to change their ways.

Frustration at continuing lack of progress with the reform strategy might lead to a strengthening of these alternatives, in the direction of broadly based movements which make links between the structure of the global economy and the power relations associated with it, on the one hand, and widespread experience of social dislocation, polarization of wealth and poverty and ecological degradation, on the other. It is unclear whether such broad coalitions can be built, or will be able to reconcile inevitable tensions between diverse sources of grievance and cultural tradition. It is, however, increasingly clear that we face an increasingly bleak global future if attempts to create such broadly based alliances to restrain the excesses of global capital should fail.

6. Nature, (Re)Production and Power: A Materialist Ecofeminist Perspective

Mary Mellor

In this chapter the theoretical foundations of an ecological political economy from a sex/gender perspective are examined. The search for an ecological political economy would, I assume, take a deep rather than a shallow approach to the relationship between humanity and the wider ecosystem and seek to reclaim elements of classical radical political economy in the face of the current ideological dominance of neoclassical economics. I argue that such an approach is problematic if the common elements that unite classical economics (even in its radical form) and neoclassical economics are not addressed.

Neoclassical economics has been widely condemned by feminist economists (Ferber and Nelson, 1993; Kuiper and Sap, 1995; Nelson, 1996) for its gender-blind, autonomous, choice-theoretic notion of 'economic man' (Mellor, 1997b). However, classical economics, the framework within which even radical political economy is based, has also been criticized as gender blind (Gardiner, 1997; Pujol, 1992). An ecological political economy that reproduces the sex/gender blindness of the past will not serve as a progressive model for the future. This is not to say that the notion of political economy is unhelpful, particularly given the current dominance of economic over political thinking, but it needs to be addressed from a feminist perspective.

Most radical thinkers have accepted that the feminist critique of male domination in human societies is valid but I do not think they have appreciated how deep this critique goes. It is not just a case of adding women to established theories. The sex/gender division goes to the heart of social life and therefore to the heart of the theories that attempt to explain it. Materialist ecofeminists like myself see this division as central to the environmental destructiveness of male-dominated economic systems (Mellor, 1997a). At the same time, I would argue that it is only *one* of the factors leading to environmental destructiveness. Class exploitation, racism, colonialism and speciesism are equally pernicious. Sex/gender does, however, differ from other structural inequalities in one key respect and that is why I am using this linked concept.

The core principle of ecological awareness is the link between the social and the natural. Sex/gender is pivotal here. Gender refers to social divisions based superficially on sex difference that are socially constructed. Gender-assigned activities vary across history, cultures and classes. Sex is the physical division of a species that reproduces sexually (which, of course, has no determinate relation to sex identity, sexuality or sexual orientation). In this sense sex is a more fundamental division than class or 'race'. It is possible to imagine (and hopefully we will one day achieve) a classless society in which 'race' ceases to have any meaning as a social categorization. Both class and 'race' are social constructs. It is also possible to envisage a genderless society in which men and women lead similar lives. However, it is not possible to envisage a sexless society unless there is some kind of radical genetic reconstruction, which presumably ecologists would oppose.

Despite the existence of physiological sex differences these *should* have no relevance for socially constructed economic relations. This is not the case, however, as sex difference underpins the main justification for women's economic inequality, the ideological division between woman-as-mother and man-as-provider. This socially constructed notion has been naturalized within society as sexual inequality based on the strong 'fatherly' capable man and the weak, ultimately fallible, woman as dependent. This assumption goes so deep that the liberal campaign for gender equality within a male-constructed world (equal opportunities) has only scratched the surface. The critique of gender inequality has to go as deep as the physiological foundations of human existence. This links the 'woman' question with the 'nature' question.

In taking a materialist ecofeminist perspective I am addressing the woman-nature issue in terms of structural relations in society rather than addressing male and female 'natures'. I have explained more fully elsewhere the relationship between materialist ecofeminism and other ecofeminist positions (Mellor, 1996; Mellor, 1997a). All ecofeminists share a concern about the link between ecological destruction and women's subordination and point to the dualistic nature of Western cultures where man-science-rationality-culture is set against woman-vernacular-emotional-nature. The basis of these dualisms is where ecofeminisms differ. Some ecofeminists stress physio-logical, cultural or psychodynamic differences while others point to historical and social contingency. Materialist ecofeminism sees these dualistic divisions as based on a structural relation of inequality rather than a dichotomous bifurcation of society(ies) or historical happenstance.

I do, however, have sympathy with those ecofeminists who see a deep psycho-cultural dynamic (Collard, 1988) or a cultural/philosophical dualism within human society (Plumwood, 1993). Women's subordination is so historically and culturally widespread that it is tempting to take an essentialist approach, not about women (as ecofeminists are accused of) but about men. Why is there this drive to dominate? In my work I have offered a material explanation which I set out below, but I do have periodic worries that there is a 'deeper' problem. I think I have read most ecofeminist literature and I do not find in it a rejection of men as such. Often there is a rejection of the 'male/masculine' as a cosmic, cultural or psycho-dynamic concept but individual men are seen as being able to choose another path. However, this optimism is not confirmed by the sexual division within radical, and particularly, green literature. Men are talking mainly to men and women to women as a glance at any bibliography will show. While many male thinkers express awareness of the sex/gender problem it rarely goes to the heart of their analysis. To save clumsy phrasing, I will use 'gender' rather than sex/gender below.

GENDER BLINDNESS IN CLASSICAL POLITICAL ECONOMY

> The origins of modern economics are to be found in classical political economy, which set out to provide an explanation of the workings of the emerging industrial capitalist system (Gardiner, 1997, p. 21).

If modern economics with all its destructive ecological outcomes is also a child of classical political economy, a radical political economy cannot develop if it uncritically adopts central assumptions shared by both. The core element for feminists is the failure of both classical and neoclassical economics to 'see' women.

The industrial system was based on the separation (for men) of home and work and the segregation of paid from unpaid work. As the system developed men became increasingly identified with the public world of paid work while women were associated with unpaid work in the home. This does not mean, of course, that women did not do paid work in the formal economy, but men certainly did very little of the remaining domestic work except as paid servants. The industrial system for working women meant a double burden of work. While the separation of work, home and leisure may make sense for most men, for the majority of women home also represents work with very little leisure. The exceptions were the wives of prosperous men who combined restriction to the home with what many felt was enforced idleness. These women formed the backbone of voluntary community work and through political campaigns forced their way into the public world of work and politics.

Along with the industrial system came the idea of the family wage and man as the 'breadwinner'. Women's work in the home and factory was either ignored or seen as secondary. More importantly, these ideas were projected back in history so that women's history as economic agents was lost. 'Man the hunter' was identified in various economic forms throughout history while 'woman the gatherer' faded from view. Feminist historians have sought to reclaim her story (Barber, 1994; Coontz and Henderson, 1986), while contemporary analysis of women's work in non-industrial society shows women have heavy levels of involvement in subsistence farming particularly in sub-Saharan Africa (Boserup, 1970; Sachs, 1996). On the basis of a survey of anthropological studies I carried out, it became clear that although male anthropologists rarely discuss women's activities, what evidence there is shows that women were central to subsistence economic life (Mellor, 1992). I was particularly struck by the report given by a missionary of Huron women's lives in seventeenth-century Canada:

> Among these tribes are found powerful women of extraordinary stature; for they till the soil, sow the corn, fetch the wood for the winter, strip the hemp, and spin it, and with the threads make fishing nets . . . they have the labour of harvesting the corn, sorting it, preparing it and attending to the house and besides are required to follow their husbands from place to place in the fields, where they serve as *mules* to carry the baggage (quoted in Anderson, 1987, p. 128).

A reading of this literature from a feminist perspective shows that male hunting often had social/ritual elements that could reasonably be defined as leisure rather than work. In many societies there was also some kind of men's house or ceremonial activities, which created public space for men away from work and women's activities. This division is clear in Aristotle's favoured separation of the public world of politics from the domestic world of women and slaves. Aristotle also differentiated between domestic provisioning and the world of trade and money-making. He saw both as inferior to the public world of the citizen, but at least he was aware of the distinction between them.

Failure to have a gender perspective leads to a confusion about what economic activity *is* and lets the contemporary capitalist market economies confuse money-making as production with provisioning as production. Feminist economists are seeking to reclaim the notion of provisioning (Nelson, 1993, 1996) as well as women's unpaid work (Waring, 1989) and the recognition of care as work (Folbre, 1994; Gardiner, 1997).

Provisioning here is defined as those activities that meet basic reproductive needs, food, shelter, body maintenance, life cycle support (birth to death), health care and emotional support. Historically women have been directly involved in the range of provisioning including food production.

Sanday has produced evidence that in rural economies where women provide a substantial proportion of subsistence needs themselves, they have more autonomy and socio-economic power (Sanday, 1981). However, women's access to resources tends to be governed by usufruct, right of use through family/communal membership. These rights tend to be lost as land becomes enclosed and commodified. In economies based on wage labour, women become dependent on either the wages earned by male family members, or the meagre earnings of 'women's wages' which assume that basic subsistence is being met from a male income (Mies, 1999).

A challenge to the male-dominated conception of the 'economic', I would argue, is essential to any development of an ecological political economy. In industrial capitalist economies capitalist patriarchy has harnessed the public world of production on a global scale (Mies, 1999). Marx in his critique of industrial capitalism explored its internal contradictions, but largely shared its definition of production and thereby the boundaries of political economy. While the social separation between the public world of men and the private world of women goes way back in history, the separation of work between the public and private worlds is much more recent. It could even be argued that it is only in later industrial society that men began to substantially increase their contribution to the total work of society (particularly in terms of basic provisioning) in comparison to women's input. In early industrial society it was, of course, women and children who first filled the factories and mines. As Marx noted, it was men who initially proved the most reluctant to accept factory discipline.

Given this background, classical political economy can be seen as the framework that describes the emergence of men as economic agents within an industrialized and commodified capitalist society. It also marks women's disappearance as economic actors. Even today women only take part in the formal economy within the professions or as core full-time workers if they present themselves as 'honorary men' denying their domestic responsibilities. As *women* they enter the workforce as poorly paid, part-time, peripheral workers deemed to be fitting their time in around their caring and domestic responsibilities even if they have no partner or children.

ECOLOGICAL POLITICAL ECONOMY AS (RE)PRODUCTION

What then, should an ecological political economy be about? It should, of course, analyse the present economic system and its ecologically destructive activities. This is what Marx did for the class exploitative activities of nineteenth-century capitalism. It should also develop the framework for a radical approach to the dynamics between humanity and non-human nature. Marx did this too in his view of labour as the interaction of humanity with the natural world. Provisioning in its broadest sense covers those activities necessary for human beings to realize their creative potential. It also covers the conversion of raw materials from the natural to the socially useful. The limitations of Marx's analysis were that he did not see the natural world as either limited or having its own 'needs'; and his failure to take account of reproductive work in the narrow sense. The bearing and raising of children was seen as unproblematically women's work. Marx assumed that there was a natural sexual division of labour. He did, however, with Engels, assume that women's labour would eventually be incorporated into the wider economy and women's equality would be achieved in that way.

The starting point for an ecological political economy informed by feminist thinking would be to break down the distinction between production and reproduction. Physically reproducing and caring for the human species is as much work as growing food and is certainly more important than producing weapons or cars. The second would be to challenge the notion of the 'economic' that has failed to recognize women's work, in particular the rationale for, and boundaries between, paid, low paid and unpaid work. The third would be to separate out provisioning from unnecessary and destructive forms of economic activity. This would challenge the assumption that the primary motivation for production is money/profit and that it is not possible to distinguish between needs and wants. The fourth would be to envisage an economic framework that would enable human communities built upon destructive economic systems (including populations which expanded on the basis of colonial exploitation) to provision themselves without exploitation of women, men, other species or the ecosystems of the planet. In a short study I cannot achieve all of these but an analysis of women's work will provide a start.

WOMEN'S WORK

For nearly thirty years, feminists have argued for the recognition of women's unpaid domestic, communal and subsistence work. They have calculated that if formally rewarded it would represent up to 50 per cent of gross domestic product (GDP) in industrialized countries and in less commodified economies women's subsistence work can represent up to 80 per cent of subsistence agricultural work (Waring, 1989). As commodified and productivist economies have emerged the centrality of women's work has become less obvious. In most industrialized economies it involves unpaid domestic, child and other caring work. However, most of women's paid work is also similar, the under-labouring work of nourishing, caring and organizing support as cleaners, caterers, nurses, teachers and secretaries.

It is becoming increasingly difficult to sustain the segregation and marginalization of women's economic activities in countries like the United Kingdom where women are more than half the workforce (although not in terms of full-time or higher paid jobs). Women entering the workforce in large numbers have followed the commodification of women's work particularly in catering and caring. In this way the confusion between provisioning and money-making becomes even more complex. With the loss of women's domestic work also comes the loss of individual skills. The population of the United Kingdom is now almost completely dependent for its basic needs on the capitalist economy. While there is increasing concern about the quality of industrially processed food, many women no longer have the time or the skills to prepare fresh food (even if they could find sufficient organic produce at a reasonable price). Within non-industrialized rural subsistence communities there is equal concern about the loss of knowledge of organic and sustainable systems of production (Shiva, 1989).

What unites women's work whether unacknowledged, unpaid or underpaid is its unremitting nature. Throughout history women have done the routine repetitive jobs, gathering, weeding, cooking, fetching and nursing. The economy of these activities is time. They never stop. There is also no means of accumulation, the products of the labour are either intangible, or immediately consumed. Where there is a surplus product (extra crops) the ownership of these, and the land they are grown on, is often claimed by the male head of household. Where they are sold by women, the money is put towards household needs, as are most women's wages when they do paid work. Where women's work is commodified it is given low status and pay. By doing the time-consuming work, women release what is arguably the first economic surplus – time.

Men's work historically has tended to be more spasmodic; building, hunting, clearing, trade and war. Hard and dangerous as this work may be, there is generally an endpoint and a reward in terms of status or tangible product. Such rewards are, of course, rarely shared equally among the men who create/produce them. Male domination of women is also accompanied by structural inequalities between men. Some women associated with privileged men also share the spoils although relatively few do so in their own right.

The material benefit of women's unremitting and repetitive work, which often takes the form of watching, being there 'in case', is to free men relatively in terms of social time and space. This space is often represented as an arena barred from women. In many cultures there is the equivalent of the 'men's house' – from the secret activities of male rites (which still exist in organizations such as the Freemasons), to until very recently, the military, government, industry and the professions. The higher echelons of these activities are still male-dominated. From this perspective the economy is not distinct from any other hierarchical social construction representing the male-dominated accumulation of time and space which rests on the hidden or low-paid world of women's work. It also rests on the work of men oppressed by 'race' and class who are forced into menial low-paid tasks. Pointing to the importance of women's work in history should not obscure the importance of slaves and bonded labour in the creation of social space, time and material wealth.

The fact that many socially necessary provisioning activities are now within the formal economy leads to the generally unchallenged assumption that commodified economies meet needs. They may do so, but this is not their primary function. Male-dominated capitalism blends necessary and unnecessary work, that is, provisioning (which includes services as well as products) with money-making. Money-making here includes not just capital accumulation but the need to have hierarchies of 'management' ensuring status which overwhelmingly benefits men. The dominance of economic thinking is so central that whenever any need is identified the first question is 'who will pay'? Similarly, the use of direct labour is seen as undermining 'real' (usually male) jobs, unless the work is community-based in which case there is little threat as there is a long history of women doing unpaid community work. The motivation for defending paid work, however, is understandable where resources are unequally shared, and money is the only mechanism by which access can be achieved.

The more important question is why systems of provisioning have become constructed into these complex structures of exchange. From a gender and historical perspective, commodified economic systems can be seen as yet another example of the elaborately constructed games played in the men's house. Money itself is the ultimate social construct, which internationally is now being built into a house of cards. The political aim should not therefore be to control economies or even to democratize them. It is to dissolve the distinctiveness of the economic itself. Why should provisioning the needs of human existence be seen as separate from other social aspects of human existence?

This would not mean doing away with money exchange or any of the other useful benefits of trade but as everyone from Polanyi onwards has been demanding, economies must be embedded within the wider social framework and, of course, in the limits and needs of the natural world. Ironically it is the 'economy' that is achieving this in reverse by absorbing increasing numbers of activities and resources (social and natural) that were formerly uncommodified. It is hard to find political ground that is free from economistic thinking, which is why the arguments from a green and feminist perspective are vital.

ECOFEMINIST POLITICAL ECONOMY

As discussed earlier, ecofeminists have argued that the subordination of women and the degradation of the natural world are linked. Some have argued that this reflects a particular aspect of the nature of women, others that it has been a contingent effect of industrialization and modernity. The basis of my analysis is that the relationship between the subordination of women and the destruction of the environment reflects a deep and pervasive material relation. In short, that the material relationship between humanity and its natural context is gendered. The pervasive and material relation to which I refer is the fact that women's work and lives have historically been disproportionately concerned with the basic means of human existence, the production of food, people and society.

I would not wish to argue that women are more naturally suited to this work, but at the same time their involvement with it is not purely contingent. The issue goes much deeper than that, humanity as a sexed species has repeatedly socially constructed its material existence on the basis of gender inequality. More specifically (most) men have subordinated (most) women and the material relation of that subordination is the sexed/gendered division of labour. However, only a relatively few men (and the women who associate with them) have managed to harness the benefits of this division of labour in the long run.

The link to environmental degradation is that if women carry out the work that represents the most basic aspects of human existence, including maintaining the human body, men will be relatively more distanced from the materiality of human existence. The more powerful the man (now joined by a few powerful women) the less likely he is to be aware of the mundane activities that make his jet-setting life possible. Even where a woman has achieved a similar position of power, she is unlikely to be able to completely shake off her domestic and linked responsibilities.

Green critics have pointed to the environmental blindness of disembedded economic systems. From a materialist ecofeminist perspective, this disembedding is not a recent phenomenon. It has been building over the generations of male use of women's 'body labour'. Concern with the impact of economic systems on the natural environment read as ecology should not blind us to the impact of economic systems on the natural as represented in the bodily lives of human existence.

If the environment has its necessary rhythms and patterns, so does human life. It has its cycles and needs, its own momentum. Ecological economists argue that economic systems externalize the natural environment and therefore avoid the costs of ecological damage. Equally, economic systems externalize the human body, its cycles of life, variations of health and capabilities and reproduction, and leave the costs to be borne elsewhere. Formal economies ignore the fact that humanity is not only embedded in its ecosystem but is also embodied in its own natural existence. It is the work of human bodily existence that has generally been left to women. Care of the young, the old, the sick and the need for daily replenishment and cleanliness.

Some aspects of this work have been commodified, but it is unlikely that it could all be integrated any more than the costs of ecological damage could be met within the formal economy. Universal care for the elderly is as unaffordable in money terms as the cost of caring for nuclear waste.

It is not the formality of payment/non-payment of women's work that is central here, however, it is the way that economic systems (capitalist and non-capitalist) have been gendered. Economic activity tends to be centred around what men do; war, trade and construction. It starts with the exceptional, exotic and grandiose, rather than the routine. In modern capitalist economies, the focus is on 'economic man', fit, mobile and resourced, and thereby deemed to be autonomous. This does not reflect the reality of women's lives. The notion of the 'economic' even for radical economists, is generally constructed within a world that represents male experience (a male-experience world, a ME-world) not the world of women's experience (a women's-experience world, a WE-world).

The starting point of an effective ecological political economy would therefore have to be the WE-world not only of ecological sustainability, but also of the human life cycle. Production would no longer be separated from reproduction, construction from care. Priority would be given to work that is currently undervalued and marginalized. Provisioning would be from the perspective of women and underprivileged people generally within the limits of ecological sustainability. Tough if there are no more golf courses or high powered cars (or any cars).

Women's work can be seen as mediating between the 'natural' and the 'social'. The natural here is taken to mean the necessary activities for the maintenance of human existence. Humans are embodied and have psychological and physical needs that must be met on a regular basis. Women have not done a disproportionate amount of this work because they are more 'natural', but because someone has to do the necessary body work and this has historically been done by women or those of low status from slaves to racially or socially oppressed groups. Those who avoid this work can exploit a much wider potential for their social activities. They can accumulate the time that is not spent in routine work and colonize the social space of those who are confined to fields, dwellings or factories.

Within modern economies the necessary work of provisioning is carried out in a variety of contexts, much of it through the formal economy, and the pattern of exploitation is much more widespread than just women's work. Within the present global economy those men (and some women) who can accumulate resources (money, property), time and space can, to a certain extent, extend the limits of human embodiedness and embeddedness. They can live well and long, travel far, enjoy luxuries and exotic goods, spend time developing social and cultural skills and build business empires or careers. In doing this they will claim to be working extremely hard and making a major contribution to the progress of humanity, and in many ways they are. Within the framework of liberal democracy they will also promise that similar life chances are available to everyone. Given the present socio-economic and environmental context, this is a lie.

The present global economy originated in the massive material and cultural wealth that developed in Western Europe on the back of trade, piracy, slavery and colonialism, as well as the sexual division of labour. Central to the European world view was the idea that humanity could dominate and transcend the forces of nature, an idea that has increasingly been brought into question. Certainly humanity can extend and manipulate natural conditions as expressed in biological and ecological processes, but it is now accepted that there are limits and consequences.

The illusions of transcendence in Western societies has been achieved by the exploitation of human labour and natural resources and the expropriation of the time, resources and space of others, including that of other species. Such transcendence is largely, although not entirely, a zero-sum game. The health and well-being of the more prosperous has been achieved largely at the expense of those whose lives are curtailed by labour and pov- erty. Mechanisms of transcendence that ignore the realities of human embodiedness and embeddedness within the ecosystem are necessarily destructive.

Far from the delusions of transcendence, I would argue that the starting point ontologically and epistemologically for an ecological political economy should be the embeddedness and embodiedness of all humanity within its physical framework, its biology and ecology. This interconnected framework imposes necessary bodywork on human activity as well as boundary limitations and consequences. None of this determines the exact nature of human activity, but destructive outcomes result from the attempt to tran- scend boundary conditions. Defining those boundary conditions is more problematic. Natural limits are not determining. 'Nature' does not have a message for us in either a mystical or a positivist sense. All we can know is that we are in an interconnected system that has its own interactive dynamic and that the outcome of that dynamic is always uncertain.

I have called this ontological and epistemological framework *immanent realism* (Mellor, 1997a). I use the word immanent/ce in opposition to the delusion of transcendence. Humanity is always immanent within the interconnected framework of its existence. That framework is real. It is not a construct of the human mind, although it is relatively malleable through human action. In pointing to the malleability of human existence, I want to avoid the extremes of naturalism/determinism and human exceptionalism.

Immanent realism is a starting point, an acceptance of humanity's cosmological status within and not outside of the whole. This compares with a starting point of transcendence, which assumes humanity stands outside and over its natural context. Immanence as used here does not mean biological/ecological determinism. Humanity is flooded with choices, but only some of them will ensure human survival in a way that enhances the potential of all its citizens. Transcendence on the basis of unequal structural relations is not one of them.

The delusion of transcendence lies at the heart of the present global capitalist patriarchal economy. A critique of this economy would start from the human life cycle and its needs, which I have called biological time. It would ask how far does 'the economy' however defined, map onto the needs of the human life cycle? Do its patterns of work, production, transport and investment meet those needs? The same questions could be asked of 'the economy' with regard to ecological time, the ecological life cycle. All provisioning would see products as having their own life cycle from raw material to disposal. This framework of analysis is very different from current political and economic theories and structures with their short timescales and 'bottom line' assumptions. It is not possible to develop an ecological political economy if the concept of the 'economic' at its heart is already disembodied and disembedded within time and space.

The question remains as to how this analysis becomes political action. Obviously it is possible to use ideas as 'theoretical practice', but the main source of change will come from the interconnections of the social and natural within human existence. While economic systems may be ideologically disembedded in the sense that they do not see the consequences of their action, they cannot be disembedded in practice. As I have argued, mechanisms of transcendence are based on structures of inequality and patterns of ecological destruction. Both are likely to affect what O'Connor (1994) has called the conditions of production. Social and environmental unrest as well as ecological dereliction will increase the costs of production or affect its political or economic viability.

Nor can the 'raw material' of those systems, the people who control it escape their embodiment indefinitely. Every human being, even economic man, lives within their own life cycle and daily being even if they obscure this fact by using the labour of others. The living breathing human person is always embedded, she or he is always 'here' within their own embodiment. As I have argued elsewhere, I do not think the political problem is getting from 'here' to 'there', to some utopian moment or alternative social structure. The more important task is to get from 'there' to 'here'; from a position of assumed transcendence to the realism of immanence. 'Here', in the interconnected whole, spatially and temporally, without delusions or mechanisms of transcendence, is where most women have been all the time (Mellor, 1995).

Transcendence is ultimately an illusion, although dominant groups can make it a short-term reality through harnessing structural inequalities. Ontologically everyone is part of the interconnected ecological whole. 'Thereness', actions that are carried out as if human economies are disembedded and disembodied, have real material consequences as transnational corporations scour the globe for profitable activities, but wherever they go they are always in somebody's 'here'. The individuals representing those companies are also 'here' in their own bodies and their own mortality. There is nothing wrong with global interaction, as such, provided it is grounded in the needs and limits of the global 'here'. To paraphrase a well-known saying, humanity should act globally, but think locally. Not just of a specific locality, but of every locality. For as immanent realism would tell us, humanity is part of the whole.

PART THREE

Ecological Political Economy and the State

7. Political Ecology and Regional Sustainability: Reflections on Contemporary Debates and Material Practices

Haripriya Rangan

Most people take for granted the fact that environmental degradation, climate change or natural resource management are profoundly geographic in their dimensions and have differentiated outcomes in various regions of the world. Yet it is a matter of great irony that critical debates around environmental issues have made little effort to explicitly state their fundamental assumptions and conceptions about geography or the nature of geographic processes. These debates have, of course, provided a variety of insights about 'nature': that it is a 'social construct'; that the division between humans and nature is a product of Western, male and scientific rationality; that nature has been colonized and ravaged by human greed; and that nature and humanity can only be saved by 'thinking globally and acting locally'. Despite the critical insights and arguments about the social construction of nature and environmental crises, contemporary environmental discourse displays a sanguine indifference towards the meaning of geography. It assumes that environmental problems, socially constructed or otherwise, can be resolved in the abstract geographical terrains of 'globality' and 'locality'. Needless to say, solutions based on such conceptions of geography have neither yielded desired results, nor provided much understanding of the ways in which distinctive geographical histories are continually shaped and altered through traditions and material practices.

This study seeks to rethink the question of environmental change and sustainability from a geographic perspective. It is based on recognizing two fundamental aspects of geographic knowledge; first, that development and change are open-ended processes; second, that geography does not merely refer to the physiographic setting in which social activity takes place, but that it is about the lived dimensions of social life that are continually reshaped through material practices and processes of differentiation, diversification and reconfiguration. The study is divided into four sections.

The first section outlines the analytical approach of political ecology, and identifies the key dimensions that provide a comparative framework for understanding the geographic dynamism of regionality and regional change. The second section then uses this comparative geographic framework of analysis to examine the ways in which issues of ecological change and sustainability have been addressed in contemporary environmental discourse. The third section focuses on the problems of constructing 'state' and 'community' as oppositional spaces in attempting sustainable management of natural resources, and examines the viability of an alternative 'regionalized' strategy that emerged in the form of 'joint forest management' in the state of West Bengal, India. The concluding section argues that political ecology not only provides a rigorous and grounded analytical framework for understanding the geographic dimensions of sustainability, but also offers new possibilities of enabling political action that seek to address issues of regionality and redistribution through substantive democracy.

POLITICAL ECOLOGY

The earliest proponents of political ecology describe it as an approach that 'combines the concerns of ecology and a broadly defined political economy. Together this encompasses the constantly shifting dialectic between society and land-based resources, and also within classes and groups within society itself' (Blaikie and Brookfield, 1987, p.17; see also Bryant, 1992; Buttel and Sunderlin, 1988; Friedmann and Rangan, 1993; Peluso, 1992 for descriptions and definitions of political ecology). They argue that the approach is regional in scope, because 'it is necessary to take account of environmental variability and spatial variations in resilience and sensitivity of the land, as different demands are put on the land through time. The word "regional" also implies the incorporation of environmental considerations into theories of regional growth and decline' (Blaikie and Brookfield, 1987, p. 17).

Blaikie and Brookfield attempt to explain the ways in which economic differentiation and environmental degradation function as mutually re-inforcing processes. For example, inequalities within society, which create conditions of marginality for some groups more than others, impose a variety of constraints on land managers which, in turn, increase the pressure on their productive capacities. The wide variation in perception regarding both social and ecological problems adds to the pressures faced by land managers who may be left with no choice but to increase production by intensive or extensive use of resources. Blaikie and Brookfield illustrate how various chains of causes and effects may lead to conjunctural outcomes that mutually reinforce the link between poverty and environmental degradation.

Although they offer a more spatially contextualized and historicized explanation of ecological and social change, some of their critics consider that their approach is not 'a theory which allows for . . . and identifies complexity' (Blaikie and Brookfield, 1987, p. 239), but rather an '*ad hoc* and frequently voluntarist view of degradation' (Peet and Watts, 1996, p. 8). Peet and Watts argue that 'if political ecology reflects a confluence between ecologically rooted social science and the principles of political economy, its theoretical coherence nonetheless remains in question . . . political ecology seems grounded less in a coherent theory as such than in similar areas of inquiry' (ibid., p. 6). They consider the lack of theoretical coherence in political ecology resulting in an approach that is 'radically pluralist and largely without politics or an explicit sensitivity to class interest and social struggle' (ibid., p. 8).

Peet and Watts' criticisms of political ecology are generally valid. The literature that falls within this broad appellation is, indeed, diverse. I would, however, challenge their criticisms by arguing that political ecology as an analytical approach has far greater theoretical coherence from a geographic perspective than other analytical frameworks that attempt to explain the processes of ecological and social change. The diversity within the political ecology literature is not necessarily a consequence of the lack of a coherent theory, but because its theoretical perspective stems from a fundamental recognition of geographic diversity. The theoretical sensitivity and commitment to geography has, by and large, remained implicit in political ecology. My intention here is to make its theoretical coherence explicit.

Let me begin with a broad redefinition of political ecology. Political ecology is an analytical approach that explains *the biogeographical outcomes of social relations* in the context of differing spatial and political configurations. The theoretical assumptions underlying this definition are as follows:

- the non-human environment (the biotic and abiotic surroundings) is a dynamic context (as opposed to a static backdrop) for the evolution of human life;
- human populations and social practices are part of the spatiotemporal unit chosen for studying change (as opposed to viewing humans and their interactions as 'alienated' from or 'external' to nature);
- the ambiguities of spatial boundaries are produced from social perceptions of place and hierarchies of geographic scale, as well as from the complexity of interactions occurring within and between recognizable ecosystems;

- spatial boundaries are dynamic, constantly changing in relation to shifting cultural values, networks of social and material practices, and political configurations over time;
- human and non-human life are linked through dynamic processes and constantly transforming relationships which may yield unpredictable or unknowable outcomes within and across networks of political and spatial configurations.

All of these assumptions highlight the distinctive geographic epistemology that informs political ecology. History is not viewed as a teleological process marching up the ladder of evolution towards a climactic state of equilibrium (Gould, 1987), but is understood as a process continually shaped by contingency and uncertainty. By acknowledging the open-endedness of social and ecological change, political ecology neither privileges 'spatiality' nor 'temporality', but focuses on the processes that continually produce diverse geographical histories.

As I mentioned earlier, political ecology's focus on regions is based on an understanding of geographies as relational spaces that people *make*, and *with which* they do various things. These *regionalities*, or the lived dimensions to social life, produce, reshape and sustain biological and material traditions. Regions, from a political ecology perspective, are not mere 'spatial settings', but geographical histories that carry both sense and sensibility of the lived dimensions to social life. They are the fluid and permeable dimensions of social experience that are produced and reshaped by the practices of everyday life (Bourdieu, 1977; Braudel, 1973, 1977). The interactions between the habitual rhythms of social and material life, and the diverse fluctuations, or *conjunctures* (Braudel, 1977, pp. 5–7; 1966, pp. 651–6), of demographic and capital movements and biogeophysical processes, create regions that become palimpsests upon which overlapping geographical histories are repeatedly inscribed and incompletely erased. Regional landscapes appear as 'structured dispositions' that carry the tension between 'objectification' and 'embodiment' (Bourdieu, 1977, pp. 86–95), between 'structure' and 'coherence'. Their identities are institutionalized through 'officializing strategies' and 'non-official' customary practices (ibid., 1977, p. 35). These processes create shared places that people reshape in familiar ways, and from which they attempt to familiarize, customize or challenge the changes brought about by conjunctures and events.

Regions are thus seen as overlapping geographical histories of common access that encompass known practices and knowable activities. They become regionalities through lived dimensions that are sustained and problematized by social practices.[1] Political ecology thus provides the means for understanding *how* rather than *why* development and ecological change occur in distinctive ways in different regional configurations.

The analytical framework of political ecology focuses on four interlinked dimensions of social institutions and instituted practices that shape the geographical histories of regionality and regional change. The first dimension centres on households. Household formation within regions is seen as diverse, encompassing a variety of social arrangements, differentially bestowed property rights and responsibilities among members. These internal relations – produced and renegotiated through customary traditions and social processes – render households as spaces of 'cooperative conflict' (Sen, 1990).

Households are seen as regional actors, engaging in diversified livelihood strategies that are not merely confined to particular localities, but carried out within broader institutional and transregional networks of social and material activity. The livelihood strategies of households are shaped by the gender and age composition of their members, and may involve, in varying combinations and degrees, activities that are generally classified as urban and rural, agricultural and non-agricultural, waged and non-waged (Agarwal, 1994; Folbre, 1986; Jackson, 1994; Peters, 1983). Social differentiation of households in these regions is produced from the mix of livelihood strategies they pursue, which both influence and change alongside the reconfiguration of regional economies, institutional networks, and transregional interactions (Levin and Weiner, 1997; Rangan, 1997b).

The second dimension of inquiry focuses on the actions of state institutions. Rather than beginning with preconceived ideas about its singular character, 'the state' is recognized as a set of nested and interlinked institutions that perform ensembles of activities encompassing a great deal more than territorial defence and coercion of its constituents. This assemblage of institutions is also involved in fostering economic activities and providing a modicum of welfare for its diversified constituency (Evans, 1995; Rangan, 1997c). As Foucault points out, 'modern' states established their legitimacy by promising and striving to act in adherence to their own laws. This was (and still is) their *raison d'état*. The *raison d'état* establishes the principles and conventions of institutional action, or to use Foucault's term, *governmentality* (Foucault, 1991). More important is that 'the state', as Foucault and others note, is not the only source or form of *governmentality*. Other 'legitimized' institutions – such as markets and 'customary' traditions – also delineate the ways in which governance occurs within particular spatial and political configurations (Bebbington, 1996; Carney, 1996; Mamdani, 1996). The analysis focuses on how governance occurs at different spatial levels, how the processes of policy making and governing are shaped by varied economic and political necessities, as well as conjunctures and events occurring within and beyond the administrative reach of state institutions. State actions are thus seen as processes that create and sustain regional differentiation through a wide range of administrative and political practices. The actions of different state institutions may appear well coordinated or, at times, intensely contentious; some may tend towards authoritarian control or, conversely, be open to capture, reform or manipulation by social groups and classes that live both within and outside their jurisdictions (Rangan, 1997c).

The third dimension focuses on the institutionalized modes of access to and control over regional resources. Here the aim is to understand management and use of natural resources, not merely as outcomes of legal ownership or property status, but rather to examine how various social groups and institutions, both within and beyond the region, exercise control over a wide array of regional resources. Juridical rights of property are seen as part of a wide variety of access regimes that shape the ways in which natural resources are used, managed or traded for profit. State agencies, market and community institutions employ differentiated ensembles of instruments and modes of control – or *access regimes* – for controlling extraction, use, maintenance and sale of natural resources within and across regions. These access regimes and instruments of control are routinely open to contestation and renegotiation (Peluso, 1992, 1995; Peters, 1987; Rangan, 1997a; Ribot, 1998).

The fourth dimension centres on examining the discursive strategies employed by institutions within regions. Discursive strategies are seen as political tools used in the process of contestation and negotiation between institutions of state, market and civil society. They may succeed in transforming particular, localized, disputes into broader social movements by redefining the identities and roles of participants in ways that gain political support for their agendas beyond their immediately known communities. But while discursive strategies may gain the attention and support of wider audiences, they may not always yield the outcomes desired by the people whose interests they claim to represent. The success or failure of any discursive strategy – that is to say, whether or not it succeeds in gaining official recognition or altering existing institutional practices – is contingent upon the malleability of administrative domains, the flexibility of dominant policy approaches espoused by different levels of government and the electoral arithmetic employed by political parties at these sites of power.

Far from lacking theoretical coherence, political ecology stems from a distinctive epistemological perspective based in geographic history and maintains its theoretical focus on regional sustainability and sustaining regionality. It provides the analytical framework for understanding how social institutions and institutionalized practices shape biogeographical and distributional outcomes in diverse regions.

The question of sustainability in its varied geographic dimensions is of central concern to political ecology. But its method of understanding sustainability differs from the ways in which this concept has been discussed in contemporary environmental discourse. Part of the current discourse about sustainability has involved protracted argument over the meaning of the term, its imprecision, ambiguity and contradictions inherent in its usage (Bryant and Parnwell, 1996; Daly, 1991b; Mitlin, 1992; Redclift, 1987). It is not my intention here to retrace these debates and pronounce judgement on their accuracy. Rather, I am interested in critically examining how dominant participants in environmental debates (Beder, 1993; Business Council for Sustainable Development, 1992; Hampson, 1990) construct the idea of geographic sustainability through their narratives.

SUSTAINABILITY AND THE GLOBAL-LOCAL

There are two distinctive features that characterize the discourse around sustainability. First, there is a shared assumption that sustainability is primarily about the biogeophysical environment, and hence, environmental sustainability. Second, that it is necessary to establish some sort of connection between the spaces of the particular and the universal for articulating the problems related to environmental sustainability. The ensuing narratives generally follow one of two trajectories, both beginning with a description of how 'the local' and 'the global' connect, then diverging in their critiques of prevailing practices pursued by states, markets and civil societies, before finally arriving at their respectively envisioned destinations of global-local sustainability.

The narratives beginning from a 'global' perspective start by outlining a range of environmental processes identified as problems by scientists, phenomena such as global warming, global population growth and global climate change. These are seen as threatening the very survival of human life on earth. The earth is variably described as a living organism, a delicately balanced ecosystem with limited carrying capacity, a whole entity whose various parts are intricately connected to support life up to a certain level beyond which survival is severely jeopardized, even impossible. Environmental problems are caused by the exponential compounding of human activities in various parts of the world: population growth creates pressures on the earth's resources as people clear forests and encroach on fragile ecosystems to cultivate more land for food;[2] industrial development aimed at meeting the needs of rapidly expanding world population results in increased exploitation of minerals and burning of fossil fuels. Hence local actions cause the global crisis of sustainability.[3]

Since sustainability represents a common good for all humans, it requires solutions that are conceived of and implemented at the global scale. It requires all governments of the world to set aside or check their national interests in favour of global environmental security, which involves endorsing policies developed by multilateral institutions and diligently seeking their implementation. Governments are thus expected to work towards the collective aim of restoring the health of the earth or the balance of the global ecosystem by reducing the rate of population growth, ending deforestation, preserving biodiversity, limiting the burning of fossil fuels and protecting the fragile habitats of endangered species within their jurisdictions.

The 'local' narratives, on the other hand, begin by identifying the crisis of sustainability as stemming from economic activities – production, consumption, exchange and waste – that occur at a global scale. In their view, the insatiable drive of global commerce and competitive pressures between countries for political and economic dominance is seen as causing irreversible damage to localities and fragile ecosystems in every part of the world. The delicate balance of the earth's ecosystem is irrevocably harmed by governments that provide succour to global forces of commerce in the name of economic development, threatening the very survival of local communities and ecosystems by allowing rampant exploitation of natural resources within their jurisdictions.[4]

Global processes exacerbate local problems, which in turn contribute to crises of environmental sustainability of global proportions. Hence problems that threaten the sustainability of life on earth need to be overcome by bringing about a change in human values and reasserting the importance of preserving local communities and ecosystems. Sustainability, in this case, requires governments to limit the powers of global commerce and organize social life within localities that are bound together by a subsistence ethic and communal sharing of political and ecological responsibility (Gadgil and Guha, 1995; Mies and Shiva, 1993, pp. 318–22).

The visions of sustainability provided by these two narrative genres may seem to offer radical alternatives to present conditions in the world. But do they really? I find at least two problems with their visions of sustainable futures. First, and this should be apparent from the preceding section of this chapter, is that there is absolutely no conception of region or regionality in these narratives. Descriptions of 'the global' and 'the local' are essentially about two spatial scales that have been stripped of geographical history. The link between global and local is tenuous at best, particularly when there is no attempt to describe how these links have been made and remade over time. Although there is little ambiguity about the spatial scope of 'the global', 'the local', despite bearing a warm fuzzy feeling, remains a poorly articulated spatial entity.

What exactly is 'the local'? Is it merely a mini-container of people at the bottom of a great pyramid of spatial hierarchies? Are individual localities linked directly to 'the global' through abstract space, or are they linked with other localities? If so, then how are these links made? The failure to articulate the meaning of 'local', to explain how this space of 'the local' is, in fact, made by social practices that are part of a broader, more fluid dimension of regionality, results in a fetishized notion of 'locality' which resembles an exclusive country club. This fetishized locality is contrasted with an equally fetishized notion of 'the global', represented as inexorable and faceless economic processes that materialize like barbarians at its gates.

The second problem concerns the role of the state. Both global and local narratives of sustainability expect states to act in both minimalist and highly interventionist ways. The global narrative requires national governments to relinquish their decision making and legislative powers to multilateral agencies, to refrain from responding to apparently populist demands and local interests, and yet somehow to maintain the political and economic power to regulate and micro-manage their populations according to globally negotiated environmental policies.[5] The local narrative requires governments to function in the exact opposite manner. It expects national governments to somehow maintain the political and economic power to impose strict constraints on transnational corporations and global financial institutions, but requires them to withdraw their presence in localities so as to allow them to manage their environments in sustainable ways (Gadgil and Guha, 1995, pp. 123–32, 190–1; Mies and Shiva, 1993).

So, on the one hand, the global narrative conjures the image of states that derive their power and legitimacy from being loyal and obedient functionaries of transnational environmental regimes,[6] rather than responding to the varied needs and competing demands of the populations within their jurisdictions. They are to function as faithful executors of a global mission to save the world. On the other hand, the local narratives invoke the image of states that are suffused with benevolence and utterly devoted to securing social justice for each individual, ensuring the ecological and social welfare of localities and communities while keeping predatory forces of globalization at bay. In this case, states are expected to behave like benign parents, providing protection without imposing overbearing authority on their offspring. The alternative futures are not only confusing, but also limited in what they offer: authoritarian 'ecoimperialism' or protective 'ecoparentalism'.[7]

The idea of national governments functioning as executors of the global will or as amiable parents (or both) for the sake of ecological sustainability may sound appealing, but practical questions remain. How are states to muster the necessary resources to perform either or both of these roles? Will they be provided with financial resources and powers of enforcement by global environmental organizations for ensuring effective implementation of policies? Conversely, will local, self-governing communities generate the resources needed with the assistance of their benevolent state to protect themselves from the rampaging forces of global commerce?

Global and local narratives seem persuasive because they present sustainability as a future state of being, abstracted from present conditions. They both fetishize 'the local' and 'the global'; they both ignore regions and their geographical histories in order to reinforce their ideal vision of sustainability. The two kinds of narratives authenticate each other through a shared vocabulary – such as environmental security, democracy, citizenship, cultural identity and so on – to present the global and the local as 'two sides of a coin' or as 'mutually reinforcing entities'. Yet their visions of sustainability are curiously conservative, exclusionary and blind to the lived dimensions of social life. Global-local narratives sketch the idea of a sustainable future through descriptions of a contemporary world faced with narrow or absolute limits – human and ecological. They employ the language of restriction, exclusion and authoritative control for the 'future survival of the planet', or for bestowing a profitable legacy (earth as property) for future generations. Such narratives seem, in fact, to speak to propertied audiences that easily understand the exercise of power through the language of exclusive rights for protecting their material interests for themselves and their progenies.

Associating sustainability with words such as 'survival' and 'legacy' invokes the need to exclude some people (usually those without property) more than others, to restrict their access to the 'commons', and to demarcate boundaries that constrain their mobility and ability to pursue their livelihoods. This kind of discourse about sustainability has little meaning for the lived dimensions of social life in regions, and even less so for marginalized households that can barely make a living from day to day in their present circumstances. How are they to go about ensuring the future survival of the planet? What property do they pass on to future generations as their legacy? The dominant discourses offer sustainability as a holistic and emancipatory goal for 'our common future', but their visions inevitably translate into conservative and exclusionary policies and practices that, from a geographic perspective, are fundamentally *un*sustainable.

By contrast, political ecology views sustainability as a geographic question of improved access to resources and social well-being in the *present-continuous*, rather than imagining an idyllic past or a utopian resolution in the distant future. It focuses on the process of sustaining regionality through social practices that enable the continuation of the lived dimensions of social life along pathways that are diverse, open-ended and open to change. Sustainable development, from a political ecology perspective, is a process that requires active, direct and continuing collaboration between regional institutions and communities to ensure that all social groups – including those that are currently impoverished, transient and politically marginalized – gain improved access to regional resources and institutional networks. It involves a fundamental commitment to *substantive democracy*, that is, the ability to actively participate and influence institutional processes that shape policy development and management of resources. The process of sustaining regionality assumes a distinctive geographic dimension shaped by social actors and groups who may articulate their needs and claims in ways that seek to influence allocation of resources, their management and distributive justice. In so doing, it becomes the terrain where the *meaning and substance* of democracy is continually put to a test through the lived dimensions of social groups.

I shall now move on to examine the ways in which the terrains of state action, market processes and community practices have been conceptualized in environmental discourse. My discussions will primarily centre on debates over forest preservation and strategies of forest management, and in particular, on the arguments put forth by those who advocate democratic and participatory approaches for sustainable management of natural resources.

'COMMUNITY' AND 'STATE' IN FOREST MANAGEMENT

Ulrich Beck is of the view that the contemporary fetish for forest preservation in the 'West' stems from the desperate desire of privileged classes to hold on to an imagined utopia of a 'nature' that never existed in the first place (Beck, 1995a). These are people who, having arrived at their desired goal of material comfort, confront with dismay an age of uncertainty and risk realized from 'a contradictory fusion of nature and society which has sublated both concepts in a mixed relationship of mutual interconnections and injuries' (Beck, 1998, p. 155).

Beck's assertions may be open to debate, but there is little doubt that the forests in poor regions of the world have been subjected to shrill scrutiny since the global environmental discourse fortuitously discovered links between deforestation and the potentially undiscriminating hazards of global warming. Forests in these regions have not only become the last vestige of nature – biodiversity and indigenous communities included – to be ferociously preserved against the juggernaut of modernization, but also the 'carbon sinks' that will save humanity at large from being overheated beyond comfort.

The global clamour for forest preservation has given rise to another set of debates regarding the role of development, science, gender and property rights in causing deforestation. Ever since Hardin (1968) propounded the dubious merits of population control and private property as the means for preventing 'the tragedy of the commons', free-market enthusiasts have argued that common ownership of forest areas inevitably distorts prices, creates inefficient markets and contributes to their degradation (Hyde et al., 1991; World Bank, 1991). Other scholars have challenged such arguments by illustrating that commonly held areas are not, either by definition or in actual fact, 'open-to-all', but function as private property for a well-specified group (Bromley and Cernea, 1989; Ciriacy-Wantrup and Bishop, 1975; Ostrom 1987). Although a great deal of useful research has come about in the process of opposing Hardin's bleak model of selfish and alienated human behaviour, it continues to struggle with the complexity of problems involved in redirecting collective actions in diverse regional contexts towards ecologically beneficial and socially equitable outcomes.

These difficulties stem, in part, from the ways in which the discourse on deforestation and degradation of forest quality describe the roles played by states, markets and communities. 'The state', of course, emerges as the most popular target of criticism. Many scholars criticize states of the so-called Third World for blindly pursuing the 'modernist' project of development (Escobar, 1992, 1995; Esteva, 1987; Gadgil and Guha, 1995; Mies and Shiva, 1993; Shiva, 1989) and thereby encouraging relentless exploitation of forest resources in the 'national' interest. Others criticize the 'scientific rationality' that undergirds development strategies adopted in these countries. They argue that the continued espousal of 'Western science' by post-colonial governments for developing forestry policies and practices further contributes to the alienation of communities from nature and intensifies the processes of deforestation and ecological degradation (Guha, 1989; Gadgil and Guha, 1992, 1995; Shiva, 1989).

The market- and community-based perspectives have, by and large, produced populist visions of alternatives that conjure a pre-colonial, pre-commercial and pre-capitalist past where communities were supposedly freed from state control and operated in a harmonious 'state of nature'. Their solutions for deforestation and degradation of forest quality are overly simplistic and deterministic, reducing history to unilinear shifts and culture to ossified artefacts of antiquated pasts. As Peters (1987, p. 178; see also Jewitt, 1995; Nanda, 1991; Pouchepadass, 1995; Sinha et al., 1997, for similar critiques) points out:

> [t]hey differ fundamentally in one critical aspect: the model positing a tragedy of the commons casts its lot with the individual actor, the social realm being at best but a context in necessary opposition to the individual's self interest. The model of

the idealized past redefines the sociocultural system and *casts the individual as a nonactor, only a figure inscribing the hidden logic of the ecocultural system* (emphasis added).

Both perspectives assert that state agencies have no right or business owning forests, and must withdraw from the sphere of forest protection and management. One argues for market control, while the other argues for devolving control of forest management to 'the community'.

How do those who make these critiques translate their arguments into strategies for sustainable forest management? International non-governmental organizations (NGOs), development agencies, and multilateral lending institutions have, under varied motivations and pressures, found it expedient to employ a mix of ecofeminist, market- and eco-populist advice for effacing the role of state agencies involved in forest management (World Bank, 1992). The intimate link between woman and nature professed by ecofeminists has enabled the assumption that peasant women in poor regions will willingly labour on various afforestation and ecological restoration projects without financial compensation; that they will, due to their innate tendency to nurture, donate substantial time and effort, and shoulder the opportunity costs for engaging in such activities (see Jackson, 1993; Leach, 1991 for critical examples).

As Jackson (1994, p. 114) points out, '[f]or the World Bank women have become the means by which environmental ends are achieved and part of this process has involved the manipulation of meaning in the vocabularies of gender and development analysis'. And, as she notes, the enthusiastic espousal of ecofeminist rhetoric by Third World NGOs stems in large part from the financial rewards for conforming 'with the expectations of bilateral and multilateral development agencies' (ibid., p. 131). On the other hand, free-market populism has further intensified fiscal crises, indebtedness and aid dependence. Here, state agencies have been forced by dire need to submit to the neo-liberal strictures of international financial organizations, to conform to the regulations imposed by international environmental NGOs brokering 'debt-for-nature swaps', or enforce norms established by global environmental regimes, all of which serve to further marginalize and alienate already impoverished populations (Hecht and Cockburn, 1989; Neumann, 1996; Peluso, 1993).

Elsewhere, states have earnestly espoused the discourse of 'small government', 'devolution', 'decentralization' and 'local empowerment' so as to reduce their fiscal burden or avoid becoming embroiled in resource-based conflicts (Diaw, 1998; Rangan and Lane, forthcoming). Yet, despite the varied responses to criticisms of state policies and actions, none of these solutions have succeeded in translating their vision into sustainable strategies of forest management (Jodha, 1998; Ribot, 1998, forthcoming). On the contrary, they made it more difficult to pursue alternative *regionally* based strategies that link state agencies and secular institutions through *collaborative* processes and material practices focused on sustaining forests.

I do not wish to present a gloom and doom scenario for sustainable management of forests. There are several instances of regions where state institutions are actively engaged in collaborative projects centred on sustaining regional ecological resources and the varied social groups that depend on them. I provide a sketch of one such example from the state of West Bengal in India, well known to foresters and scholars of common property resources as the Joint Forest Management (JFM) experiment. My intent is to illustrate the workings of this region-based strategy by setting it in the context of its geographical history, and to highlight the ways in which it negotiates the process of sustaining regionality.

JOINT FOREST MANAGEMENT IN WEST BENGAL, INDIA

The history of state intervention in forest control and management in various regions of India spans more than two centuries (Smythies, 1925). Systematic efforts to incorporate forest conservation and management as part of state economic policy under British rule occurred around the mid-nineteenth century (Brandis, 1897). Even at the time, the question of state ownership and modes of controlling access to forest resources were subjects of heated debate (Ribbentrop, 1900). Competing perspectives regarding the need for state intervention initially led to the creation of various classes of forests which were to be controlled for a range of purposes by different agencies (Stebbing, 1922). These forest categories were reclassified in various regions through conflicts and disputes between local inhabitants, traders and different government departments. The conflicts centred on who could gain access to forests and the instruments and methods of control used by institutions – state, market, and customary – to mediate access to, use and sale of forest resources (Rangan, 1995, 1997a).

Soon after India's independence from British colonial rule in 1947, state governments were urged by the Indian government to implement land reforms for providing poor and socially disadvantaged rural households the means of securing livelihoods and increasing agricultural productivity (Government of India, 1952). Although the redistributive outcomes of land reform were largely dismal in most states, the ceilings on land ownership set by legislation allowed many state governments to transfer large, privately owned forests to their forest departments following due compensation to owners. Private forests were a minuscule proportion of the total forest area, and, following transfer to state government ownership, came to be known as Vested forests. Most of these forests were severely degraded because landowners had stripped them of all commercially valuable resources before the transfers took place (Lal, 1989).

In the following decades, policies outlined by successive Five-Year Plans of the National Planning Commission increasingly focused on self-reliance in the production of raw materials for industrial development. The Commission advised state forestry agencies to pursue afforestation strategies that centred on strict protection of existing forests undergoing natural regeneration, and extensive plantation of fast-growing tree species in degraded public lands and other forest categories (Government of India, 1976).

This policy shift faced severe criticism from various quarters. Scholars and activists accused state forestry agencies of working against the needs of the poor and socially disadvantaged sections of Indian society (Gadgil and Guha, 1995; Shiva, 1989). Numerous uprisings and disputes erupted in various parts of the country: forests were burnt, plantations uprooted and forest officers faced threats to their lives (Anderson and Huber, 1988; Banerjee, 1984; Corbridge and Jewitt, 1997). In 1976, the Indian government responded by passing a constitutional amendment that made forestry a 'Concurrent Subject'. (Forestry had previously been part of the agriculture sector, which was considered a 'State Subject' by constitutional law, that is, under exclusive control of state governments.) This meant that the role of the national government, which had previously functioned in an advisory capacity on forestry matters, expanded to include direct involvement with state forest departments in policy formulation and programme development.

The Indian government justified this action as a necessary response to several problems: the need to check state governments from pursuing short-term gains from natural resource extraction; to prevent them from succumbing to pressures exerted by powerful regional trade and business interests; and to help them achieve the national goals of social equality and distributive justice. The national populist agenda set by the Prime Minister at the time, Indira Gandhi, was translated in part into the Fifth Five-Year Plan. The plan advocated 'Social Forestry' as an alternative approach to be followed by state forest departments. The document argued that destruction of India's forests would not cease until rural and indigenous forest-dependent communities participated in their maintenance. The term 'social' was used in both descriptive and normative sense, indicating public involvement in forestry programmes as well as fulfilling people's material needs. Social Forestry comprised two distinct components: the first, farm forestry, provided incentives to farmers for planting trees on their lands for supplying the raw material needs of industries; the second attempted to involve rural communities to plant fuelwood and fodder trees on public lands for meeting local subsistence needs (Saxena and Ballabh, 1995).

Social Forestry programmes received willing and generous financial support from international funding bodies (Tiwary, 1998). The outcomes were mixed. Farm forestry projects proved successful in expanding the sheer volume of tree crops (Saxena and Ballabh, 1995). But this expansion was criticized by environmentalists who argued that the benefits accrued mainly to wealthy farmers, that it led to a reduction of food-crop production and that the fast-growing species planted on these lands (largely eucalyptus) were environmentally undesirable (Chowdhry, 1985; Shiva and Bandyopadhyay, 1985). Other scholars observed that farm forestry reduced demand for seasonal employment in agriculture and further marginalized poor rural households and landless labourers (Someshwar, 1993). On the other hand, social forestry on public and degraded lands remained largely unsuccessful for several reasons. The programmes depended on voluntary contributions of labour and capital from local communities, thus increasing the opportunity costs for poor and marginal rural households (Saxena and Ballabh, 1995). In other situations, the preference for planting single tree species reduced the variety of commercially valuable non-timber forest products in public lands, leading to further immiseration of indigenous groups and communities dependent on petty commodity extraction from these areas.

Despite these reversals, the broad policy emphasis on social forestry created conditions for other related experiments. In the state of West Bengal, it was attempted in conjunction with an innovative approach to agrarian reform adopted by the Left-Front government that came to power in the mid-seventies. The Left-Front launched a special programme in 1979 called 'Operation *Barga*' for securing the legal rights of *bargadars*, or sharecroppers, and landless labourers by recording their names in the government land registry, and using this registration as the basis for extending access to credit and agricultural inputs for cultivation. It provided landless households with leases on public lands for raising tree crops (Singh and Bhattacharjee, 1995).

The main emphasis of the government was on developing group action among potential beneficiaries, and on direct interaction between the organized groups of beneficiaries and government officers responsible for programme implementation. The Left-Front government also sought to strengthen local governance and accorded village councils the power of decision making for rural development (Dréze and Sen, 1996; Lieten, 1992; Williams, 1997). It fostered reforms in the forestry sector by encouraging the West Bengal Forest Department to engage in collaborative projects with forest-dependent villages and communities.

Between 1980 and 1986, the West Bengal Forest Department undertook the first collaborative social forestry experiments in Midnapore – an impoverished region with a substantial proportion of *adivasi*s (the Indian term for aboriginal groups) who had suffered the brunt of intense rural violence in earlier decades – with 'forest fringe' communities for managing and improving the quality of degraded forest areas. It issued a number of facilitating resolutions for JFM. Beginning with financial incentives for tree protection, the experiments expanded to include joint decisions regarding the choice of tree species, their plantation and maintenance. Later, these were extended to include sharing net profits from the sale of forest products between the Forest Department and village councils (Government of West Bengal, 1996).

During this period, the Left-Front government re-emphasized the importance of ensuring equitable access to forest resources for all rural communities. It created a statutory body called the Forest and Land Protection Society and issued directives that safeguarded the rights of Scheduled Castes and Scheduled Tribes (the official term referring to those historically disadvantaged groups identified in the Schedule of the Indian Constitution), and expanded their role in JFM committees (Sen, 1992). The JFM committees were required to identify economically disadvantaged households within these populations and include them as member beneficiaries. The state-sponsored West Bengal Tribal Cooperative became the intermediary institution for marketing forest products traditionally harvested by indigenous communities, sharing 25 per cent of net profits with its members (Society for the Promotion of Wastelands Development, 1993). The share of net profits accruing to JFM committees was renegotiated with the Forest Department and increased from 25 per cent to 50 per cent in new forest plantations (Poffenberger, 1996; Tiwary, 1998).

JFM committees comprise regional and local forest officers, elected village representatives affiliated with regional and national political parties, members belonging to economically and socially disadvantaged groups, members of local, non-political voluntary institutions, as well as individual households who hold membership in forest protection committees. They are charged with multiple duties and functions, delineation of usufructuary rights and concessions for households belonging to member villages, and the distribution of financial benefits from the sale of forest produce (Poffenberger, 1996; Society for the Promotion of Wastelands Development, 1993). They are responsible to each other *and* to their respective cultural affiliations, political constituencies and institutions at various levels of government. The involvement of women in committees has so far been voluntary, but may well increase with a proposed legislation which, if approved by the Indian parliament, mandates village- and district-level councils to reserve a third of their electoral seats for women candidates.

JFM is thus a *state-initiated* strategy that emerged within the broad rubric of social forestry policies set out by the Indian government. The West Bengal Forest Department and local communities have, within this framework, collaborated to find ways of expanding access to forest resources for disadvantaged social classes, improving forest quality and management systems, and negotiating the shares of net income earned from harvesting resources produced through their shared efforts.

The JFM process has run into many unavoidable problems that are part of any endeavour involving diverse actors within civil society. It encounters new problems relating to redistribution, and unforeseen conflicts arising from the multiple political affiliations and social identities of its members. It appears extremely successful in some areas of the state but not in others (Tiwary, 1998). Despite these mixed outcomes, JFM continues to function as a pragmatic approach that is firmly grounded in its regional context. It requires direct interaction between diverse institutions of government and civil society for negotiating needs and demands in relation to changing political configurations and broader economic conditions. It attempts to reshape and sustain the region through processes of substantive democracy by ensuring that local communities, as well as socially disadvantaged households and indigenous groups, have some means of access to and control over state-owned forests for securing their livelihoods (Sarin, 1996).

I do not wish to uphold JFM in West Bengal as an exceptional example of virtuous state action or as the prescribed path to a Marx-inspired utopia. Indeed, there is plenty of emerging evidence from studies to indicate that this approach is being decontextualized from its geographical history of regional engagement, and being represented as the ultimate victory of 'community' management over 'state-involved' strategies. JFM's partial success in West Bengal can, from a political ecology perspective, be seen as emerging from the collaborative efforts of state institutions and regional communities that attempt to address the question of sustaining regionality through substantive democratic processes that reshape access to resources, modes of redistributive justice and political representation. In this sense, JFM in West Bengal constitutes a fairly radical process that has redefined conventional (liberal) notions of property rights for the purpose of improving economic, ecological and social resources in the region. It reveals the ways in which state agencies and their diverse constituents are engaged in a substantive democratic process that requires them to constantly negotiate, accommodate and readjust their needs alongside changing economic and political conditions.

SUSTAINABILITY AND SUBSTANTIVE DEMOCRACY

My geography-centred perspective regarding the question of environmental change and sustainability may appear as an outlandish argument to those who view geography in conventional ways. They are likely to argue that the contemporary processes of globalization have undermined the possibility of adopting a geographic-historical approach, and that regional governments no longer have the political or fiscal capabilities for expanding and strengthening the spaces of access for all inhabitants within their jurisdictions. But it is necessary to remind oneself that governments and their constituents have always been mutually dependent in the process of creating and maintaining spaces of production, political life and legitimizing cultural identities. In the more recent past, many nation-states and their constituents emerged from colonial domination by mutually reshaping and legitimizing their roles and identities around ideas of freedom, self-rule and democracy.

These experiences suggest that while globalized processes of accumulation and consumption can generate tremendous economic uncertainties and environmental risks, they can also produce possibilities that compel states and civil societies in different regions of the world to re-examine, and actively renegotiate the meanings of glibly used terms such as global democracy, neo-liberalism, freedom, universal citizenship, 'private' property and 'public' domain in the context of their distinctive geographical histories. There is no better time than the *continuing present* for governments and their constituents to rework these concepts in enabling, rather than exclusionary, ways for sustaining regions.

There are many examples of such activity in different parts of the world, where institutions of state and civil society are engaged in sustaining regional households and communities. The process of JFM in the state of West Bengal is one such example where attempts to address the question of regional sustainability has locked diverse institutions of state and civil society into a bittersweet liaison that requires them to constantly negotiate, accommodate and readjust their practices as they deal with economic conjunctures and political events. Such collaborative strategies and practices are integral to sustainable regional development because they regard sustainability as part of the practices of social institutions which grapple with questions of enabling access to resources, redistributive justice and political representation. Insofar as they remain committed to practices that do not seek to exclude those that are poor and politically marginalized, they ensure that regions and regionalities continue to be sustained by substantive democracy.

NOTES

1. I am, in a sense, re-articulating what many scholars in the disciplinary traditions of geography and regional development have been saying about regions and regionality. See, for example, Friedmann (1988); Harvey (1996); McGee (1997).
2. I cannot possibly list the innumerable books and articles written in this vein. Readers may wish to revisit such neo-Malthusian classics written by Ehrlich (1971); Hardin (1968); Meadows et al. (1974); and their more recent writings Ehrlich and Ehrlich (1990); Meadows et al. (1992). For enthusiastic opposition to Ehrlich and other 'green doomsdayers', see Simon (1994).
3. For critical accounts of this perspective, see Agarwal and Narain (1991); Taylor and Buttel (1992).
4. The writings in this vein are as voluminous as the former, with an equally long tradition. For examples written during the past few decades, see Bookchin (1980); Callenbach (1978); Lovejoy (1974); Sale (1985). For an overview, see Bramwell (1989); Pepper (1984). Some classic examples, particularly with respect to the so-called Third World, are Gadgil and Guha (1995); Mies and Shiva (1993); Shiva (1989).
5. See Peluso (1993), who argues that the rhetoric of global environmental change, deforestation, and ecological collapse has allowed 'globally concerned' environmental groups to tacitly support coercive conservation tactics that weaken local claims to resource access for sustaining livelihoods. She observes that some of the conservation programmes introduced by international conservation groups in Indonesia and Kenya have not merely 'armed' local non-governmental organizations with symbolic and financial support to 'empower' local users, but have directed the bulk of their efforts towards influencing state policy.
6. See, for example, the recent collection of essays edited by Young (1997).
7. See Agarwal and Narain (1991); Corbett (1995). Charges of 'environmental imperialism' also occasionally emerge from unlikely quarters such as the General Agreement on Tariffs and Trade (GATT) and the Organisation for Economic Co-operation and Development (OECD), multilateral institutions not commonly renowned for viewing the world through Trotskyist lenses. See Dodwell (1992).

8. Beyond the Statist Frame: Environmental Politics in a Global Economy

Ken Conca

Economic globalization undermines the quest for an ecologically and socially sustainable future. The constant threat of international capital flight strips individual governments of important domestic regulatory powers. The transnationalization of production makes it easier for high-consumption societies to export ecological costs onto distant, less powerful, or less organized communities. Debt burdens and intense pressures for 'competitiveness' turn traditional public goods and common resources into commodities ripe for plunder. Traditional practices that provision local communities are undermined by powerful transnational forces operating through disfunctional, oligopolized global markets. The fabric of community, a key resource for any serious programme of sustainability, is torn by social dislocation and turbulent change.

Proposed mechanisms for global environmental governance have been slow to adjust to these challenges and controversies. Almost ten years after the Earth Summit and almost three decades after the 1972 Stockholm Conference, appeals for global sustainability have been fashioned into an institutional monoculture of environmental diplomacy, in which supposedly authoritative governments bargain over the allocation mechanisms to limit their national contributions to global environmental harm, one issue at a time. In this manner the problem of global ecology has been reframed as a collective-action problem among the two hundred or so entities with sovereign standing in the interstate system.

These 'actors' are said to be drawn to environmental diplomacy because they are locked into a Hardin-style tragedy of the commons. Because pollution ignores borders, we are told, even the best of intentions on the part of one state are quickly foiled by the actions of others. States, therefore, bargain to realize the mutual gains that lie on the other side of this collective-action problem, with some operating as 'leaders' and others as 'laggards' in the process. In this highly stylized world, power, wealth and agency are properties of states; justice, responsibility and accountability are measured in the relations between states.

The powerful hold of the state on global imagination was apparent in *Our Common Future*, the influential report of the Brundtland Commission. The report, which placed the issue of sustainability squarely on the global agenda and laid the foundation for the Earth Summit, presents 23 principles for environmental protection and sustainable development. After an initial principle defining an individual's right to a sound environment, the remaining 22 principles each begin with two words: 'states shall' (World Commission on the Environment and Development (WCED), 1987, annexe 1).

The hegemony of this statist frame is by no means limited to the élites who fashioned the Brundtland Report. Much of the energy of ecological social movements has been spent in pushing and prodding governments to negotiate and ratify international treaties on specific environmental problems with an international dimension, such as the loss of biodiversity, climate change or depletion of the stratospheric ozone layer. As we have seen in the recent furore around persistent organic pollutants ('endocrine disruptors'), advocates of aggressive global action move quickly and seamlessly from sounding the warning to calling for a new international regulatory framework consisting of interstate cooperation (Colborn et al., 1996).

Obviously, governments are central to any meaningful action for global sustainability – just as they have been central to the processes of modernization, marketization and enclosure that have delivered us to our current circumstances of ecological peril. Governments cannot be ignored as part of the problem, and the state's capacity to redress the power imbalances at the heart of environmental problems must be seized upon as part of the solution. The problem is not the efforts to improve interstate relations and the behaviour of governments, but rather with the reification of the state as the sole form of political authority in the modern era. This process of reification makes the 'country' the logical unit of analysis when weighing questions of responsibility, justice, risk and opportunity. The state is viewed overwhelmingly as the agent of global sustainability, and interstate bargaining mechanisms are seen as the pathway to change.

I argue below that viewing the problem this way – as one of sorting out the relations between separate, sovereign countries – distorts our thinking about both causes and solutions in several important ways. Important forms of inequality, injustice and concentrated power become harder to see. I also argue that, as economic globalization deepens, analysis that moves beyond this limiting, distorting statist frame has become a critically scarce intellectual resource for social change in the direction of sustainability.

I begin by sketching a few of the key changes that underpin the trend towards economic globalism, with particular emphasis on the changing organization of global production. I then examine some of the more important distortions that come with seeing the ecological dilemmas of a globalizing world economy through the traditional lens of interstate relations. I conclude with some thoughts on the resulting challenges of conceptualization and practice for scholars, citizens and social movements seeking ecological sanity in the context of economic globalization. Although a comprehensive 'post-statist' paradigm remains elusive, the chapter identifies a few promising pathways for moving our conceptualizations of global political ecology beyond the statist frame.

THE CHANGING CHARACTER OF THE GLOBAL ECONOMY

A popular understanding of economic globalization focuses on the deepening and quickening of the interdependence that has marked international economic relations since the end of the Second World War. This limited view of the concept emphasizes the growth of transactions across borders; its hallmarks are international trade and global capital mobility. Trade has indeed flourished, growing far more quickly than the world economy since the 1960s. The drivers of this growth include negotiated tariff reductions, aggressive attacks on such 'non-tariff' barriers as health and environmental regulations and, most recently, the expansion of the global free-trade regime of the General Agreement on Tariffs and Trade (GATT) and the World Trade Organization (WTO) to previously excluded sectors such as agriculture, services and so-called intellectual property.

The second pillar of this transactions-based view of globalization is transnational capital mobility. Invocations of capital mobility may refer to any of several trends: growth in the overall volume of transnational investment, the deepening integration of capital markets, the rise of 'offshore' capital sitting beyond the effective reach of national regulations and the growing speed with which transnational capital can relocate in response to short-term fluctuations in economic conditions. These globalizing trends in trade and finance are often described as the product of technological innovation, although it is sometimes acknowledged that they have also been unleashed by policy changes such as aggressive trade liberalization and the widespread relaxation of restrictions on short-term capital movements.

What this popular rendering of globalization misses is that the process is also characterized, indeed driven, by underlying changes in the global organization of production. Among these changes, three stand out: the rise of increasingly complex transnational commodity chains in products as diverse as automobiles, personal computers, athletic footwear and garden vegetables; the shift in many of these chains towards so-called 'post-Fordist' forms of industrial organization; and the increasing role of advertising, retailing, marketing and other 'downstream' nodes in shaping the activities of the entire chain.

To be sure, these changes in the global organization of production would not be possible without the trends of trade liberalization and capital mobility discussed above. But the global reorganization of production has profound impacts on work, community, power, the sustainability of specific places and livelihoods and the relationships among different communities, classes and regions that cannot be understood solely through the lens of trade and financial transactions. In other words, globalization means not only quicker and more frequent transactions among separate units but changes in their relations of power and authority and, in many cases, reconstitution of the units themselves.

An increasing share of global production can be thought of as consisting of transnational commodity chains (Gereffi and Korzeniewicz, 1994). The stages of production that form the nodes in these chains – extraction, component manufacture, assembly, packaging, marketing, advertising, retailing and myriad associated services – are globally dispersed, meaning that the production process crosses borders several times on the road to consumption of the commodity being produced.

The growth of international trade merely hints at a process of transnationalization that is at work across all stages of the chain. Brazil and Mexico, for example, saw a net inflow of foreign direct investment of $14 billion and $12 billion, respectively, in 1997, with much of this money gravitating towards export-oriented industries (CEPAL, 1998a, p. 3). These changes affect both new and traditional economic sectors. Again, taking the example of Latin America, obvious examples of this process are the proliferation of free-trade zones and the growth of high-tech and consumer-nondurables industries.

But the effects can also be seen in more traditional sectors such as the auto industry, which has been a linchpin of regional industrialization since the 1950s. Foreign investment has been the dominant force in the region's auto industry for several decades. But whereas the emphasis was once on production by multinational subsidiaries for protected local markets, the new trend is towards integration into global production systems in the context of trade liberalization and global competitiveness (CEPAL, 1998b). The domestic content of Mexican automobiles manufactured for export has fallen from 60 per cent to 30 per cent as Mexico's auto industry has shifted from car production for the local market and the free-standing export of auto parts to a more integrated role in the global auto commodity chain. Auto-industry exemptions in both Mercosur and the North American Free Trade Agreement (NAFTA), which basically shift protectionism from the national to the regional scale, may have slowed but have clearly not prevented this restructuring process.

A second important trend is that, in many sectors, these globalizing chains are marked by the rise of so-called 'post-Fordist' forms of industrial organization based on 'flexible specialization'. Reynolds (1994, p. 145) summarizes the shift:

> According to a great many authors, the Fordist model of production has broken down since the 1970s and is increasingly being replaced by a more flexible, post-Fordist pattern of production. Piore and Sabel argue that the new production model is based on flexible specialization – batch production in small firms that are linked through dense networks and produce for niche markets. They suggest that post-Fordist production can out-compete the Fordist model because of flexibilities in work organisation, product specification, and marketing strategies. Many studies have found that large manufacturing firms are undergoing a process of vertical disintegration whereby production is increasingly undertaken by small specialized firms linked through production contracts.

Observers disagree as to the extent of 'post-Fordization' of the world economy. They also disagree on whether the difference between Fordist and post-Fordist modes of production is as clear-cut and significant as is sometimes claimed. Nevertheless, one important ramification of this shift appears to be that, within many commodity chains, leverage is increasingly exercised not by industrial capital but rather by retailers, brand-name firms, advertisers and other 'downstream' nodes in the chain. A classic example is Nike, a firm that owns no production facilities but instead a powerful marketing symbol (the Nike 'swoosh'), a set of marketing and advertising relationships, and the public images of Michael Jordan and Tiger Woods. According to Gereffi, 'buyer-driven' commodity chains of the sort that Nike is involved in are closely tied to the rise of flexible specialization and are particularly common for labour-intensive consumer goods industries (Gereffi, 1994).

More generally, the shift in global demand from materials-intensive to knowledge- and symbol-intensive industries as varied as telecommunications, media, fashion and entertainment also strengthens the hand of these downstream nodes. At the same time, increasing capital mobility and integration across national capital markets means that power in many commodity chains has shifted upstream from the factory to the increasingly liquid (and thus powerful) financial capital of well-heeled global specu-lators and institutional investors. This simultaneous upstreaming and downstreaming of power has displaced the classic vertically integrated, production-centred multinational of the 1960s and 1970s across an increasingly wide swath of the global economy.

Some have suggested that the changes wrought by globalization are more apparent than real. Critics of globalization hype and 'globaloney' are quick to point out that we have had a highly integrated capitalist world system since the age of empire and colonialism. They are sceptical that claims about transnational corporate power, a global logic of capitalism, and the tight coupling of the contemporary system represent anything particularly new. These are valid observations. For example, the popular observation that today many large corporations have annual earnings rivalling the gross national product of mid-sized nations overlooks the history of the international system – after all, during the age of empire most of the countries today being compared in size to corporations were not countries at all, but rather resource colonies and captive markets exploited by alliances of state power and corporate power in the imperial states. We would do well to remember this history before concluding that economic transnationalism is anything new for most of the world's peoples. But qualifications of this sort must not be allowed to obscure the fact that very real changes are occurring in the organization of production, creating new problems and new challenges for social movements seeking to promote ecological sanity.

THE COUNTRY AS DISTORTED LENS

The discipline of international relations has been moving steadily away from its emotional and intellectual commitment to an overconstructed and insufficiently critical view of the state. It is no longer controversial or novel to suggest that states are not the sole important actors in world politics, that the sovereign character of states cannot be assumed, that national identity is often a tenuous construct or that most states face crises of authority and governance. Nowhere is this more apparent than in international environmental affairs. Corporations, non-governmental organizations, social movement groups and other non-state actors have always been influential in shaping the positions of their home governments in international diplomacy. But the rise of globalization, economic interdependence, regional integration and transnational networking have meant that these non-state actors can increasingly exert more direct forms of influence in the international sphere. A growing body of evidence shows their ability to encourage, resist or otherwise shape emerging mechanisms of global environmental governance (Barker and Soyez, 1994; Clapp, 1994; Keck and Sikkink, 1998; Kuehls, 1996; Lipschutz, 1996; Princen and Finger, 1994; Wapner, 1996).

But the newly found freedom to think in terms other than the state has not left us entirely free to think in terms other than the country. Discussions of what is possible, what is needed and what is fair in global environmental governance almost always presume that countries are still the logical units for comparison and analysis. Debates about regulating global pollution invariably use aggregate national data to illustrate the sources of the problem. Debates about distributive justice, including efforts to establish acceptable levels of pollutant emissions, invariably devolve into proposals for country-level allocation mechanisms. The language employed in these debates, which personifies countries as unified, strategic actors, reflects these underlying assumptions: What will China do? What does Brazil want? Can Russia implement? Why does the USA resist?

The hold countries have on our imagination is no surprise. Most of the available information for analysing contributions to global environmental problems derives from nationally aggregated data, making it difficult to draw a comparative global picture in any units other than national aggregates. But the limits of data also reflect an underlying political assumption; a mythic notion of the state still lies at the heart of the international relations paradigm. It is generally assumed that, challenges to state power and legitimacy notwithstanding, states are still the most authoritative implementers of any agreed-upon environmental measures.

The statist frame distorts our thinking in at least four important ways:

1. *The myth of the average citizen* The statist frame reinforces the myth that countries are meaningful units of consumption. This masks enormous domestic inequalities rooted in income disparities, class rigidities, regional variation or gender inequality.
2. *The arbitrary allocation of responsibility* The statist frame arbitrarily disaggregates global production systems into geographic locations. This blurs the interests actually served by production in a particular geographic location.
3. *The misidentification of power* The statist frame obfuscates the linkage effects of transnational commodity chains and their tendency to concentrate power. This misidentifies where power and the capacity to adjust actually reside.
4. *Hiding the sustainable middle* The statist frame reifies a simplistic global class structure of affluent North and impoverished South. This draws attention away from the wide array of relatively sustainable lifestyles and livelihoods that lie between over-consumption and desperate poverty. It also hides the enormous challenge of sustaining those communities in the face of the twin eroding effects of over-consumption and economic marginalization.

The effect of these distortions is to hide certain forms of power and injustice in our current ecological dilemmas and in proposed solutions to those problems.

The Myth of the Average Citizen

One obvious problem with the statist frame is that countries are fictional units of consumption. National averages mask enormous domestic variability in consumption levels, particularly in societies marked by great income inequality, rigid class structures, urban-rural disparities, regional antagonisms or gender inequality. The myth of the average citizen, whose global responsibility is calculated in per capita terms, masks enormous variance in how different individuals or social groups in any given country actually live.

That the average citizen revealed in per capita data is in fact a myth can be seen in a quick perusal of basic quality-of-life and human-development indicators. A review of recent human-development reports for four large 'developing' countries – India, Indonesia, Turkey and Egypt – illustrates the point (Conca, 1998a). These reports makes it possible to identify internal disparities at the regional level by looking for the highest and lowest figures for a given indicator among Egypt's 26 governorates, India's 32 states and union territories, Indonesia's 27 provinces and Turkey's 76 provinces. The biggest gaps within a single nation included a life expectancy gap of more than 10 years within India and Indonesia, a sevenfold difference in infant mortality within India, a more than twofold disparity in literacy rates within all four countries, a more than threefold disparity in gross educational enrolment rates within Turkey and fourfold disparities in income levels within India and Turkey.

One of the most pernicious effects of the myth of the average citizen is that it hides the very different distributional consequences of different approaches to solving global environmental problems. If the state is not an instrument of redistributive justice, then changing the distribution among states will not resolve the question of justice within societies, and may even exacerbate existing inequities. Injustice in this case is not being eliminated by international cooperation, but merely shifted to the subnational level, where it is rendered less visible to global society.

The Arbitrary Allocation of Responsibility

A second problem with the statist frame is that it systematically misallocates responsibility. By stressing the geographic locale ('country') where pollution, ecosystem degradation or resource scarcity is manufactured, interstate diplomacy arbitrarily disaggregates global production systems. National data and interstate bargaining stress the geographic location of isolated segments of production rather than the locus of demand that the entire commodity chain serves. This, in turn, blurs the interests actually served by production in a particular geographic location.

The phrase 'shadow ecologies' has been coined to describe the process by which centres of production and consumption cast a shadow of environmental effects on the hinterlands from which they derive their raw materials (MacNeill et al., 1991). The recognition of such transnational effects has also informed efforts to calculate a society's ecological footprint, or the amount of the Earth's land surface area that is required to sustain that society's level of consumption. No society lives solely on the resources within its borders, but some clearly cast much longer shadows and make much larger footprints than others. Thus, for example, Rees calculates that the city of Vancouver, with an area of 11 400 hectares, imposed an ecological footprint in the early 1990s on the order of 2 million hectares to sustain the consumption of its 472 000 residents (Rees, 1996, p. 2).

As economic globalization deepens, some shadows grow longer and some footprints grow larger. The allocation of ecological responsibility to the geographic location of production is increasingly a distortion of both responsibility and the capacity to change. The resulting disjuncture has both a spatial and a temporal dimension. Spatially, a moment in the production cycle located in a specific place cannot be isolated from choices and market conditions both upstream and downstream. In many cases – those Nike tennis shoes made in Southeast Asia – what we are seeing is a shift of power downstream, in which US or European consumers and the large retailers, advertisers and marketers that stimulate and feed their demand have most of the power to define what happens upstream at the production end of the commodity chain of athletic footwear.

This does not mean that a purely consumption-based allocation of environmental responsibility is preferable to a purely production-based one. Societies reap a complex and unevenly distributed set of goods and bads from both production and consumption. The end consumer of those Nike athletic shoes benefits, entailing responsibility. But the responsibility is not total, if for no other reason than the fact that not all of the benefits accrue to the final consumer. Rather, those benefits are distributed in complex fashion across the various nodes in the transnational chain of production and consumption. But the key point here is that the production-based view of environmental responsibility, which underlies the dominant frame of international environmental diplomacy, assigns none of that responsibility to the end-user or to the agents who reap the bulk of the profits from that final consumption.

This spatial disconnect between current environmental diplomacy and the changing world economy is accompanied by a temporal disconnect, in which countries are wrongly assumed to be relatively fixed and static producing units over time. For example, this flawed assumption underpins the idea that 1990 baseline figures on greenhouse gas emissions are a reasonable target for emissions in 2010. For many countries, two decades of highly transnationalized economic change – including an increasing share of gross national product (GNP) linked to trade, the growing role of foreign direct investment, the acceleration of transnational portfolio investment, major fluctuations in currency values, a substantially different profile of external debt and increasingly transnational labour mobility – will have rendered the 2010 economy almost unrecognizable in 1990 terms.

The Misidentification of Power

Along with the misallocation of responsibility comes a flawed map of the distribution of power and the capacity to change. Here, perhaps most obvious is the problem that transnational commodity chains resist the reach of national regulation. Capital mobility shifts bargaining power away from the regulatory state, and flexible specialization facilitates the rapid shifting of activities among any of a myriad of subcontracting firms in any of a number of countries. As the global financial crisis erupting in Asia during the second half of 1997 demonstrated clearly, the new global structure of production has intensified the dependency of even rapidly growing and diversifying Third World economies on external conditions and decisions they do not fully control. The weak links that triggered the crisis were countries either previously exalted as newly industrialized (South Korea) or part of the next wave of so-called Asian tigers (Thailand, Malaysia, Indonesia).

The fictional world of environmental diplomacy blurs this power shift away from the state by focusing instead on the euphemism of 'state capacity'. Discussion of the 'capacity' issue is usually limited to how to build it in the global South, with primary emphasis on the technical and administrative dimensions of state capacity. This framing avoids the most fundamental question: How many governments have the economic autonomy, political foundation and policy control to regulate, through national means, the climate-impacting activities in the transnational commodity chains that pass through their border? Even if current political trends could be reversed and regimes intent on reasserting regulatory authority came to power in a wider spectrum of countries, the realities of enhanced capital mobility and the almost infinite substitutability of production sites and material sources raise genuine doubts.

The shifting locus of power is more complex than merely public-private, however. The advantages enjoyed by flexible production umbrellas such as Nike, when compared to the traditional, vertically integrated manufacturing multinational, alter the power distribution both within and surrounding the commodity chain. Within the chain, downstream activities such as marketing, retailing, advertising and distribution gain in power and influence relative to upstream activities of extraction, manufacturing and assembly. Surrounding the chain, social movement groups are forced to shift attention away from protests and policies targeted at the point source of pollution or ecosystem degradation. Instead, they are increasingly challenged to engage these newly powerful downstream activities – and the diffuse, societally based attitudes, ideologies and consuming practices those downstream nodes seek to stimulate. Working the halls of international treaty negotiations and tinkering with the allocation mechanisms embedded in those treaties are not effective leverage points for these new and fundamentally different tasks.

Hiding the Sustainable Middle

A final ramification of the statist frame is its effect in hiding the current global pattern of consumption and the effects of globalization on that pattern (detailed in Conca, 1998a). Despite the popularity of North/South, rich/poor dualisms, large numbers of people exhibit consumption practices that fall somewhere between the dubious excess of a billion over-consumers and the desperate acts of a billion marginalized poor. To be sure, a global stratum of marginalized poor does exist, and their actions – a product of desperation, dislocation and the destruction of traditional communities – do hurt the planet's environmental health.

At the other end of the spectrum, a global stratum of over-exploiters do far greater damage. As Alan Durning has pointed out, a few simple indicators distinguish these global extremes: over-exploiters get most of their protein from grain-fed meat, work in office buildings that are air-conditioned even in winter, and transport themselves, typically alone, by automobile. The marginalized, in contrast, face protein deficiencies, suffer in the heat or cold and walk (Durning, 1992).

But what lies in between these extremes? A majority of the planet's population, at least for now. To be sure, this group is far too diverse to be romanticized as a planetary middle class – just as the rich and poor are too complex to be thought of simply as global underclass and ruling class. But the size of this middle stratum suggests that there are many ways of living that offer alternatives to both the pollution of excess and the pollution of poverty. To the extent that this is true, this middle stratum in all its diversity is where the potential global foundations for a more sustainable future are likely to be found.

The problem of building on this potential foundation is twofold. One major aspect of the global problem of sustainability is the erosion of this potentially sustainable middle from both ends as part of the wrenching changes of the globalization process – with the upper middle being sucked into the global class of over-exploiters and the lower middle threatened with marginalization (Conca, 1998a). These effects are being felt in the so-called South, where euphemistic 'emerging markets' are being dragged into the world economy through capital mobility and trade liberalization. They are also being felt in the so-called North, where global economic integration, de-urbanization, corporate relocation and the destruction of rural communities have had such disruptive effects.

But the fact that these squeezing effects are felt by millions does not mean that those millions are seen. Indeed, quite the opposite: the statist frame and the myth of the average citizen push us towards highly polarized and dualistic images of North and South. Instead of seeing the problem as the destruction of sustainable communities and livelihoods, we are presented with cartoons: fears that uncontrollable Third World disintegration and ecoviolence will spill over to undermine what are presumed to be sustainable consumerist societies (Kaplan, 1994), or false promises that neo-liberal growth will help impoverished societies scramble up the Kuznets curve of greater demand for environmental protection (Reilly, 1990).

BEYOND THE STATIST FRAME: CHALLENGES FOR SCHOLARS AND SOCIAL MOVEMENTS

Globalization and its consequences pose serious challenges of adaptation for ecologically minded social movements. Scholarship has an important role to play in this process of adaptation. The central intellectual task is to create a new conceptual frame for global governance, rooted in the trans-nationalization of production, the complexity of global ecological class structure and consumption patterns and the changing locus of power in global society. This frame is needed to counter the dominant narrative which I have called the statist frame, with its imagery of separate societies engaged in increasingly dense but still arm's-length and voluntary transactions while sovereign governments bargain over the terms of collective action. Without an alternative frame, it remains easy to misallocate responsibility for environmental harm, to render underlying patterns of production and consumption more difficult to see, and to misidentify where the power to change actually resides.

What are the elements of this new frame? One of the most important intellectual tasks is to trace the shift in power inherent in the changing global organization of production. There are at least two distinct dimensions to this power shift. First is the shift in the balance between public and private power, as 'flexible' production systems become better able to resist the regulatory reach of the state. Second, and just as important, is the dispersal of power away from the factory – upstream to the increasingly mobile capital of profit-taking investors, and downstream to marketers, advertisers and brand-name retailers sitting in the commercial and symbolic nodes towards the consuming end of the production chain.

These power shifts demand new tactics and new targets – and therefore new maps of the global economy/ecology nexus. The power shift appears to be most advanced in sectors that have not been the central focus of environmental campaigns – apparel, footwear, textiles, toys, produce, household products and other consumer non-durables, as well as large chunks of the burgeoning service and information-technology sectors on the other hand. Transnational campaigns focused on these sectors are important laboratories for ecological social movements, in that they address how an ever larger swath of the world economy is actually organized. They also offer rich opportunities for coalition building, because these sectors are central to labour struggles over de-unionization and offshoring at the same time that they form the front lines of a new ecological agenda centred on toxics, pollution havens in free-trade zones, environmental health in the workplace and the export of consumerism.

Maps of these commodity chains that cut across national aggregate data to tie their ecological damage to their centres of decision-making power within the chain are vital. For example, national emissions data constitute the dominant way of toting up the 'sources' of human-induced climate change. A jarringly different way of looking at the problem might begin with the observation that a relative handful of firms control the bulk of the world's fossil fuel production. Where does power reside in the global commodity chains for fossil fuels? What fraction of a country's fossil energy use serves the export sector? How does the picture of responsibility change when we adjust national emissions for the energy embodied in international trade?

A second and related intellectual task is to develop new ways of thinking about issues of distributive justice. As suggested above, the statist frame arbitrarily disaggregates global production by geographic location. This skews the allocation of responsibility towards nominal 'producers', while deflecting attention away from consumers. It also deflects attention away from power dynamics among the many nodes within the production chain, not all of which are located at the point of ecological harm where responsibility is fixed. This allocation of responsibility clearly favours centres of global financial and consuming power, while leaving the world's poorer regions with the stark choice of leaving the talks or asking for exemptions from responsibilities they do not fully deserve to be saddled with.

An alternative frame of distributive justice might work instead to implement responses along the multiple nodes of global production chains. Consider the problem of climate change. Currently fashionable in the global climate talks are various abstract emissions trading schemes, which would allow countries to buy and sell emissions credits or take credit for transnational investments in emissions reductions. These abstract, market-based mechanisms do nothing to tie together the stages of production, the financing mechanisms of production and the consuming interests served by production. Mechanisms to combat global warming that trace the offshoring of pollution back to the consumption centres and profit centres reaping the bulk of the benefits of production would constitute a fundamentally different frame for distributive justice than abstract, atomized market mechanisms that facilitate the trafficking of responsibility.

Third, we need to think more systematically about the links between production-centred and consumption-centred modes of analysis. In a world marked by the downstreaming of power across a wide array of global commodity chains, a purely production-centred political ecology risks ignoring the importance of 'control of the means of consumption'. Similarly, a consumption-centred approach, disconnected from questions of structural power and the transnationalization of production, yields little more than a disempowering individualization of guilt and decontextualized calls for 'voluntary simplicity'.

The key is to link these production- and consumption-centred views. The commodity-chains approach I have employed in this chapter can be useful in this regard. So too is the idea of the spatial and social 'distance' between production and consumption (Princen, 1997). Much of the popular analysis of globalization emphasizes the shrinking distances of a supposed global village. This ignores one of the main effects of globalization – an increase in the spatial and social disconnect, or 'distance', between production and consumption as global commodity chains grow longer and more complex. The effect of this distancing is to disrupt or distort important signals between producers and consumers that would otherwise serve as useful negative feedback. The task for social movements is to reduce these distances through transnational citizen action, global networking and the creation of alternative institutional channels (a task that some aspects of globalization may facilitate). An interesting example is the Forest Stewardship Council and the ecocertification movement, which seeks to shorten the 'distance' between timber harvesting and the consumption of forest products (see Chapter 11 by Gale). If the political challenge is to build these networks and shorten the distances and disconnects of globalization, then an important intellectual challenge is to map these distances and develop ways to measure or anticipate their rates of change.

CONCLUSION

Some suggest that globalization is propelling us beyond a politics of place. Spatially based institutions such as the state are dismissed as quaint, nineteenth-century arrangements in a twenty-first-century world of speed, virtuality and post-material identities. This strikes me as an overreaction: it extrapolates non-linear changes as though they will follow a constant trajectory, and it understates the importance of a sense of place in the formation of collective identities. The struggle for state power has not become entirely irrelevant; few states have been stripped completely of the capacity to act on environmental problems. My purpose in arguing for a 'post-statist' frame is not to dismiss the state as irrelevant so much as to relocate our understanding of it as we seek to create the transnational architecture for meaningful, ecologically attuned governance. The nation-state has never been the sovereign, neutral reflection of the popular will that it is presented to be in much of the mainstream analysis of global environmental politics, and ongoing processes of global economic reorganization make it ever less so.

As a direct result of these changes, we are seeing the emergence of a wide array of non-state-based approaches to global environmental governance. Some of these, consisting of countless protest groups, citizens' organizations and social movements, seek to reconstitute a public realm with a richer transnational dimension. Others, in direct contrast, seek to take environmental governance further into the private realm – be it through the codification of private, voluntary standards of corporate environmental management through the International Organization for Standardization, or the efforts to enclose and privatize traditional common goods ranging from breathable air to germ plasm.

Conceptual models that misallocate responsibility, misidentify power and hide the communities and livelihoods where truly sustainable models most likely reside are not neutral in the struggle to build these diametrically opposed visions of global environmental governance. The enormous tasks of global sustainability demand not only new institutions for political action but also new conceptions of politics in a global economy.

PART FOUR

Ecological Political Economy and the 'System'

9. Ecological Sustainability: Some Elements of Longer-term System Change

Gar Alperovitz, Thad Williamson and Alex Campbell

How might we begin to develop an overview of political-economic structures that could in principle form an ecologically sustainable system? And if we were able to do this, how might we begin to develop a coherent path that could get us from here to there? This dual problem, of course, is at the heart of a vast literature on ecological matters – and, too, of a great deal of political and citizen activity. Direct analyses of the underlying structural features of political-economic systems, and the impact of these features on a society's ecological practices, however, are still relatively rare, even though the need for a thorough rethinking of the building blocks of a truly sustainable society has never been more urgent.[1] A start, we believe, can be made by recognizing, first, that these questions are inherently 'system' questions (not simply policy and political questions); and second, that they take us well beyond some of the structural and dynamic principles associated with both capitalism and classical socialism.

CONFRONTING THE SYSTEM PROBLEM

There is a growing consensus that to avoid compromising the needs of future generations, any political-economic system must significantly reduce ecological stress, repair past environmental damage and generate sufficient political and policy momentum so that net environmental deterioration can be halted.[2] Although precise definitions vary, many now recognize that 'sustainability' requires both an institutional structure and a culture with the capacity to achieve these bottom-line results in an ongoing fashion (Milbrath, 1996).

It has also become increasingly obvious that neither of the two major 'systems' of the twentieth century – capitalism and socialism – are organized in a manner compatible with achieving these goals. This is not to say that modest and occasionally substantial goals cannot be achieved within the existing structures. But if the larger judgement is correct, then the conventional debate will obviously need to push much deeper to confront the underlying design characteristics of these and other systems to see if any are – or might be – sustainable.

Socialism

Throughout Eastern Europe and the former Soviet Union, the push for cheap energy and maximum industrial production – together with a wanton disregard for public health – created vast ecological wastelands in which dirty air, polluted water and heavy toxic emissions despoiled ecosystems and threatened human life. In 1988 (just before the collapse of the system), air pollution in more than a hundred cities in the former Soviet Union was more than 10 times the legal standard. Sixty-five per cent of Poland's river water was deemed too polluted even for industrial use, and large segments of the Polish population were not served by any waste treatment facilities (French, 1990). Energy efficiency in each of the former socialist countries of Europe lagged 50 per cent behind even modest US levels. Much energy was produced by filth-generating, brown coal plants, many without any pollution controls whatsoever.

At the end of the 1980s it was estimated that one out of every seventeen deaths in Hungary was due to air pollution. 'Wherever you point your finger on the map', observed one Russian scientist shortly after the breakup of the Soviet Union, 'there is another horrible place' (Shapiro, 1993).[3]

In Asia, 8 Chinese cities are among the 10 with the worst air pollution in the world according to World Health Organization studies. Acid rain, the result of sulphur oxide and nitrogen oxide pollution, affects nearly one-third of the Chinese land area. Severe water quality problems face the majority of the population: perhaps 700 million Chinese drink water contaminated with animal and human waste. While most industrial wastewater receives some treatment, only 65 per cent of the industrial wastewater released in 1998 met standards set by the government. China also faces severe soil erosion, solid waste and desertification problems (Ash and Edmonds, 1998; Wang, 1999).

Behind such statistics – many more could be cited – are domineering, growth-at-all-costs centralized government bureaucracies and an ideology which suggested that nature could and should be bent to human will whatever the consequences. The governing authorities of the socialist states lacked the will – and probably the capacity – to hold economic operations accountable to true social costs; and local communities had no means of contesting the anti-ecological values of central power. As ecological economist Ken Townsend has observed, 'rationality' converted forests of rich diversity into monocrop fields and attempted to reverse the flow of entire river systems (Townsend, 1993).

The difficulties of the Soviet Union and China, of course, also derive from development problems common throughout the world, and, too, the consequences of militarized economies. However, the results can also be traced to certain basic properties or design features of the state socialist system.[4] For instance, the Soviet Union, with its emphasis on expansion of productive capacity and its need for centralized coordination among different activities, placed great pressure on managers of state-run enterprises and other state agencies to meet output goals as an overriding priority. Enterprises and agencies were often compelled to cut ecological corners. Moreover, when ecological damage took place, there were few countervailing mechanisms to challenge abuses. Real-world socialist systems have typically concentrated the political power of the state while simultaneously weakening and suppressing civil society.[5]

Capitalism

We have little difficulty recognizing large order, underlying structural characteristics when we look 'outwards' towards another system. But what of our own system? Are the environmental problems of capitalism also inherently structural and systemic? Is the trend towards environmental degradation and the continuing escalation of resource consumption a minor side effect of the system? Or is it a necessary result of the system's inherent design?

The trends are not encouraging to those who would prefer to avoid facing the implications of these questions. Consider natural resource consumption. The World Resources Institute (WRI) has recently noted that major capitalist industrial economies consume between 45 and 85 tonnes of material per person each year. For example:

> fabricating the automobiles and other metal-intensive products for which Japan is well known requires mining and processing a yearly per capita equivalent of about 14 metric tons of ore and minerals. Growing the food required to feed a single US resident causes about 15 metric tons of soil erosion annually. In Germany, producing the energy used in a year requires removing and replacing more than 29 metric tons of coal overburden for each German citizen, quite apart from the fuel itself or the pollution caused by its combustion (Adriaanse cited in the World Resources Institute (WRI), 1998).

In 1995 the United States consumed nearly nine times as much commercial energy as India; per capita emissions of carbon dioxide, a principal greenhouse gas, are over 20 times those of India (WRI, 1999, pp. 333, 345). The United States consumes 333 kilograms of paper per person per year, compared to approximately 15 kilograms per year in the developing world (WRI, 1999). Deforestation world-wide has left only one-fifth of the planet's original forests intact (WRI, 1999). (Americans also consume a highly disproportionate quantity of the world's meat: 118 kilograms per year per person, in 1996, compared to just 24 kilograms per year in the developing world (WRI, 1999, pp. 333, 345)). Alan Durning reports that between 1940 and 1976 alone Americans used up as large a share of the earth's mineral resources as did *everyone* in history previously (Durning, 1992, p. 38).

The trends are no more comforting when one looks at pollution. US yearly production of synthetic organic chemicals grew one-thousandfold – from 150 million kilograms to over 150 billion kilograms – between 1935 and 1995. Studies by the National Academy of Sciences demonstrate that we lack sufficient information for even a 'partial health assessment' of 95 per cent of the chemicals that have already been released into the air, water and soil. A thousand or more new chemical substances are put on the market each year, many of which are likely to be harmful, even in small quantities, by themselves or in combination with other substances. But the US conducts only 500 product tests per year – not enough to test the constant stream of new chemicals, let alone make a dent in the backlog of untested chemicals. Literally millions of tests would be required to assess the potential health risks of these chemicals in combination (Mitchell, 1997, pp. 32–3).

Confronted with such data illustrating the ecological consequences of our current development path, a common response of many environmentalists has been to emphasize the 'greed' of corporate and other economic actors in generating such problems. It is important, however, to recognize that growth in capitalist systems is not motivated simply by hunger for profit but by fear that derives from the central logic and dynamics of the capitalist system: companies for the most part *must* cut costs if they are to withstand competition. They *must* externalize: if a company willingly spends money on a pollution reduction problem and then must raise its prices to cover the cost, it risks finding its market share reduced or destroyed by a less conscientious rival firm.

Communities often face similar pressures in deciding, say, between continued logging of declining forests or loss of jobs. We see cities and states commonly prostrating themselves in order to attract corporate investment, because the consequences of not doing so are so severe: high unemployment, tax losses, continued social breakdown, and, of course, negative political outcomes for incumbent government officials. For communities as for capitalist firms the built-in system logic is obvious: very often it is simply a matter of 'grow or die'.

The same propositions unfortunately commonly hold for many individuals as well. Consider the life cycle of a typical middle-class American: one goes to college in order to get ahead and thereby incurs debt; paying off the debt requires accumulating as much money as possible; then it is time for a family, children and if you are lucky, a mortgage – more responsibilities, and more pressure to accumulate as much as possible – now; parents come to realize that if they do not live in the right neighbourhood, their child's education will suffer, and they had better start saving for college; by the time that is over the question 'Who will take care of me?' in old age or sickness becomes central.

For the vast majority of Americans whatever security one achieves is fragile at best. At any time – and this is now as true for white-collar managers as for blue-collar workers – one might be laid off as a result of a downturn in the economy, a corporate buyout, a new technology or even simply a change in the exchange rate. In his recent book *Illusions of Prosperity* Joel Blau underscores the perverse nature of the current situation: despite low unemployment, the massive pressures of the economy (layoffs, downsizing, corporate buyouts, low-wage jobs and so forth) result in intense feelings of insecurity:

> Although many employees continue to have what are nominally permanent jobs, contract work has become the metaphor, if not the fact, for much of the labor market. Whether they sign up for a couple of weeks or a couple of years, more and more Americans know that their work at any particular job is time-limited, and their future probably includes a period of unemployment. Employees have always looked for jobs; employers have always done the hiring. Now, however, it is different. Search, hire, and fire; search, hire, and fire: not since the Great Depression has the constant churning of the US labor market engendered such intense feelings of economic insecurity (Blau, 1999, p. 43).

In such situations the only way to obtain any real security is to avoid falling – and indeed, to keep climbing. In the absence of job or income security, it is always wise to strive for 'more' – more income, more power and prestige at work, and commonly, more hours – *now*, since tomorrow may well bring 'less'.

In addition, status differences based on income and consumption – which are endemic to the system – exacerbate the drive to consume (Duesenberry, 1949; Frank, 1999a; Hirsch, 1976; Lichtenberg, 1995; Schor, 1991, 1998, 1999). In a society of massive inequalities and growing insecurity, and in which the media make very visible the lifestyles of the affluent (both through advertising and the content of programming), it is hardly surprising that there is general adulation of the rich and the secure in the system, or that the capacity to consume so often becomes a measure of self-esteem and status.

These pressures towards increased consumption by individuals and families are also tailored, of course, to supporting continued growth and expansion in the economy as a whole. As the billions of dollars spent each year on advertising so clearly suggest, firms have an obvious interest in creating 'needs' and shaping consumers' tastes and interests to sell their products. Indeed, capitalism can continue to expand within advanced economies only by continually generating new needs. At the same time capitalist development undercuts individual economic security and increases inequality it also undermines the basis of community integration and support as a matter of course: companies come and go, jobs appear and disappear. Often as not the social fabric is allowed to unravel, the local culture disintegrates, the community fragments and young people leave. There is little 'community' left to nurture a less materialist orientation; individuals must face the powerful influences of our corporate-driven media largely alone.

Finally, and not least, there is the political power and political culture which accompanies advanced capitalist economies – and the impact both have on ecological policy making (and, indeed, democratic practice in general). Countless studies – and common observation – indicate that corporate institutions have the capacity and interest to wield disproportionate political influence, to manipulate regulatory agencies, thwart citizen action groups and impact both electoral politics and legislation.[6] A recent study found that several polluting industries out-contribute all environmental political action committees (PACs) by an order of magnitude, and also spend one billion dollars a year on corporate advertising and 'greenwashing' (Dowie, 1995; Stauber and Rampton, 1995, p. 128). Largely in response to corporate pressures the US government has regularly intervened in the economy to promote ecologically inefficient and destructive practices.

Two examples among a multitude serve to illustrate: while allocating a pittance to the development of solar and wind power, the Federal government sank $100 billion into nuclear power between 1950 and 1990, and it continues to subsidize the fossil fuel industry with billions of dollars each year (Friends of the Earth, 1999).[7] Similarly, in what amounts to an indirect subsidy for private automakers, the government has lavished billions on the Highway Trust Fund and created the interstate highway system, while allowing public transit of most types to decay.

Distinguishing Outcome Realities

We have been dwelling on such widely recognized and self-evident features of our own system for a reason. We all know very well that our system is characterized by such institutional, structural and power 'design features'.

That they are 'system properties' is obvious. The problem is that we rarely call a spade a spade. *Most important, the implications are seldom incorporated into analyses of the challenge of long-term sustainability.*

Part of our difficulty in confronting the systemic nature of the problem is that we often have trouble distinguishing between reforms which help ameliorate the worst aspects of environmental degradation and changes that actually result in altering *trends*. At the most general level, it is obvious that positive movement that diminishes harmful impacts on the environment regularly occurs within capitalist systems. Legislation is passed which helps control pollution, 'progress' is made in eliminating lead and chloro-fluorocarbons, there are improvements in the reduction of sulphur oxides, carbon monoxide and particulates.

It is absolutely essential, however, to discriminate much more clearly among the following three categories of change: type 'A', reforms and gains that mitigate but do not end specific ecological problems; type 'B', that include occasional breakthroughs on a particular issue or substance (such as the complete removal of lead from gasoline); and type 'C', that occasion *significant, comprehensive long-term trend reversals in an entire category of ecological concern* (such as a much hoped-for but little accomplished reversal in the generation of greenhouse gases in order to minimize the risk – or at this stage, in all likelihood, mitigate the consequences – of global climate change).

Although most of our environmental debate is focused on fostering occasional breakthroughs, token reforms and 'gains', the fact is a great deal of evidence points to the conclusion that the A- and B-type improvements do not lead to reversals of the basic *outcome trends* that matter most in terms of sustainability. We have noted some of the most obvious consumption/ resource indicators that clearly show continued negative trends above. Defenders of the US regulatory system often point to successes in two areas in particular: air and water pollution. Even here, however, the evidence suggests that despite some major achievements, especially with regard to a few particularly hazardous pollutants and some high-profile successes like the recovery of Lake Erie, real problems remain in both areas.[8]

Even more disturbing: a 1995 study of long-term trends in 21 environmental factors compiled by the National Center for Economic and Security Alternatives confirmed (with limited exceptions) a general worsening of various ecological outcomes in each of nine industrialized countries surveyed over the past 25 years. This despite the fact that the quarter-century began with the first Earth Day and extended through a flurry of legislation, reform, green planning, the establishment of environmental ministries and growing ecological consciousness and grassroots activism. Had economic growth been anywhere near the levels that business and government leaders hoped for, the general trend towards environmental degradation would have been substantially worse (Alperovitz et al., 1995). And, of course, since the heyday of environmentalism, a conservative anti-environmental political backlash has occurred in many countries (Rowell, 1996; Switzer, 1997; Tokar, 1997).

John Dryzek has pointed out that even our environmental 'solutions' often tend to shift pollution across space or time, but do not actually eliminate many problems. For instance, smokestack scrubbers can remove pollutants from air emissions, but leave us with toxic sludge as a new threat (Dryzek, 1987a). Similarly, in our search for cheap or non-air polluting power, we have often created new problems: nuclear waste in the case of nuclear power, and vast habitat destruction in the case of hydroelectric dams.

Dynamic characteristics of the system give a particular edge to the problem: first, there is often a time delay in connection with remedial actions due to the complexity of the natural systems involved (consider global warming). Second, technological innovation is constantly creating potential *new* difficulties, and only after they are discovered does the tortuous process of building the political will to force a response begin. The United Nations Environmental Programme's (UNEP) recently released *Global Environmental Outlook – 2000* lists the following 'emerging' environmental problems (among others):

- nitrogen's harmful impact on ecosystems;
- increased severity of natural disasters;
- species invasion as a result of globalization;
- increased environmental pressures caused by urbanization;
- the impact of refugees on the natural environment (UNEP, 1999b).

Will the next generation of environmental problems emerge from biotechnology, cold fusion developments, nanotechnology, space junk, attempts at desalination or another area of technological advance (Yoon, 1999)? 'Normal accident' theory suggests that the various elements of complex processes are likely to interact with each other – and with the very safety systems with which we attempt to protect ourselves – in highly unpredictable ways (Perrow, 1984). (For instance, the Chernobyl meltdown was caused by a safety test of the back-up power sources) (Sagan, 1993, p. 39).

The implications are not pleasant to consider. Whatever one thinks of the regulatory system's ability to handle ecological issues, a further question remains: does the political-economic system generate *new problems* at a faster rate than it generates the capacity to solve them? (See also French, 1995.)

ELEMENTS OF AN ALTERNATIVE

Many have long been aware, at least in a 'background' sense, of the ways in which not only state socialism but also our own system work against achieving ecological sustainability. More novel is the suggestion that the best response to this situation is not simply to continue to 'muddle through' and hope for the best. We believe that it is not only essential, but also possible to begin to sketch at least some of the properties of a system that might reduce the underlying pressures that generate the negative outcomes.

If unsustainable growth patterns are encouraged by the reality of widespread economic insecurity, it follows that a first principle of an ecologically sustainable society is that it must provide economic security for individuals and communities. So long as most citizens are only a few paycheques away from insolvency, and so long as they worry that their income may be taken away, economic expansion and job creation will be a higher political priority than environmental protection for large numbers of people. At the community level, so long as localities remain dependent on uncertain investment decisions for their economic health, protection of the environment will take a back seat.

A second principle is reducing the dominance of consumerism. This in turn requires reducing the pressures of inequality-driven status envy on the one hand and, on the other, building up sources of social and community support for individuals which begin to offer satisfactions from interactions with people rather than from consumption of goods. A long-term alternative path would also include a reduction in work time, a concomitant reduction in consumption and an expansion of free time (or a shift to more intrinsically rewarding – though possibly less technologically advanced – work) (Lane, 1993). This is also inextricably linked to the first principle (economic security): people are unlikely to seek any reduction in work time as long as they face insecurity.

A third requirement of an ecologically sustainable society is that producers who damage the environment should bear the costs of their damage. Since the true costs of production are not reflected in the prices of goods on the market, firms benefit by externalizing costs such as pollution cleanup (or lack thereof) to the public (Underwood, 1998).

Finally, and perhaps obviously, a fourth requirement of an ecologically sustainable economy is simply that growth should no longer be a top priority. Economic growth *per se* need not be eliminated entirely: one way to reduce resource use and pollution is to cut production and shrink the economy; another is to make productive systems more efficient (England and Harris, 1997).[9] If the nation decided to hire more elementary school teachers – and at the same time to buy fewer sports utility vehicles – ecological damage could decline even as the size of the economy stayed roughly the same.[10]

TOWARDS A SYSTEMIC RESPONSE

These – and other (for a representative listing, see Daly and Cobb, 1989) – requirements of an ecologically sustainable society might be easy to deal with if we imagined an all-powerful state which enforced strict ecological standards on both individuals and businesses. Not only is such a vision unattractive on its own terms, it probably would provide only a temporary solution to the ecological problem: permanence is not a characteristic of authoritarian regimes (of any stripe), and we would expect widespread resistance to top-down environmental measures implemented without the support of public opinion.[11]

Our strategy for a first stage response proceeds on several levels. We begin by emphasizing the fundamental need to rebuild – and add to – the basis of enforceable ecological norms 'from the bottom up'. This in turn involves four issues: achieving greater local economic stability; nurturing local civic environmental culture; building new forms of embedded and democratized capital; and altering the larger structures of inequality and time availability (which in turn forces the analysis upwards towards larger institutional issues). A fifth issue – to which we turn subsequently – involves the matter of scale.

Ecological Norm Building

First things first: norms are ultimately the driving force behind policy. Survey research reveals major shifts in public attitudes over the past 25 years. For instance, the number of Americans who judged that we should 'sacrifice economic growth in order to preserve and protect the environment' grew from 38 per cent in 1976 to 64 per cent in 1990 (Cambridge Reports cited in Kempton et al., 1995, p. 4). A particularly revealing illustration is offered by Gregg Easterbrook: President Clinton, he notes, was more responsive to environmentalists than labour unions in negotiating side-agreements to the North American Free Trade Agreement (NAFTA): 'This is a shift of the first magnitude. Had you told a political scientist 20 years ago that by the 1990s environmentalists would be taken more seriously in a Democratic White House than the AFL-CIO, you would have been advised to seek professional care' (Easterbrook, 1995, p. 446). In 1996, pollsters Quinlan and Greenberg (1997) found that the 'expectation of a clean environment has evolved into a virtual norm – a near universal belief in the country that this is the right way to organize society'. Modern improvements in acceptable air and water standards – and many other recent achievements – are inconceivable without the change in norms that preceded them.

The work of political scientist Ronald Inglehart and others suggests the trend of growing environmental concern will continue. Most significant among Inglehart's findings is evidence that ongoing long-term trends in overall economic abundance tend to increase the relative prevalence of 'postmaterial' values, that is, a growing concern with democracy, the environment, and quality of life. His research also suggests intergenerational shifts in values towards increasing postmaterialism in younger age cohorts – together with shifts in the predicted direction in nearly every one of 44 countries examined (Inglehart, 1997).[12]

For the various reasons previously reviewed, we believe it unlikely that the past and ongoing process of norm evolution is – or can be – sufficiently powerful on its own to achieve significant ecological trend alteration (as opposed to type 'A' and type 'B' changes). Hence, a strategic requirement over the long haul may be defined as *adding to, enhancing, supplementing and ultimately transforming* the already-building developmental line of norm evolution. If this can be done, the basis of civic and political culture – the ultimate precondition of lasting policy and structural change – may perhaps be fuelled steadily and expansively.[13]

Stability

What can be done, concretely, to facilitate the further evolution of strong ecological norms, starting at the local level? A first step is to increase individual and community economic stability.[14] One set of strategies involves traditional local, state and national tax, loan, regulatory, procurement, and other efforts to keep jobs in communities and to reduce the pressure of globalization and destabilizing trade. Other policies to encourage stability include economically targeted investment by pension funds, trade adjustment assistance, worker training, Community Development Block Grants and Empowerment Communities/Enterprise Zones, rural community assistance and brownfield redevelopment. Related to this is the need to manage trade in a manner that does not undermine communities. Various strategies have been suggested by such experts as Jeff Faux and Dani Rodrik. Others have been proposed by a number of coalitions.[15] The bottom line: stabilizing communities is more important than abstract theories of neoclassical trade management.[16]

A second line of defence involves the development of 'anchored' community industries that inherently increase stability. These include community-owned firms, small businesses, employee-owned companies,

community development corporations, non-profits in business and so forth
(see below for further details). The key characteristic of such firms is that
they are owned by local people and are much less likely to 'get up and go'.
Traditional policies can also be used to support such inherently community-
friendly institutions. Local and state governments are also experimenting with
specific technical assistance programmes for anchored firms.

The Northeast Ohio Employee Ownership Center (OEOC), for instance,
conducts feasibility studies for potential worker buyouts. Since its founding in
1987 the OEOC has coached numerous firms in employee-ownership
strategies (since 1988 it has done this work under contract with the state)
(Louge, 1998, pp. 34–5).

A third strategy is to attempt to enhance local 'multipliers', that is, the
number of times a dollar recirculates within a particular local economy. 'Buy
local' strategies and enhanced local supplier networks also tend to increase
local stability. Another approach is based on new forms of local currency,
such as 'Ithaca Hours' in Ithaca, New York, that is, 'money' that can only be
spent at local businesses.

Still another strategy entails the strategic placement of public facilities
including universities, hospitals and government agencies. Many struggling
localities dream of landing a major public asset or facility as a development
anchor: hundreds have bid on the siting of new federal facilities and even new
prison construction. With government economic activity approaching 40 per
cent of gross domestic product (GDP), opportunities for careful targeting of
such activity to enhance local community stability abound.[17]

Possibilities for rooting and stabilizing economic activity in local
communities may be increased by a trend that has traditionally (and quite
rightly) been viewed as debilitating to community – the decline of
manufacturing in the United States. The manufacturing sector today employs
less than 14 per cent of the workforce and is projected to shrink to
approximately 9 per cent by the middle of next century (US Bureau of
Economic Analysis, 1995).[18] The economy of the future will be dominated by
the service sector, a sector that is much more locally oriented, enjoys fewer
economies of scale and has far less need to agglomerate around central
locations (such as ports or rail connectors) than the manufacturing sector.

The trend offers new opportunities for strategies aimed at local stability.
Indeed, a recent study by Wiewel and Persky (1994, p. 129) already reveals
'not a decrease but an accelerating increase' in the 'percentage of economic
activity . . . [that] serves local markets' between 1979 and 1989. Economist
Thomas Michael Power has also documented a 'growing localness':

> About 60 percent of US economic activity is local and provides residents with the
> goods and services that make their lives comfortable. This includes retail
> activities; personal, repair, medical, education, and professional services;

construction; public utilities; local transportation; financial institutions; real estate; and government services. Thus almost all local economies are dominated by residents taking in each other's wash . . . This figure represents an increase from 52 percent over the last two decades, an increase that has occurred largely because the aggregates of retail and wholesale sales, services, financial and real estate, and state and local government are making up a larger and larger percentage of total earnings. In 1940, locally oriented production represented just 42 percent of total earnings (Power, 1996, pp. 37, 49).

Given these and other trends it is no longer unreasonable, even in narrow economic efficiency terms, to speak of rooting economic activity in particular places as an achievable goal in the new century. Taken together, the various strategies offer the possibility of a slow but steady enhancement of local economic stability – the precondition of many other changes at the level of the community.

'Embedding'

Stability is a necessary but clearly not sufficient condition of further development. A second is the systematic embedding of economic activities in local communities so that they can be shaped by democratic accountability in general and ecological concerns in particular – both in order to deal with problems locally and to help nurture a longer-term norm structure which can constrain larger regional and national activities.

A slow build-up at the local level of a variety of embedding mechanisms requires rooting capital in communities so that there is a community of responsibility for the consequences of economic activity, and wherever possible also some form of local democratized ownership. As we have noted in connection with community stability 'anchoring', there are many possibilities along these lines: non-profits in business, municipal enterprises, worker-owned firms, locally owned corporations, and so forth. In addition, new legal structures can enforce a return to the original concept of the corporate charter, that is, that incorporation is a privilege to be reserved for entities that meet public needs (Behr, 1999, p. E1; Mokhiber and Weissman, 1998).

One of the most important developments occurring just below the surface of public awareness is the growth of new economic institutions which democratize capital in some way, and which are potentially more capable of being embedded and made accountable to community ecological concerns. The growth of such institutions is well known among specialists. However, those not familiar with this field are often surprised at its range and extent. For instance, currently functioning in the United States alone there are:

1. Some 3500 to 4000 Community Development Corporations (National Congress for Community Economic Development (NCCED), 1995, 1999).
2. More than 48 000 cooperatives generating over $120 billion in annual economic activity. (The National Cooperative Bank estimates that one-third of all Americans – roughly 100 million people – are directly served by at least one type of cooperative) (National Cooperative Bank, 1998, p. 9).
3. More than 15 000 significantly worker-owned firms whose employees own 9 per cent of corporate equity in the United States (National Center for Employee Ownership (NCEO), 1997; Rosen, 1998).[19]

The remaining three categories are less well developed and less well known. There are:

4. Some 120 community land trusts in 32 states and the District of Columbia, the vast majority of which have got off the ground in the past 15 years (Orvis, 1998).
5. A wide range of municipally owned enterprises, from the 2000 municipally owned utilities to municipally owned recreational facilities and transportation systems to such less traditional ventures as cable television, internet provision, retail stores, hotels and baseball teams. Indeed, local governments typically use municipal enterprises to bring in nearly half of their total self-generated revenue (Stumm, 1997, pp. 498–515).
6. More than 350 community development finance institutions (including community development banks, community development loan funds and community development credit unions) (Howard, 1999, pp. 24–7; Howard and Rusch, forthcoming).

Another emerging model for local-level governance and 'embeddedness' of economic activity – 'civic environmentalism' – offers additional possibilities for future development. The traditional regulatory state approach has been applied to only a limited set of environmental problems – mainly those that are most amenable to monitoring compliance. A typical example: the Clean Water Act has done a reasonable job of limiting concentrated dumping – but little formal regulation has been applied to the more difficult problem of 'non-point source' pollution, that is, releases from widely dispersed locations, such as farms.

Locally negotiated, flexible approaches have been adopted in numerous areas as alternatives to traditional 'command and control' regulation – in, for instance, habitat preservation, forestry, toxic release control, green space preservation, land trusts and so on. Some authors see the trend as a vital way forward in dealing with some of the most deeply intractable environmental problems (Abel, 1999; Sabel et al., 1999, pp. 4–11). From the perspective of political-economic design, the most interesting 'Civic Environmental' experiments are those which provide for sustained citizen input into local corporate decision making.

Barbara Scott Murdock and Ken Sexton of the Center for Environment and Health Policy at the University of Minnesota report one particularly interesting example: in Manchester, Texas, the Rhone Poulenc chemical plant, a local environmental group, and representatives of the community met in the wake of a serious chemical release in 1991. The company felt pressure to negotiate because it needed its permit to incinerate hazardous wastes renewed. The plant signed a binding agreement to allow a health and safety audit by an expert to be chosen by the community; to open company documents; to sponsor a study of health effects of the plant; and to improve the emergency notification system. Ultimately, Murdock and Sexton argue, 'where community members hold veto power, voting power, or the ability to block a permit, they can have substantial power to affect a company's environmental decisions', regardless of which particular form they use to negotiate with the company (Murdock and Sexton, 1998).

Some experimentation with civic environmentalism undoubtedly consists of public relations measures undertaken by companies in order to gain credibility by involving local activists – without allowing them any real authority or traction on the problems they seek to address.[20] Nevertheless, in combination with other capital embedding strategies, such experiments and innovations may also offer promise for the long haul.[21]

Income, Wealth and Capital

Community economic stability and embedding economic activity in a local culture of ecological sustainability are two major thrusts in the direction of enhancing the basis of long term norm evolution at the community level. The problems of individual economic security, inequality and free time force us to reconsider the way larger economic activity is owned and controlled.

It is now a commonplace that wealth and income inequality have increased dramatically over the past quarter century. Since 1973 the top 5 per cent of families has seen its share of national income increase by more than one-third (from 15.5 per cent to 20.7 per cent); the top fifth has seen its share increase by 15 per cent (from 41.1 per cent to 47.3 per cent). Meanwhile, the share of *every other income group* has fallen: the rise in the top share has come at the expense of all households in the 'bottom' 80 per cent (US Census Bureau, 1999).

Disparities in wealth are much greater and have grown much more dramatically. Professor Ed Wolff of New York University has shown that the top 1 per cent's share of household wealth has more than doubled since the mid-1970s: from 19.9 per cent in 1976 to 40 per cent in 1997.[22] The top 1 per cent now owns more than the entire bottom 95 per cent of Americans combined. Bill Gates alone owns more than the bottom 45 per cent combined (more than 120 million people) (Shifting Fortunes, 1999, p. 8). If one removes equity in owner-occupied housing from the picture and looks simply at financial wealth (which includes all forms of business ownership, bonds, real estate and so on), the richest 0.5 per cent of households alone possess 42 per cent (Shifting Fortunes, 1999).

Even more challenging: these relative comparisons ignore the much larger *absolute* income and wealth gap, which is growing annually (even at times when relative inequality stays the same). Thus, if we make $10 000 and you make $500 000 one year and we make $20 000 and you make $1 million the next, relative inequality has stayed the same (a ratio of 1 to 50), but the real-world, absolute gap between us has increased from $490 000 to $980 000! The absolute inflation-adjusted gap between the average family in the top 5 per cent and the average family in the bottom 20 per cent grew from $137 365 in 1979 to $233 994 in 1998 (all in 1998 dollars).

Current trends of income and wealth distribution have produced what may be described as a 'perpetual envy machine'. As Schor (1999, pp. 37–50) observes:

> As a result of their increased income, the rich and super-rich began a bout of conspicuous luxury consumption, beginning in the early 1980s. Members of the upper middle class followed suit with their own imitative luxury spending. (Thus began the so-called decade of greed.) The 80 percent below, while gaining some ground in absolute terms, lost relatively to those above them. Not surprisingly, they emanated dissatisfaction and pessimism and engaged in a round of compensatory keeping-up consumption.
>
> As members of the bottom 80 percent of the population have fallen behind relatively, they have become more inclined to imitate those in the top income group. The difference between what they aspire to and the income they have available to spend – what I call the 'aspirational gap' – has increased enormously . . .

Not only does growing inequality drive status insecurity, it encourages consumption by creating new needs. Frank (1999b) has noted that the 'arms race' among car buyers is not simply a matter of taste or status indication: to the extent drivers of small, relatively fuel-efficient cars face the possibility of collision with a 7500 lb. Ford Expedition, they are very much encouraged to buy a larger car for the sake of safety alone. In addition, inequality helps generate urban decay, which in turn has played an important role in driving suburbanization and its concomitant auto-centred (and expensive suburban) economy as residents move to escape urban woes and to place their children in better schools (Segal, 1995, p. 27).

Traditional tax-and-spend policies aimed at reducing inequality not only are in trouble in the current period, but except in extremely unusual moments they have never achieved sustained improvement in either relative or absolute inequality. At best, traditional approaches have on the whole served to slow down a deep-seated century-long trend towards ever-greater inequality. As MIT economist Lester Thurow has noted, only 'great social shocks such as wars and economic depression' have actually been able to (temporarily) halt or reverse the trend. However, as Thurow writes, 'no one knows how to engineer such changes in less extreme situations.'[23]

Recent studies illuminate in statistical detail how obstacles to income redistribution follow in most Organisation for Economic Co-operation and Development (OECD) countries directly from the simple fact that the relatively affluent have – *as a function of their affluence* – disproportionate political power to block redistributive measures (Rodriguez, u.d.). As a consequence, a growing number of analysts at various points on the political spectrum are coming to accept that tax-and-transfer measures are simply not likely ever to succeed in stemming the inequality tide. Reich (1999, pp. viii–ix) explains: 'Trying to redistribute income from those relatively rich to those relatively poor through specific federal program . . . has become next to impossible, as evidenced by the difficulties of funding everything from Head Start to housing subsidies'.

The difficulties facing tax-and-transfer policies have forced a steady stream of authors to propose new remedies – especially those that are asset- or wealth-based rather than income-based. The underlying idea is that allocating capital may ultimately be more politically feasible and more efficient than trying to compensate for inequality through redistribution. As Harvard economist Richard Freeman (1999, p. 14; see also Bowles, 1999) observes, 'Equality of income obtained in the first instance via greater equality of assets, rather than as an after-the-fact . . . state redistribution of income from rich to poor, would enable us to better square the circle of market efficiency and egalitarian aspiration'.

Many writers both in the US and abroad have also begun to explore models of larger-scale economic activity that move beyond the corporation as we commonly know it. For instance, the late Louis Kelso; Cambridge University Nobel Laureate, the late James Meade; and the radical American economist John Roemer have all put forward carefully worked out proposals for quasi-public corporate structures which pass profits on to citizens as a matter of right. Other scholars are revisiting the very early vision of the

Tennessee Valley Authority – a regional public enterprise structured along grassroots participatory principles. In another area entirely, many have noted that approaches to Social Security reform which include stock market investment point ultimately towards some form of public management or oversight on behalf (minimally) of unsophisticated poor and low income Americans, and this in turn (as conservatives fear) is likely to lead to greater public control of capital investment.

An intriguing and potentially suggestive approach is that of the Alaska Permanent Fund. The state fund manages an income flow derived ultimately from oil exploitation so as to provide each individual citizen a dividend (well over $1000 in recent years) (Alaska Permanent Fund Corporation (APFC), 1991). (Alaska's general revenues are also provided in large part by earnings from mineral rights.) Of course, from an ecological perspective this example is deeply flawed because it depends so heavily on the exploitation of oil, which involves environmental degradation of many kinds. However, the institutional mechanism for providing at least some additional support to individuals suggests practical possibilities that might one day be developed in other areas.[24]

We believe an answer to increasing inequality will ultimately require some form of democratization of capital at the national level, which builds on such ideas, and perhaps on other examples (from municipally owned firms to public land ownership). Interesting precedents also include state and local government investments in local firms through venture capital funds. (A 1996 survey found that more than one-third of responding city governments had used venture capital investment strategies and 52 per cent had engaged in some form of equity participation) (Clark and Gaile, 1998, p. 84). State governments are also involved – more than 20 regularly participate as venture capitalists in start-up companies (NASDA, 1998). The Federal government, of course, owns one-third of the nation's land.

A new institution to democratize wealth would likely allocate income flows to individuals, building on the precedent of the Earned Income Tax Credit and the Alaska Permanent Fund. It would derive its funds directly from earnings rather than taxation. In addition to direct support for individuals, funds could also be used to support public functions such as local education, public universities, health care and environmental protection.[25]

Getting a handle on growing inequality and even beginning to reduce the vast disparities will probably also ultimately require an income and wealth cap (or very high taxation) of some form for the very rich, either through traditional taxes on income and wealth or through much more stringent taxation of large sums of inherited wealth (Alperovitz, 1994, pp. 31–6).[26]

Technology, Productivity and Time

Clearly what Kelso once called a 'second income' that flowed through to individuals could not only help reduce inequality and achieve greater personal economic security: it would also feed back into local community stability strategies. Again, a second line of income could open up the possibility of greater free time and of increasing satisfactions other than those provided by consumerism (Lipietz, 1995). The most interesting options, indeed, involve trading money for time and translating the trajectory of productivity increases over the coming century into a reduced work week.

A small number of privileged Americans now have sufficient wherewithal, financial and psychological, to personally attempt to live lives of 'voluntary simplicity'. However, as Segal (1999, p. 92) has argued, a key requirement of any serious approach to reducing the work week for the vast majority is the provision of a stream of income unrelated to work. This could be done either via an approach like the Alaska strategy of direct income payments or a modification of the current Earned Income Credit, or alternatively through indirect subsidies similar to those currently used in France.

Significant opportunities for change in this area are likely to emerge as the economy changes. The basic fact is that the productive potential of the US economy is already massive: If the output of the American economy – today – were to be divided equally among all families (or groups) of four, each would receive over $125 000. Even Social Security Administration projections, based on very conservative assumptions, suggest the economy will produce $308 000 per family of four by the end of the next century. The slightly more optimistic assumptions used by the Council for Economic Advisors generate an estimate of $538 000 per family of four by the year 2100 (all figures in current dollars). The economy of the twenty-first century is likely to be so productive that instead of taking future gains in the form of more 'goods', it would be rational to reduce time worked.[27] Indeed, the work week might well be trimmed to half the current norm (Segal proposes 25 hours) or less – even as families enjoy the same or greater economic abundance as today.[28]

There is a reciprocal relationship between the structural arrangements inherent in any large national institution which can alter the ownership and control of capital so as to permit greater redistribution of time and income, and the impact of that time and income on such institutions. New norm patterns are necessary to control the ecological thrust of any large scale economic entity and make it accountable to the public. But the development of these norms in turn requires that citizens have the time and income to participate in democratic oversight – time and income that only such larger institutions can provide. If the 'virtuous cycle' inherent in the relationships here described can be achieved – and bolstered community-by-community through 'bottom-up' norm evolution – the larger system structures can potentially be organized in a systematically sustainable manner.

Scale

This preliminary set of proposals has so far proceeded at two levels – the local and the national. However, ultimately, we believe a different level of scale is important to consider. Americans have mainly failed to directly confront the gigantism of the continental scale of the United States. Many discussions of social and political theory related to sustainability, and many proposals for change, utilise comparative European models: the Scandinavian countries did this, the Germans did that, the Dutch did this. However, these European countries are of a geographic scale so vastly different from the United States as to make most comparisons questionable. For instance, Germany could be tucked into the states of Washington and Oregon. France could fit inside Texas. The Netherlands is minuscule.

The United States is so large today that it is extremely difficult to generate a social consensus in favour of expanded ecological protection. If we agree that the size of a polity has implications for consensus-building (Dahl and Tufte, 1973; *The Economist,* 1998; Hayek, 1944; Katzenstein, 1985; Simons, 1948), then we ultimately need to look to entities that are smaller than the continental national government: states or groupings of states within a region, for example. Smaller-scale and semi-autonomous regional polities with increased powers and responsibilities *vis-à-vis* the national government are ultimately likely to be another important element in a reconstructed ecologically sustainable system.

At the very least, a reconstructed system would need mechanisms at the state or regional level to ensure that one community does not pollute another. There would also inevitably need to be a planning mechanism to help allocate sufficient capital to each community to guarantee local-level economic stability and to help communities adjust when some industries decline due to market shifts.

CONCLUSION

The general line of potential development we have suggested in this study involves the slow reconstruction of local economic and social patterns together with slow changes in institutions of capital ownership at all levels. It is possible, of course, that no significant changes may ever occur even over very long stretches of time. On the other hand, it is not inevitable that all positive change will be slow. An illustration of how ongoing activity may erupt into new power is the new – and largely unpredicted – explosion of efforts to limit sprawl in many urban areas: for decades wasteful land use, transportation and other destructive and unplanned urban development went largely unchecked in many parts of the nation.

Suddenly, however, a movement of surprising strength emerged during only a very few years: in the autumn of 1998 alone over 70 per cent of 240 ballot measures were approved at the state and local level for 'capital investments in green [anti-sprawl] infrastructure' (Myers, 1998). The powerful new citizen activities to limit growth are phenomena of importance in their own right. They also suggest that long-term norm, institutional and system change may be more open in the future than many now think.[29]

NOTES

1. For an annotated listing of some attempts, see Williamson, 1998.
2. Sustainability as a central concern can be traced to the Club of Rome report (Meadows et al., 1974). Usage of the term has become so widespread, in fact, that some question its usefulness (Lélé, 1991).
3. Facts on Eastern Europe from French (1990, pp. 11, 12, 23).
4. One study found greater environmental degradation in command economies than market economies, even at similar levels of GNP, see T. Zylicz, 'Environmental Policies for Former Centrally Planned Economies: A Polish Perspective', Mimeo (Poland: Warsaw University, 1990), cited in Hubbell and Selden (1994).
5. For a comprehensive overview of environmental failures in the Soviet Union, see Feshbach and Friendly (1992). For discussion of the priority given to industrial goals, see Jancar (1987). For a theoretical model which suggests self-interested central planners are likely to overproduce consumer goods (versus environmental goods) and seek to minimize public awareness of environmental problems, see Hubbell and Selden (1994). For accounts that emphasize the lack of oppositional political culture, see Peterson (1993); and Sobell (1990). For a discussion of the problems of effectively regulating economic activity in a socialist economy, see Taga (1976). For a discussion of the dangers of combining centralized state power, ideology and a weakened civil society, see Scott (1998, pp. 88–9). For a discussion of these issues in relation to China, see Vermeer (1998).
6. Olson's (1965) observations on the incentive structure of interest group politics suggest that this will be an on-going and unresolvable problem. On the ability of corporations to minimize the enforcement of environmental laws, see Worth (1999, pp. 36–41).
7. Shifting the 'path' of technological innovation, of course, can have a very significant impact on long-term environmental outcomes: see Goodstein (1995).
8. In regard to air pollution, dramatic reductions in lead emissions have been made and US emissions of volatile organic compounds, sulphur dioxide and carbon monoxide are all down approximately one-third since 1970. This is a reversal of trend: emissions are no longer increasing. However, they *continue* at high levels. Other emissions, particularly those contributing to ground-level ozone, remain at levels that threaten human health in numerous cities. Additionally, little progress has been made with regard to nitrogen oxide emissions and hundreds of other air pollutants are entirely uncontrolled (Council on Environmental Quality, 1998, p. 282; UNEP, 1999a). The Environmental Protection Agency reports that a far larger percentage of rivers and estuaries now support 'designated

uses' (fishing or swimming) than in the early 1970s – between 55 per cent and two-thirds currently as opposed to about 25 per cent 25 years ago. Bodies of water such as Lake Erie are no longer 'dead' (Council on Environmental Quality, 1997, pp. 225–31; Easterbrook, 1995, pp. 628–9; Ehrlich and Ehrlich, 1996, pp. 51–3). Beyond such successes, however, a recent report by Public Employees for Environmental Responsibility (PEER) (1999) has questioned the validity of the data upon which EPA bases its claim that overall water quality is significantly improved. On the negative side of the ledger, water pollution from agricultural run-off is clearly worsening (Davies and Mazurek, 1997, p. 19; UNEP, 1999a). Similarly, despite legislation to protect wetlands, their net loss persists in the United States, and not even the most optimistic environmental activist imagines that wetlands' acreage can be restored to the 1970 level. While the rate of loss of wetlands has been cut significantly, net losses continue at more than 100 000 acres per year (Council on Environmental Quality, 1998, pp. 304, 306).

9. This issue is also related to revising the measurement of the GDP. Only a measure that takes into account a significant portion of pollution and resource use costs can effectively assess whether the growth taking place is real, and/or environmentally benign. See England and Harris (1997).

10. Commoner (1993, pp. 519–39), for one, has argued that the technology of production is the single most important factor in total pollution produced.

11. One can also question the likelihood of success of such an approach, given the severity of information problems in authoritarian government structures. See Dryzek (1987a).

12. For a review of literature on postmaterialism, see Deth and Scarborough (1995).

13. For discussion of the importance of building alternative norm systems at the local level, see Hoff (1998), Orr (1999) and Prugh et al. (1999).

14. In addition to providing a basis for norm development, local economic stability is important for the development of locality-specific knowledge – see DeWitt and Mlay (1999); Scott (1998); Sirianni and Friedland (1997, pp. 14–23). A negative corollary, pointed to by Schor (1998) is that a loss of community stability has increased the 'aspirational gap': Americans are becoming more likely to compare their levels of getting and consuming to public figures or their superiors at work rather than the more achievable levels of their neighbours.

15. A number of environmental writers and activist organizations now advocate measures to assure that, minimally, US environmental regulations are not side-stepped or overturned either by permitting goods made in environmentally harmful circumstances to enter the US market duty-free or by making US laws (especially at the state and local level) subject to challenge by other nations under free-trade agreements or multilateral agreements on investment rules. The most far-reaching proposals aim at a systematic, upward harmonization of baseline environmental laws and practices among trading partners (such as the United States and Mexico) over time. For a comprehensive treatment of trade issues by a leading ecological economist, see Daly and Cobb (1989); for critical discussions pertaining to globalization in general by an academic economist, see Rodrik (1998, 1999); and for a representative proposal from activist groups, see the Alliance for Responsible Trade (1997).

16. For a comprehensive listing of policies and their potential, see Alperovitz et al. (forthcoming).

17. The usual figure (30–33 per cent) does not include such government activities as utilities, universities, and other direct facilities, see US Census Bureau (1998, pp. 307, 451).

18. Even much of traditional manufacturing is shifting towards a service-manufacturing hybrid, which can also call for more localized economic activity. See Panchak (1998, pp. 96–105).

19. 'Worker-owned firm' here means companies that distribute ownership broadly to all or most employees. The criterion is not that employees necessarily have majority ownership. For an analysis of variations among firms, see Howard (1999).

20. See the responses to Sabel et al. by Lowi and others in *Boston Review* 24:5 (October/November 1999).

21. Robert Frank suggests another reason that community stability is vital for reducing the drive to consume: material consumption as a means of indicating status is particularly important among strangers (Frank, 1985). Accordingly, greater instability in personal relations may increase the importance of status-oriented consumption.

22. Ed Wolff's preliminary data for 1997 is cited in Collins et al. (1999, p. 10).

23. For a rigorous and systematic new analysis of this problem, see Rodriguez (1998). See also Roemer (1998); Olson (1984); Thurow (1980). For a history of inequality in the United States, see Williamson and Lindert (1980).

24. A related approach is the recent proposal of Bruce Ackerman and Anne Alstott to grant every American an $80 000 'stake', to be paid in four annual increments starting at age 21 to all high school graduates. (The money could also be accessed at age 18 to help pay for college.) Ackerman and Alstott frame their proposal, which would be funded by a 2 per cent national wealth tax, as a way to ensure that every young American has the means to make substantive choices about their future. In the long term, they also believe that the 'stakeholder' proposal would generate more attachment of Americans to the community at large as each person growing up realizes they have a concrete stake in the society (Ackerman and Alstott, 1999). Others have presented similar schemes: Kuttner (1998, pp. 30–6) has proposed that newborn babies be given capital ($5000 to each infant, plus $1000 a year, so as to produce a stake of $50 000 by age 18 – more if held longer. Michael Sherraden has proposed 90 per cent matching allocations of capital assets for poor people who save. These Individual Development Accounts (IDAs) are currently being experimented with by many state governments and some NGOs, using foundation funding. Legislation has been proposed in the US Congress to spend $100 million funding IDAs (Canedy, 1998, pp. 4–7).

25. For a discussion of different mechanisms to make this efficient, see Putterman et al. (1998, pp. 861–902).

26. Very high marginal tax rates were, of course, common during much of the most successful post-war economic boom period in US history.

27. France is already moving towards completion in the year 2000 of a government-mandated shift to the 35-hour week, see *Société Générale France* (1999). Many German workers are already working 35 hours or less through voluntary agreements, see Lipietz (1995, p. 50). Workers in Norway work only 1400 hours a year, or the equivalent of 40 35-hour weeks, suggesting significant room for improvement given even current technology, see *New York Times* (1999, p. A15). A 32-hour week has recently been proposed in Canada, see Willis (1998, p. 4).

28. Greater free time also makes possible less consumption-oriented means of providing human satisfaction. More time-consuming patterns of travel, recreation and consumption are often inherently less resource-intensive (Sachs et al., 1997).

29. The emerging anti-sprawl movement is suggestive in other respects as well: (1) it reflects the importance of experiencing a problem in one's own locality and of citizen action; (2) it serves as another civic learning opportunity specifically related to the need to democratically delimit market behaviour; and (3) many of the more successful strategies involve community or regional control or ownership of land.

10. Equity, Economic Scale and the Role of Exchange in a Sustainable Economy[1]

Patricia E. (Ellie) Perkins

INTRODUCTION

Environmentalists who are critical of 'free trade' often point to the accelerating resource depletion, rampant pollution, reduced government power to regulate ever-growing corporations, and threats to democratic decision making which can be seen to result from increased international trade as facilitated by institutions like the World Trade Organization and the North American Free Trade Agreement (NAFTA).

The alternative that is sometimes put forth by environmentalists – calling for more local economic autonomy and self-sufficiency, reduced international trade and closer spatial links between production and consumption so that environmental impacts are clear and can be factored into democratic political-economic decision making – is attractive in many ways. It evokes a pre-industrial, human-scale, pre-fossil fuel type economy, adapted to a post-fossil fuel world, which also makes use of postmodern information exchanges, technological development and design to maximize human potential (Aberley, 1994; Douthwaite, 1996; Milani, 1999; Morrison, 1995; Schroyer, 1997). Such localized 'green' economies are nascent in some places, and the institutions and consumption patterns necessary to build such local economies are in fact emerging throughout the industrialized North (Hudson, 1996; Perkins, 1996a, 1999; Roberts and Brandum, 1995).

However, many observers are still very doubtful whether the juggernaut of globalization will be substantially affected by such 'green-fringe' activity, even when rising fuel costs make traded goods much more expensive than they are today. Technological optimism holds sway in many circles, and the politics of a democratic switch to a lower-consumption, reduced-variety economy are problematic.

Moreover, there are two major issues that need to be addressed in principle before the local-economy solution can be termed a progressive or utopian one. Both problematic issues relate to *equity*. In the first place, local production for local consumption is usually more expensive than exploitative and polluting production mediated by transnational corporations and international trade; higher prices hurt low-income people most; so is this approach not, in some senses, regressive? Whether it is the rising cost of fossil fuels, the cost of internalizing environmental externalities, or the cost of fair labour practices that pushes up the prices of traded goods and thus makes locally produced ones more competitive, the impact of these price increases on those who are most vulnerable economically must be a concern for anyone advocating local-economy sovereignty.

Most emergent local-economy institutions (such as Local Employment Trading Systems (LETS), organic food co-ops, community shared agriculture schemes, and energy-efficient housing retrofit programmes) are aimed at middle and upper-middle class people – those who own their homes, are able to travel farther and pay more for vegetables, and are in the market for massages and music lessons offered (along with other things) on the LETS. So is the 'green' local-economy alternative really an alternative for everyone?

Secondly, the implications of reduced trade for international and North-South equity are also very problematic. While trade has doubtless contributed to environmental depletion, political repression and human rights abuses in many places, especially in the South, it has also contributed to an absolute increase in living standards, health care, education and international mobility for many. More important, it is virtually the only existing mechanism with some potential to bring about increases in the equity of global income distribution (despite the fact that absolute income inequality has been increasing over the past 20 years, fuelled, some argue, by cut-throat trade patterns).

If we are unhappy with current North-South and other global inequities, a system for reducing these inequities and ensuring a more progressive dynamic in global interchanges must be posited. The local-economy alternative, viewed only from the perspective of the North, externalizes the pressing issue of global intra-generational inequity.

This study explores these theoretical and practical issues, considering the question of the environmental and ecological impacts of economic activity from the viewpoint of the scale at which this activity takes place and the exchanges across time and space which affect its sustainability. Following a consideration of the dynamics of economic change in the next section, the meaning of trade/exchange, economic scale and political/ecological/economic boundaries are discussed before returning in the final section to the two equity-related issues outlined above.

NEGATIVE FEEDBACK AND GLOBALIZATION

Much of the current literature on globalization stresses the snowballing impetus of trade patterns controlled by multinational corporations, who increasingly make global production decisions (which are also consumption and resource-depletion decisions) with very little input from the political process in any jurisdiction.[2] The steps along the 'positive-feedback loop' of globalization include advertising, increased consumer demand and waste, long-distance transport of goods, pollution, high profits, strategic political influence, reduced local institutional control, mechanization, reduced demand for labour and centralized private decision making. Each step tends to reinforce the effects of the others and create the conditions for an expansion of trade and of the global economy.[3]

However, there are also 'negative-feedback loops' at work in the global trading system – processes which, like a pituitary gland, work to limit the growth of trade and to counter its insalubrious effects on income distribution, resource depletion and local political systems. The economics of self-limiting systems is not well developed, but – flowing from work in ecology and biology – new theoretical approaches to understanding self-limiting economic systems are becoming more widely known.[4] The essence of the concept of a negative feedback is that one step in a process leads to a second step which has an opposite effect on the overall system. For example, in a plant or animal, increases in age and physical size eventually lead to hormonal changes that halt further growth in stature. The factors involved in natural negative feedback include biochemical changes, hormones and genetic coding, which spark changes in response to environmental signals such as light, solar and lunar cycles, nutrient availability and biochemical signals from within or outside the organism itself. Often these processes are subtle, complex and delicately balanced.

The primary negative feedback in a competitive market system is that of prices, whose rise induces a fall in the quantity demanded of the good in question, which causes more of it to be available, causing the price to fall again and so on. Insofar as the price of natural resources and energy is competitively set, price increases can induce technological change which reduces the demand for increasingly scarce resources, thus perhaps causing production processes to become more sustainable. Likewise, to the extent that negative 'externalities' such as pollution or labour exploitation can be internalized in competitive markets (through, for example, well-enforced government taxation or other policies), the effect will be to make production processes more sustainable than before. Since most global markets are not competitive and are growing progressively less so, the actual impact of these feedback mechanisms is probably minimal. They do, however, perhaps have resonance for anyone who has studied economics.

Consumer pressure represents another negative feedback process at work, even in non-competitive markets, which can be a strong motivator for progressive environmental and social movement by corporations. Especially in Europe, 'green' consumer pressure has brought about many progressive changes in production processes.[5]

There are two other negative feedback processes which facilitate the development and adoption of 'green' and socially positive technological change in the face of globalization.

1. The spread and democratization of scientific knowledge, via the Internet and other means, allows technological solutions to local problems to be developed by the people who need them, in response to their own resource constraints, social situations and awareness of global potentialities as well as inequities.[6] In other words, globalization leads to the international dissemination of ideas that can permit some people to remove themselves from the global market if it does not meet their needs. Smaller-scale and more appropriate technological development, and the use of 'green' technologies developed in one place by people in other places, can result.
2. Globalization of markets also makes consumer boycotts, 'whistle-blower' actions and international campaigns for corporate responsibility much more effective and powerful than they would be in segmented national markets. Environmental, health and human rights concerns arising in one place can receive international attention, and large firms may devote extra attention to product testing, worker safety and pollution control to ensure that they do not receive uncontrollable negative publicity.[7]

Both of these mechanisms, while given impetus by the momentum of globalization, have the effect of generating beneficial changes in both production processes and the social effects of production, from a sustainability viewpoint. They are effective primarily because they cause changes in international trade patterns, generally in the sense of reducing the kind of trade that is most harmful to sustainable economies.

As the global implications of fossil fuel and other resource depletion, climate change, biotechnology risks and toxic waste generation become clearer (and/or as crisis situations bring these dangers into focus for many people), there will be increasing pressure for the kind of technological change that will allow reduced material throughput with no loss in use-value of the goods produced. This redefinition of the meaning of productivity growth –

instead of more output per unit input of a factor, more *use* (for example, longer product life, or more consumer satisfaction) per unit of output produced and sold – leads organically to a second redefinition, of the meaning of consumer satisfaction itself. Instead of positing insatiability, and equating greater consumer satisfaction with higher consumption as measured in dollars spent, economists must continue to explore and theorize the non-material, and indeed the non-consumption, component of human satisfaction.[8]

Meaningful work is clearly a primary determinant of human satisfaction. Because most 'green' production processes require more labour and less capital in comparison with traditional production processes (since they use less energy and fewer machines, and take more effort to reduce wastes), they often have the side effect of creating more jobs, which is a crucial need in both North and South.[9] This is another negative feedback in the global system: for both ecological reasons and for social ones, the limit to mechanization of production processes is becoming apparent; a switch to greener and more labour-intensive production processes implies positive effects both environmentally and socially.

Fine, but what is the real potential of all of these feedback mechanisms to actually reduce the overall volume of world trade or to slow globalization? And would that be a good thing? Would it not harm those in both the South and the North who are already the worst off? The following section takes up these important questions.

GLOBALIZATION, TRADE AND EXCHANGE

The idea of sustainability encompasses a number of components. In the context of trade and its effects, three elements stand out:

1. Resource depletion and the environmental effects of producing, distributing and consuming traded goods and services instead of local goods and services.
2. Income distribution or the effects on different social groups of their participation or non-participation in a global trading system.
3. Political equilibrium or the impact of trade on the institutional infrastructure of the countries involved.

Much of the literature on 'Trade and Environment' focuses on the first of these elements, and concludes that the Ricardian efficiencies associated with trade lead to economic growth which makes possible environmental protection strategies such as pollution taxes and emissions control mechanisms, which would be too costly for autarchic economies. Natural resources are also used more efficiently via trade, it is argued: more economic benefit can be derived from a given level of resource throughput, with less pollution, when trade allows factors to be used efficiently. Because of technological change and substitution possibilities, resource depletion is not seen by some as an important issue.

Dissenters in this discussion argue that trade skews incentives towards the use of new natural resources and over-consumption rather than reuse of goods and materials, and that the beneficial environmental policy effects of trade-related economic growth are limited to a few kinds of pollution control in a few countries. Crucial global environmental questions, such as climate change and trade in toxic wastes, require urgent attention. Unlimited resource substitution is not possible, due among other things to the laws of thermodynamics; trade contributes dramatically to the depletion of fossil fuels, accounting by one estimate for about an eighth of all fossil fuel use (Ekins, 1995, p. 309). Thus, even considering only the 'environmental' effects of trade, opinions in the literature are mixed but tend towards the negative regarding trade's implications (Daly, 1993; Daly and Goodland, 1992; Jackson, 1993; Johnstone, 1995; Lang and Hines, 1993; Steininger, 1994).

When social and political effects are added to the question, this tendency is reinforced. Income inequality within countries seems to increase with globalization, which puts some people out of work in the North and puts increasing competitive pressure on other workers in the South. Income inequality is also increasing internationally, in part as a result of trade expansion, as the rich become better able to take advantage of global market opportunities (Krugman, 1995; Van der Stichele, 1997). According to United Nations statistics, the gap between the richest 10 per cent and the poorest 10 per cent of the world's population increased almost tenfold during the 1980s; between 1975 and 1990 the volume of world exports nearly doubled (French, 1993, p. 7; Gill, 1995, p. 77). Gender-based inequality also increases with trade in many instances (Cameron, 1994; Cohen, 1992; Elson, 1993; Gabriel and Macdonald, 1996; Ward, 1990).

For some commentators, however, the most insidious effects of increasing trade are those on political institutions and the policy-making system. 'Regulatory chill', reduced government revenues and provision of social and other services, lowered emphasis on enforcing environmental regulations, international competition for foreign direct investment, increased currency speculation and financial/monetary instability, and growing unanimity between corporate and government agendas, are some of the aspects of this process (Campbell, 1993; Low, 1997; Perkins, 1996b).

From a thermodynamic viewpoint (in which global entropy unavoidably increases over time and this can only be countered by the use of solar radiation), sustainable economic growth can be viewed as the amount of incoming sunlight and its capture through photosynthesis. Trade can thus allow ecological constraints on economic growth to be avoided *spatially*, just as leaving mountains of waste behind for future generations avoids ecological constraints *temporally*. But the potential for such avoidance of eco-logical constraints is absolutely limited also by thermodynamics, and 'ecological limits turn into social limits and finally into barriers to economic rationality' (Altvater, 1993, p. 230; see also Jackson, 1996; Rees and Wackernagel, 1994, p. 377). The distinction between trade that allows 'entropy-shifting', and trade that does not, therefore becomes important in assessing its sustainability.

Taking all the above considerations into account, we are left with the issue of how much trade is 'sustainable'. The stronger one's definition of 'sustainability', the less trade seems to be desirable (Perkins, 1997). Moreover, far more than environmental impacts must be considered if true long-term sustainability of the economic (and also the social and political) system is the goal. These trade-related effects include those at the local or community level as well as at the national and global levels (Huq, 1985; Norgaard, 1995, p. 82; Nozick, 1993).

In effect, the sort of trade which does no harm to a sustainable economy might be defined as follows. It is an exchange of goods or services across national or bioregional borders which involves and requires only renewable physical resources and energy supplies, does not exceed the natural generative and assimilative capacities of the ecosystems where it takes place, is engaged in freely and voluntarily by all (even indirect) participants, contributes to the potential, interest and diversity of people's lives without undermining their own productive abilities or independence and has no deleterious effects on social structures, political institutions, culture or democracy in the areas involved. This definition, by its very contrast with the reality of the current global trading system, points up the political challenges inherent in transforming the global political economy to allow for the possibility of sustainable local, or larger than local, economies.

In fact, for trade (or exchanges of goods among bioregions) to be 'sustainable', what is needed is *congruence among the ecological, political and economic scales* at which these exchanges are taking place. In other words, the environmental costs of production (be they resource depletion costs or pollution costs) of goods or services destined for use outside the bioregion must be acceptable to those within the bioregion, and these residents must have a way of debating, deciding and implementing their choices about production methods and exchange patterns.[10]

Where the political scale at which production decisions are made (for example, the nation-state) does not correspond to the ecological scale at which the impacts of production and waste disposal are felt (the bioregion, watershed, airshed, aquifer, migratory zone or other space), there is a disjuncture between the environmental impacts of economic activity and the society's ability to address them in a satisfactory democratic way. The spatial impacts of economic activity vary with each production process: a factory's emissions plume affects its airshed while its effluent is mainly felt downriver; agriculture affects entire watersheds and aquifers; a fish-processing plant may draw its 'raw material' from the high seas but cause local water-pollution problems. Transnational corporations in fact may exploit differences among jurisdictions' regulations, shifting production to least-cost areas while doing their best to avoid public interference in their internal decision processes.

Trade – exchanges among nations or bioregions – exacerbates these disjunctures by adding the complication of global money flows and economic impacts to the already-complex picture.

In the face of the incredible welter of spatial and institutional scales which exists, environmentalists' advocacy of localized economies can be seen as an attempt to bring the political, economic and ecological scales of economic activity together at the local (and therefore perhaps more manageable) level. A global ecological democracy could also unify the scales of production, consumption and waste disposal, and since many of the environmental impacts of production processes are clearly global in impact anyway, perhaps this is the only reasonable goal. But effective, well-functioning democratic institutions on a world scale seem a long way off.

Whether the feedbacks listed above are actually causing reductions in trade overall is a matter for empirical investigation, which as far as I know has not been done. More important than these mechanisms' general effects on trade volumes, however, are their implications for the *kinds* of goods traded. As previously noted, trade which is more sustainable than at present will involve 'greener' goods, produced using 'greener' production methods by workers who live 'greener' lives. The effect of all the mechanisms listed above is to shift overall production and trade in a more sustainable direction.

This shift will be driven by a combination of price changes, financial and ecological crises, social and environmental policy innovation, consumer demand, local economic development and 'delinking', technological and organizational change and political pressure. Whether it will be fast enough and effective enough to forestall global social and ecological disaster remains to be seen. But the key to understanding this process lies in deconstructing the category 'trade' into its component parts, from the standpoint of its sustainability implications. This involves much more than just the traded goods themselves; the whole nexus of social, ecological and political conditions surrounding their production is also important.

For workers and consumers in the South as well as the North, this shift is a positive thing. As noted by Leff (1996, p. 82; see also Leff, 1995) with regard to Mexico:

> emergent environmental movements are internalising the environmental conditions for sustainable production, based on the productivity of nature and the values of social equity and cultural diversity. As these movements deploy their power strategies to construct an alternative productive rationality, resources will be removed from the sphere of market economy, imposing a limit to the capitalisation of nature.

While a generalized 'delinking' from global markets is not frequently espoused from a Southern perspective, due perhaps to the need for economic growth as an engine of international income redistribution, a few Southern theorists have extensively explored and advocated development strategies focusing on national self-reliance in the South. They include Clive Thomas, Samir Amin, Raul Prebisch and Osvaldo Sunkel (Hudson, 1997, pp. 103–26; Khor, 1993).

Whether in the North or the South, it is local-level (not national) policy initiatives, and community-based or non-market actions, which are central to many of the feedback mechanisms discussed above. Usually these measures are undertaken by people who are well aware of the specifics of trade's impact on their communities, and the reasons for these impacts. In the Toronto area, for example, the FTA- and NAFTA-related job losses caused by factory closings in the early 1990s led to an upsurge of interest in the Toronto LETS, which allowed people with reduced money incomes to continue to be economically active while building the institutions of a less-trade-dependent 'local economy'.[11] What this indicates is that the specific information needed to analyse trade's effects *is* available at the local level, for those who look. There is growing theoretical support for such disaggregated, specific and contextual study of economic processes.[12]

CONCLUSION: EXCHANGE, SCALE AND EQUITY

In a steady-state economy based on renewable inputs, the dynamism and change that are necessary to avoid stagnation and perpetuated inequities must come from exchanges and innovation. Development, viewed as the ongoing process of obtaining economic value in new ways from a limited and sustainable amount of throughput, depends on the spread and exchange of ideas, innovations and their benefits. It is possible to envision a positive feedback cycle in which social diversity leads to ongoing innovation, pockets of difference within a context of exchange, respect, communication and inquiry, discovery of new ways of using renewable resources and human potential and increasingly equitable distribution of the shared benefits of economic and social development. Trade (viewed as 'sustainable exchange', among production regions where decisions are made democratically and the ecological impacts of production, consumption and waste are internalized) is vital for the dynamism that is necessary to sustain human development.

Both the green local-economy movement and the movement for global equity are aspects of an inevitable readjustment of world institutions and production systems in the face of ecological realities. The undemocratic privatization of production decisions that have global social and environmental implications, in the hands of a few corporate managers, is what is unsustainable.

NOTES

1. Acknowledgement: This study has benefited from a number of insightful and helpful comments offered by Hilkka Pietilä and by participants in the 'Nature, Production, Power' workshop. An earlier version of this study entitled 'Trade, Transition Paths and Sustainable Economies' appeared in the *Canadian Journal of Development Studies*, XX (3) (1999), 594–608.
2. Global capital flows, which dwarf goods trade in monetary terms, have related but distinct effects and implications deserving of a separate analysis, which is not undertaken in this study.
3. For an elaboration of the positive feedback cycle by which 'the past and present degradation of nature impedes economic development in the future' (Altvater, 1993, p. 183; see also Arthur, 1990, pp. 92–9).
4. For a discussion of negative feedbacks and their economic implications, see Peet (1992, pp. 75–6). See also Allen (1994, pp. 1–17); Krugman (1996, pp. 2–5); Leydesdorff and Van Den Besselaar (1994, p. 16); Magnusson and Ottosson (1997, pp. 44–50).
5. Examples include the high demand for recycled paper and vegetable-dyed textiles in Europe, as well as the package recycling systems supported by taxpayers and consumers there.
6. For example, in The Netherlands, community groups' science research needs are addressed through a network of 'Science Shops' run by volunteer university researchers; in Peru, PRATEC (the Andean Project for Peasant Technologies) develops indigenous blends of cultural and technical solutions to local agricultural problems resulting from the Green Revolution. See Appfel-Marglin and Addelson (1997); Sclove (1997).
7. Examples include the Nestlé boycott related to infant formula marketing practices in the South, the Nike boycott protesting exploitative labour practices in Asia, negative publicity for Dow following the Bhopal incident, protests in Europe against Canadian forestry practices and the seal hunt and boycotts on the use of tropical hardwoods. Consumer products corporations, which are vulnerable to such boycotts, have responded by disguising their production chains, keeping information on the location and operation of production facilities secret, and 'downstreaming' control over production by dealing with franchised or licensed suppliers instead of fully owned subsidiaries. The organizing and sleuthing techniques of non-governmental organizations and environmental and human rights activists also continue to evolve.

8. Examples of this new kind of theorizing include Altvater's (1993, p. 228) redefinition of use-value as 'lower entropy with higher order'; Norgaard's (1995) inclusion of cultural values, diversity and sufficiency as elements of consumer satisfaction; and Gandhian economists' 'doctrine of non-possession' (Diwan and Lutz, 1985, pp. 76–85).

9. The kinds of work created, whether it is paid or unpaid work, and who does it, are all important distributional issues that arise in this connection. See Macgregor (1996).

10. The anthropocentrism of this discussion is apparent and glaring, given the use of the term 'bioregion'. In a sense, the concept of economics itself is inherently anthropocentric. Hopefully the day will come when 'economics' is understood to encompass non-human species (and women) as well as *homo economicus*.

11. The reverse can also happen: when the global economy is thriving, it sometimes absorbs workers and resources from formerly localized economic activity. The imperatives of globalization, however, mean that workers and resources *somewhere* will always be bypassed in favour of cheaper alternatives elsewhere; globalized production processes cannot exist without an 'away' to throw their wastes into and draw their resources from. The impetus for a more sustainable political economic system lies in moving beyond the segmentation that makes it possible to externalize costs and hide exploitative economic behaviour.

12. See the work of Paul Krugman (1995, 1996), Richard Norgaard (1995) and Amartya Sen (1990); also O'Hara (1997, pp. 141–54); Funtowicz and Ravetz (1994, pp. 197–207).

11. Regulating Accumulation, Guarding the Web: A Role for (Global) Civil Society?

Fred P. Gale

INTRODUCTION

In this chapter, I develop a framework to justify the increasingly necessary involvement of civil society actors in global politics. I place the concept of a 'socionatural web' at the centre of my framework to capture the emerging global space of mutually constructed natural and social production, transportation, display and consumption relations. I argue that the present hegemonic regime of accumulation that dominates the web (based on the private factory, the free market and a proprietary system of technological development and diffusion) is incapable of ushering in an era of genuine sustainable development. This is because its two central institutions – the state and the corporation – benefit too greatly from unsustainable growth. It is this growing realization of the incapacity of representatives of states and markets to curb the regime's expansionist logic that has motivated civil society actors to intervene at every level (local, national, regional, global) and in many sectors (forests, fisheries, agriculture, and so forth). As an example of the kind of civil society involvement required, I outline the structure and operation of the Forest Stewardship Council (FSC) and its role in promoting sustainable production and consumption of global forest products. I argue that if globalization is to be sustainable, the institutional innovations of the FSC must be extended to other production/consumption sectors.

THE SOCIONATURAL WEB

My starting points in developing an ecological political economy are the ecological and social processes that compose the multidimensional spatial and temporal web of socionatural relations. Conversion of matter/energy is the central feature of this socionatural web, such conversion being a consequence of four basic activities: production, transportation, display and consumption. In the production process, matter is transformed and energy is released. Plant and non-human animal production (which I term here 'ecological production') have been dominant throughout the ages. Plants, via the process of photosynthesis, transform sunlight, air, water and soil nutrients into fibre. In this way, food is provided for other animals, carbon dioxide is fixed and oxygen released; and these processes enter into the creation and maintenance of the conditions for the further development of oxygen-dependent life forms (Capra, 1996; Chiras, 1988; Lovelock, 1988).

Production by humans (which I term here 'social production') is a more recent phenomenon from the perspective of geological time. It involves both direct appropriation by humans of the fruits of ecological production (as in the harvesting of wild mushrooms, for example) and indirect appropriation (as in the use of technology to produce flour from wheat). Until recently, the ratio of total social to ecological production was insignificant, because small human populations met their subsistence needs using unsophisticated technologies. In the last 300 years, human population and technological capacity has grown enormously and large-scale manufacturing plants appropriate directly and indirectly huge quantities of oil, ore, timber, fish and other material to meet a growing list of social needs/wants.

In contrast to production, in the consumption process living things absorb external inputs to maintain their self-organization. From the perspective of biological history, plants and non-human animals constituted the vast majority of consumers, the scale of ecological consumption being constrained by biogeochemical feedback loops related to ecosystem carrying capacity (Chiras, 1988). The agricultural revolution that occurred about 10 000 years ago loosened this hitherto stable relationship between biology and consumption. Technological developments in the last three centuries have severed the link completely. A single species, *Homo sapiens*, formerly only one among many, is now a partner with the rest of nature in consumption appropriating, according to one estimate, more than 40 per cent of net primary production (Hawken, 1993, p. 22).

Transportation is the movement of matter from one place to another within the socionatural web. Historically, most transportation has been both ecologically determined and undirected. Winds transported seeds; waters carried animals to distant shores; and birds and animals spread plant seeds on their fur and in their faeces. While humans also played a role in the transportation process throughout history, their role was modest until recently. Although long-distance trade was a feature of Athenian Greece (Andrews, 1967), the scale of transportation that took place then was insignificant compared to that occurring ecologically. Today, things are very different. Companies take exclusive responsibility for the movement of goods via networks of roads, railways, seaways and airways. The coordination of such transportation is increasingly facilitated by the new communications technology – telephone, fax and e-mail.

Finally, the process of display involves making available and communicating to others the existence of goods and services. Display is a social innovation that emerged with the development of agriculture and the establishment of settled communities. Displayers are a necessary result of the division of labour when producers began to transmute matter/energy not for their own consumption but for the consumption of others. Only humans have been capable of systems of production beyond subsistence and of a division of labour beyond the tribe. Thus displayers are essentially a human phenomenon. Display has existed at least since classical Greek times, in the form of traders and shopkeepers (Andrews, 1967, pp. 130–60). In the modern world the activity is carried out chiefly by owners and managers of retail outlets, newspapers and advertising and marketing companies. Anywhere, in short, where goods from producers and transporters are marketed, made available or sold to consumers.

A SENSE OF PROPORTION

For most of world history *ecological* conversion has dominated. *Social* conversion has, until recently, been of minor importance. The human population was small, technology, simple and demands, basic. In hunter-gatherer societies, for example, human production, transportation and consumption activities (displaying had not yet emerged) were carried out within the tribe. Although in many cases tasks were assigned on the basis of gender and/or age, the division of labour prevailing within the tribal unit lacked breadth and depth. By and large the same individuals that caught, gutted and transported fish were those that cooked and consumed them. In prehistoric times, ecological conversion dominated the socionatural web and social conversion was checked. Droughts, floods, disease and plagues combined with simple technologies kept population growth rates and overall population levels low.

The development of agriculture, the domestication of animals, the establishment of settled communities and the improvement of transportation technology altered the fabric of tribal life, creating the basis for more sophisticated societies with wider and deeper divisions of labour. While most people worked in the fields, producing, transporting and consuming the produce locally, settled agriculture permitted the generation of an economic (agricultural) surplus that was used in part to encourage specialization.

In addition to gender and age, new divisions of labour emerged based on caste, rank, property and skill. The social structure of settled societies could vary widely, although many were based on slavery. In classical Greece, for example, slaves undertook a great deal of the production and transportation work, while a disproportionate amount of consumption was reserved for the élite citizens of Athens and other city states (Andrews, 1967).

The extent of social conversion taking place within the socionatural web in classical Greek times was certainly greater than that which had occurred in prehistoric tribal communities. Long-distance trade developed, specialists in the transportation of goods emerged; and displayers began to grow in number and sophistication. Social conversion in classical Greece was certainly capable of generating local and regional ecosystem damage. Significant deforestation occurred in the region around Athens and Sparta, for example, as the population expanded and human demand for housing, fuel, shipbuilding, public construction and security increased (Perlin, 1991, 93–4). However, regionally and globally, if not locally, the ratio of ecological conversion continued to exceed social conversion by several orders of magnitude.

Despite some significant developments from classical times to the fifteenth century, the proportion of ecological to social conversion remained relatively constant. The intervening period certainly saw population growth, technological innovation and the establishment of a larger number of settled communities. However, the rate of growth in social conversion was slow and punctuated by significant reversals, such as the arrival of the bubonic plague in the fourteenth century. It is only in the past three hundred years or so, therefore, with the advent of the factory system, the growth of the market and the systematic application of the science and technology to production, that there has been a significant decline in the ratio of ecological to social conversion.

The factory system was built on the twin principles of specialization and the division of labour. It necessitated, in its turn, a social institution to distribute the vastly increased number of goods produced. For many, the appropriate institution was the market, which required widening and deepening to ensure that there was sufficient demand for the increased volume of goods and services (Smith, 1776). And the growth of the market in turn promoted the emergence of more and more specialized units, including those that could transport goods from one location to another. Such developments were accompanied by a huge growth in storage, marketing, advertising and retail activities designed not only to make the produce available, but also to stimulate consumption.

At the outset, these developments were centred in Europe. The development of the sciences, stimulated by the thirst for profit, led to the exploitation of coal and oil reserves, vastly increasing the scope and scale of production and transportation activities. Botany and genetics led to the development of strains of seeds that produced more grain per bushel, which, coupled with the application of science to agricultural, led to increased grain production, raising average nutrition levels and decreasing infant mortality rates. Medical research improved understanding of the functioning of the body and surgical interventions began to save significant numbers of lives and to prolong life expectancies.

Such knowledge interacted with developments in chemistry, generating a pharmaceutical industry that also reduced mortality. In short, the competitive structure of the factory system required and depended on the market to valorize past investments. It necessitated also the continuous application of science via technological innovation to maintain individual factory competitiveness. The consequence has seen a reweaving of the socionatural web over the past 300 years, as humans emerged from a subordinate position to become a partner with the rest of nature in the totality of all matter/energy conversion activities.

SOCIONATURAL CONVERSION AND THE LOGIC OF THE PRIVATE FACTORY/FREE MARKET/PROPRIETARY TECHNOLOGY REGIME

The environmental movement is united in its view that the recent expansion of social conversion threatens the integrity of the socionatural web. There is, however, no agreement within the movement on what elements of this expansion are most salient. Some focus largely on technological solutions (Hawken, 1993; Lovins et al., 1999), others on a critique of capitalism (O'Connor, 1988) and others again on the desirability of self-sufficiency (Sale, 1985). These different perspectives articulate very different ideas about what needs to be done to make the social matter/energy conversion 'sustainable', resulting in three radically different conversion regimes for sustainable development. These are (a) the tweaking of the private factory, free market, proprietary technology conversion regime; (b) the (re)-establishment of public factory, state, public technology conversion regime; or (c) the establishment of a craft production, community, appropriate technology conversion regime.[1]

This study focuses on the conversion regime dominated by a private factory, free market and proprietary technology logic. This is the dominant regime today, largely responsible for reconstructing the socionatural web in its own image. In only a very few locations (for example, Cuba, North Korea) and as a subordinate form of production elsewhere (for example, utility companies), do we now find conversion regimes that operate according to the logic of the public factory, state ownership and public technology. And, despite some examples of production organized according to a craft/ community/appropriate technology logic (in community forest management, for example), pure forms of organizing matter/energy conversion according to this logic remain elusive (in Amish communities, perhaps?). Elsewhere, this conversion regime remains subordinate to the logic of the private factory, the free market and proprietary technology.

To better understand this private factory/free market/proprietary technology regime and its role in structuring and restructuring the socio-natural web, consider the set of natural and social relations that enable us to drink a cup of coffee when we choose. The set of non-human production, transportation and consumption activities that maintain the biosphere in dynamic stability (ensuring the continuation of the ozone layer, a tropical climate, adequate rainfall and sunshine, stable soils, biodiversity and so forth) constitute the preconditions of all social conversion activities. It is in this context that privately held companies (individually, family and shareholder owned) engage in the production, transportation and display of coffee. The larger companies involved in the conversion of coffee plants into coffee products harness sun, air, water and earth to transform seeds into seedlings into plants into beans and leaves. They do so often by establishing large-scale monocultures that require additional technological inputs (such as fast-growing, high-yielding, genetically altered seeds, chemical fertilizers, herbicides and pesticides).

Production occurs through specialization and the division of labour, with low-paid employees working in the fields tending and harvesting the plants and higher-paid employees in local, regional and head offices involved in managing these and other components of the production process. Such private factories incorporate into their own production system and/or outsource necessary transportation services. Transportation companies specialize in the movement of goods, in this case coffee, from one location to another. Once again, in the larger companies, the specialization and division of labour enables individuals to self-define themselves as truck drivers, stevedores, sailors and baggage handlers; and as junior, middle and senior managers. The former use their physical labour to move the coffee from one location to another, while the latter determine when, where, how and at what cost such movement shall occur.

This conversion regime depends on the successful displaying of the goods, ensuring their consumption. Large-scale retail outlets obtain the coffee from transporters and place it on shelves in supermarkets and specialty stores.

Advertising companies work with production, transportation and display companies, orchestrating campaigns to convince consumers that coffee is pleasurable to drink and that one brand is better than another. Consumers, under the combined influence of biology, advertising, culture and family/peer group, purchase and drink the coffee, obtaining 'utility' from its consumption.

The central element linking these private factory conversion activities together is the market. That is, it is through market relations that the network of companies evolves, stabilizes and transforms itself. Each company participating in this network seeks at a minimum to maintain its own internal coherence and position in the network. The means to achieve such internal coherence is to ensure that the commodities produced by the company are sold in the market at a price that covers all of the costs of production, including a return to the owners of the company. A failure to earn an adequate rate of profit results in takeover or bankruptcy.

While this private factory/free market/proprietary technology regime literally 'delivers the goods', its central tendencies are socio-economic crisis and ecological stress. Once the private factory system based on specialization and the division of labour is in place, the logic of the market asserts itself, and society become oriented towards the production of those goods and services for which there is an effective demand (Heilbroner, 1985; Smith, 1776).

Effective demand for products can be stimulated by paying higher wages, dividends, interest and rent to a pool of consumers and by increasing the number of consumers. It can also be stimulated through advertising, encouraging those who might otherwise save their money to purchase the goods displayed. The production process is stimulated, in turn, by the potential returns to be earned by providing goods that meet effective demand and by constant competition among production units in terms of price, quality and timeliness. Competition fuels the search for new market niches, brand-name recognition, cost-cutting technologies, union-busting, low wages and minimal levels of taxation. Although there is general recognition within this socially constituted matter/energy conversion regime that those participating in it require a return for their efforts, there are no mechanisms to equitably structure this return. Consequently, each company relies on its own resources, practices self-help and forces others to become equally innovative or risk takeover or bankruptcy.

In addition to the constant danger of a realization crisis (Lipietz, 1987), which threatens to plunge this private factory/free market/proprietary technology arrangement for matter/energy conversion into recession and depression, there is the inevitability of ecological degradation through indiscriminate expansion of throughput to meet growing effective demand, a second contradiction of capitalism (O'Connor, 1988). That is, there are few 'negative feedback' mechanisms within this matter/energy conversion regime to constrain resource overuse, block the hasty adoption and diffusion of not fully tested technologies, and dampen effective demand for matter/energy-intensive throughput.[2] What restraints exist have, historically, been implemented by the nation-state, with the nature of those restraints conditioned by domestic political institutions of authoritarianism, corporatism and democracy.

In addition to a generalized lack of feedback mechanisms, the private factory/free market/proprietary technology conversion regime undervalues the making of qualitative distinctions between different types of growth. It is evident that the result of stimulating effective demand *under current conditions of production* is increased throughput of resources. Yet it is conceivable that increased demand could be met without any increase and possibly with a decrease in resource throughput, if more attention were paid to the design of the matter/energy conversion process (Hawken, 1993; Lovins et al., 1999). Whether an increase in matter/energy throughput occurs depends on the nature of the social needs/wants and the manner in which they are satisfied. For example, people's understandable transportation require-ments, under a private factory/free market/proprietary technology regime, have been largely met through the private purchase of automobiles.

This resource-intensive solution to the social problem of transportation has placed a huge load on the socionatural web, requiring massive amounts of matter/energy throughput and resulting in significant problems in waste disposal and atmospheric pollution (Freund and Martin, 1993). While many currently advocate the development of integrated transportation solutions, especially to manage the daily movement of commuters in urban and suburban areas, the institution of such alternatives is external to the logic of this conversion regime. Even worse, the provision of such integrated transportation alternatives is not in the perceived interests of car companies and their workers, or those consumers who have come to define themselves as integral members of the car culture.

If such integrated transportation policies were introduced on a grand scale (assuming they could garner broad political support), they would result in significant ecological benefits to the socionatural web. Their social benefits, however, could be very negative, depending on how the transition was managed. The sudden introduction of such policies could lead to a significant shift in investment out of the automobile industry, leading to plant closures and corporate restructuring. Given the political-economic importance of the automobile sector in most economies, financial support would be needed to manage this restructuring process. Otherwise, one conceivable outcome could be a sudden, precipitous drop in general effective demand, inducing a recession.

GUARDIANS OF THE WEB

While the full ramifications of the dominant regime of matter/energy conversion for the socionatural web remain elusive even to the most persistent inquirer, it is nonetheless possible to gain a good understanding of its logic and central tendencies through critical study and analysis. Unfortunately, such critical inquiry is discouraged by those holding power and with a vested interest in the regime's maintenance. Consequently, most people have a rudimentary and distorted understanding of its logic and dynamics. This rudimentary understanding is reinforced by the tendency of practical people to take an interest in those matters that most directly affect their livelihood.

Workers struggle to obtain secure jobs, decent pay, reasonable time off, good overtime allowances and safe and healthy working conditions. Factory owners struggle to maintain a good rate of profit, flexible hiring practices, low levels of taxation and attractive investment incentives. Politicians are preoccupied with fire-fighting the issue of the day within an electoral system that privileges short-term compromise over long-term ecosystem health.

The parochial view fostered by the factory/free market/proprietary technology conversion regime would matter not at all, if there were strong natural and social negative feedback mechanisms in place to reduce the current imbalance between non-human and human matter/energy conversion. This is not the case, however (see Perkins, Chapter 10). In fact, the central tendency of the complex is to create positive feedback mechanisms, as when improved nutrition, health care and education lead to improved health, reduced infant mortality rates, longer life expectancies and an increase in population. Such positive feedback is also evident in the regime's constant stimulation of effective demand, which promotes continuous matter/energy throughput without any qualitative distinction made between the resource intensity of inputs and outputs. It is also evident in the rush to introduce technological innovations into the production process without adequately examining their impact on natural ecological cycles.

The inability of those in the work-a-day world to perceive the deficiencies of organizing social production, transportation, display and consumption according to a private factory/free market/proprietary technology logic would matter less too if other powerful social forces could intervene successfully to ensure the socionatural web's dynamic stability. As yet, however, the socionatural web has few guardians. Historically, people have looked to the state as the institutional vehicle to safeguard their wider interests. In modern liberal and pluralist political theory, the state is viewed most often as capable of transcending and/or arbitrating particularistic interests for the benefit of the general good.

Confronted with conflicts in civil society that pit social forces against each other – industry against workers against environmentalists against indigenous peoples – the modern state continues to play, and be expected to play, this mediating role. The key assumption that underpins this expectation, the potential autonomy of the modern state, is untenable, however. As the neo-Marxist debate on the state in the 1970s and 1980s demonstrated, the state achieves at most only a relative autonomy from powerful societal forces, remaining structurally dependent on capital in a globalizing political economy (Mahon, 1991; Miliband, 1969; Poulantzas, 1976).

Environmentalists have largely adopted liberal and pluralist conceptions of the state, viewing it as the rightful guardian of national ecosystems. In the 1960s and 1970s, therefore, they put pressure on their respective democratic states to introduce legislation to ameliorate the impact of the private factory/free market/proprietary technology conversion regime on the socionatural web. Such pressure ushered in the era of legislative environmentalism that led to a reduction in point-source pollution from identified industrial plants, an increase in the number of parks and protected areas, improved protection in some jurisdictions for endangered species, and better screening through environmental impact analysis of large-scale industrial projects. Despite such successes, however, the socionatural web continues to show signs of being stressed beyond its adaptive capacity, and the era of national environmental legislation must be declared a failure.

The failure of the legislative approach to safeguarding the environment is also the failure of the modern state to function as an effective guardian of the socionatural web. The explanation for the state's defeat lies in its contradictory position, requiring it to 'balance' the web's socio-economic and econatural demands. This, the modern state is singularly ill-equipped to do, given its past and present role in fostering matter/energy conversion, whether according to the private factory/free market/proprietary technology regime or the public factory/state/public technology regime of the former Soviet Union.

The state has been the institutional mechanism that constituted the national space over which it reigns as a sovereign power linking together a population large enough to support a division of labour deep enough to create significant economies and efficiencies in the production of goods and services. The legitimacy of the modern state has been founded on its role in expanding and deepening the process of matter/energy conversion through the construction of roads, railways and canals; the creation of navigable shipping lanes; the expansion of power facilities (including nuclear power); and more recently the development of the telecommunications infrastructure.

In addition to its role in facilitating the process of socio-economic development, the state has at certain times responded to pressure from below from workers. As a consequence of this social pressure, minimum wage laws were instituted; workers' rights to organize, protected; welfare and social security payments, established; and public health care systems, inaugurated. The state contributed risk capital to launch new ventures when private capital was not forthcoming and rescued private business from bankruptcy when the negative socio-economic and political consequences threatened the accumulative logic underlying the private factory, free market and proprietary technology regime. The state engages in these activities not only because its representatives are under the sway of the regime's dominant logic, but also because it receives its own share of the economic surplus generated in the form of tax revenues.

Another reason for the poor performance of the modern state as a guardian of the socionatural web relates to the structures of modern representative democracy (Johnston, 1996). In representative democratic societies, there is a contest for control over the state between representatives from two or more political parties. Politicians running for office must develop popular political platforms that appeal to the needs/wants of their electorate. People in most societies are preoccupied with their standard of living, which they equate not unreasonably with the health of the private factory, the existence of a free market and the use of proprietary technology. Consequently, policies are demanded and supplied that foster the regime's expansion. Both the electorate and politicians have an interest in discounting the future. The likelihood of ecological disasters many years hence and many miles away weighs less heavily than does the immediate socio-economic dislocation that attend the policies required to avoid those disasters.

Finally, because the modern state is a spatial institution, its capacity to safeguard the socionatural web is compromised by the expansion of this matter/energy conversion regime beyond its borders. The processes of political, economic, social and cultural globalization are having profound societal and ecosystem consequences. States are responding to this seismic change in interstate relations by signing wide-ranging international trade and investment treaties to ensure access to foreign markets and to make their own states attractive to foreign investment (Hart, 1995). While strong agreements are forthcoming in trade and investment, notably weaker agreements are negotiated on environmental and social concerns.

In short, the fragmentation of authority at the global level legitimated by the principle of sovereignty; the existence of deep inequities within and between states in terms of citizens' living standards; the constraints on politicians, who are structurally bound by the electoral cycle and constituency interests; a generalized popular incapacity to perceive the mutual and complex socio-economic and econatural interdependencies of the socionatural web; and an overall structural dependence on tax revenues, all constitute insurmountable barriers to the state's capacity to take a leading role in modifying the regime's logic in the interests of ecological sustainability. Something must be done, but the institutional capacity to do it is lacking.

INSTITUTIONAL INNOVATIONS

The modern state must be situated within a broader context, which, as we have seen, is dominated by the logic of the private factory, the free market and proprietary control over technology. With most states now societally and structurally predisposed to favour this logic of accumulation within and outside their borders, there is constant interstate rivalry over each state's share of the total global product. Such interstate rivalry makes international cooperation both desirable and difficult, even in issue areas such as trade, investment and money that are of vital importance to the maintenance and expansion of this matter/energy conversion regime. Interstate rivalry has its counterpart at the corporate level in inter-firm competition, and both drive the process of accumulation and consumption forward, winding up ecosystems to provide more resources over the short term to satisfy societal needs/wants and generating increased pollution, waste, loss of biodiversity and generalized ecosystem stress.

This is the context in which the environmental movement emerged within civil society in the latter part of the twentieth century. Initially rather narrowly focused on 'purely' environmental questions such as nuclear power, toxic waste and species extinction, the movement's understanding of the dynamics of the conversion regime's logic has grown in sophistication in the past three decades. In its conceptual struggle to have the environment taken seriously, the movement has generated the sub-disciplines of environmental and ecological economics.

Environmental economists build their conceptual apparatus within the discipline of neoclassical economics, and accept the private factory, the free market and the proprietary technology complex as the context in which policy must be conceived. Their objective is to reform the regime's operation to ensure that prices reflect the full costs of production, transportation, display and consumption activities, including externalities. Hence, those working within this perspective focus on the need to eliminate perverse subsidies, restructure tax policy, cost the disbenefits of waste and pollution, and adopt environmental accounting and environmental management systems (Tietenberg, 1997).

While such proposals constitute important policies in any future ecological society, environmental economists, lacking a structural analysis of the state operating within a matter/energy conversion regime dominated by the logic of the private factory, the free market, and proprietary technology, are misled about the transformational capacity of both states and corporations. The policies they advocate are invariably watered down when consumers and producers mobilize to ensure that their convenience and profits are protected. Such policies are further weakened during interstate negotiations, as national state industry (and sometimes worker) corporatist coalitions struggle to ensure continued accumulation within their own domestic borders (see Dauvergne, forthcoming, for an example of this process in the forest sector).

Ecological economists adopt a more explicit understanding of the economy's dependence on the environment. Where environmental economics tends to reduce environmental problems to malfunctions of the price system, ecological economists see the need for a more fundamental restructuring of economics to cope with environmental questions. Hence, ecological economists have introduced key environmental concepts into their economic analysis such as entropy, ecosystem, carrying capacity and population. The policy recommendations of ecological economists go much further than those of environmental economics, and include more than getting the prices right.

Many ecological economists have favoured a large role for the state in instituting policies that usher in a steady-state economy, one which reduces society's ecological footprint to a sustainable level (Daly, 1973; Daly and Cobb, 1994; Wackernagel and Rees, 1996). Thus, implicit in many of the policies promoted by ecological economists is an autonomous view of the modern state, which takes issue with the relative autonomy critique, outlined above. This perspective on the state generally remains implicit in the ecological economics literature, and the discipline has defined itself in such a way as to avoid dealing with the messy question of social power (Gale, 1998c).

Environmental and ecological economists need to give more serious attention to the new institutional forms that are emerging from grass-roots experiments at every level (local, provincial, national, regional and global). These experiments in institution building are constituting themselves as new centres of social power, modestly challenging elements of the logic of the private factory/free market/proprietary technology regime in a variety of ways. Space does not permit a comprehensive discussion of all these new institutional forms, although many of them are outlined in other chapters in this book.[3]

In this section, therefore, I analyse one important example at the global level: the Forest Stewardship Council (FSC). In order to make this analysis as meaningful as possible, I will compare the FSC's approach to forest certification with that sponsored by the Standards Council of Canada (SCC)/Canadian Standards Association (CSA). The SCC is an arm of the Canadian state, charged with promoting the development of voluntary standards within Canada. The CSA is an industry-dominated organization that develops standards in many different product sectors. This comparison illustrates the relative weakness of state and industry responses to the forest crisis and the relative strength, in contrast, of a global civil society-led alternative.

THE FOREST STEWARDSHIP COUNCIL VERSUS THE SCC/SCA

The FSC is the outcome of dissatisfaction among environmental organizations participating at biannual meetings of the International Tropical Timber Organization (ITTO) (Gale, 1998a). The concept of ecocertification and labelling, already well established in the field of organic agriculture, was transplanted to forest products by Koy Thompson of Friends of the Earth UK (FoE) in the mid-1980s. FoE and the Oxford Forestry Institute lobbied the British Government to put forward a proposal at the ITTO to study the feasibility of ecocertification and labelling. The proposal, considered at a 1989 ITTO Council meeting, was greeted with hostility and ridicule and proved completely unacceptable to many First- and Third-World delegations, to the forestry profession and to the tropical timber export and import industry. Under heavy pressure not to proceed, the British delegation caved in and modified its proposal so greatly that the subsequent consultants' study almost completely ignored the original topic of certification and labelling (Oxford Forestry Institute, 1991).

Environmental NGOs, however, continued to believe in the concept's merit and the World Wide Fund for Nature (WWF) began to work with progressive members of the forest industry and academia to create an ecocertification and labelling organization. The eventual result, the FSC, was officially formed in 1993 at a conference of parties in Toronto, Canada (Dudley et al., 1995, pp. 145–52).

In subsequent years, the FSC has grown in terms of membership, budget, organizational capacity and volume of forests certified and timber labelled. It is a unique institution across several dimensions. First, it is civil-society led, constituted by a General Assembly that is divided into three equal chambers representing environmental, social and economic interests (Dudley et al., 1995; Elliott, 1999). Although it has received funding from several states and regional bodies (including the European Union, the Netherlands and Austria), states are not members. Second, a North/South balance is achieved by electing members from developed and developing countries to each of the chambers (Hansen and Juslin, 1999, p. 12).

Third, the FSC builds on a much more elaborate, ecosystem understanding of nature and natural processes, embodying many of the elements of an ecosystem-based approach to forest management in its 10 forest principles (FSC, 1999). Fourth, FSC is a highly decentralized and devolved organization, embodying the principle of subsidiarity through its national level FSC working groups and network of independent, accredited certifying organizations (Upton and Bass, 1995). Fifth, the organization promotes a market-based, voluntary instrument (ecocertification and labelling), as opposed to either free markets or state protectionism. Finally, the organization's mandate is global, rather than national, regional or local, aiming to promote forest certification and labelling in all of the earth's major forest types.

There is a stark contrast between the FSC's history, structure and ethos and Canada's Sustainable Forest Management System (SFMS), promoted through the SCC (1998) and the CSA. The SCC is a Crown Corporation that reports to Parliament via the Ministry of Industry (SCC, 1998). Its mandate contains several objectives, two of which are key.

The first is to 'co-ordinate and oversee the efforts of the persons and organizations involved in the National Standards System'. The second, to 'develop standards related strategies and long-term objectives, in order to advance the national economy, support sustainable development, benefit the health, safety and welfare of workers and the public, assist and protect consumers, facilitate domestic and international trade and further international cooperation in relation to standardisation' (SCC, 1998). In order to achieve these and related objectives, the SCC works with four Canadian standards' development organizations including the CSA, which took the lead in the development of standards in the forest sector.

Elliott has set out the history and evolution of the SCC/CSA standard for a sustainable forestry management system (Elliott, 1999, pp. 296–321). In 1993, the Canadian Pulp and Paper Association (CPPA), concerned about the establishment of the FSC, announced its own certification initiative with the CSA. In early 1994, the CPPA formed the Canadian Sustainable Forestry Certification Coalition to promote a 'made in Canada' solution and contributed $1.5 million to the CSA to set up a Sustainable Forest Management Technical Committee (SFMTC).

The membership of the SFMTC, which met nine times between July 1994 and May 1996, was heavily biased in favour of government and industry participation, with token environmental and indigenous peoples representation (Elliott, 1999). In developing its sustainable forest management system standard, the SFMTC built on the International Organization for Standardization's (ISO) environmental management system's approach (ISO14000). This decision was at least partially strategic, the longer-term objective being to have the Canadian approach adopted by the ISO as *the* international management standard for forestry (Elliott, 1999, pp. 296–310).

The SCC/CSA's approach to standards' development contrasts starkly with that of the FSC. First, unlike the FSC, the evolution of the CSFMS standard was industry and state driven, with marginal participation from key civil society groups including the environmental movement. In addition, First Nations' interests were significantly under-represented and no attempt was made to involve non-Canadians. Third, the CSFMS was developed using an industrial conception of 'sustainable forest management' that necessitated no fundamental changes in Canadian forest practices, permitting continued clearcutting of old-growth timber. Fourth, the system focused on process not performance, with responsibility for initiating and implementing the management system in the hands of industry. The responsibility of the certifying agent is to ensure that the company properly implement/document the process by which it arrives at its management plan, including its public consultation process. Finally, the SCC/CSA viewed its approach first and foremost as an instrument of Canadian trade policy, despite the customary gratuitous reference to support for sustainable development. Its purpose is to preserve market access for Canadian products, especially in Europe where demands for certified wood products are increasing.[4]

These differences in organizational history, structure and ethos are crucial from the perspective of this study. It is only when institutional forms mirror those developed by the FSC (that is, civil society controlled, inclusive, equitable North-South participation, an ethos of ecosystem-based management, and devolution of responsibility down to appropriate regional and local levels) that there is the possibility of sound, environmentally sustainable policy. In contrast, when the institutional form mirrors that of the SCC/CSA (that is, control by industry and state, participation exclusively by country nationals, an ethos of industrial forest management, a focus on competitiveness and centralization of decision making), then policy and practices will reflect specific spatial and socio-economic interests.

When the state-based, nationalistic process inherent in the SCC/CSA approach to certification is transposed to the global level, we observe precisely the same level of dysfunction in the development of a global policy on certification and labelling. At international meetings of the ITTO, for example, no agreement could be reached on the desirability or feasibility of ecocertification and labelling, despite endless discussions stimulated by numerous reports between 1988 and 1994 (Elliott, 1999; Gale, 1998a). Several reasons can be adduced to explain why the ITTO was unable to deal successfully with ecocertification and labelling.

First, the organization was dominated by two coalitions representing the interests of developed and developing countries. The individual members of each coalition aimed to protect their own nationally defined economic interest, leading to weak intra-state, lowest common denominator, compromises especially within the European Union (Gale, 1998a). These internally weak intra-coalition agreements were then further watered down through a process of intercoalition negotiation.

In addition to its domination by state/industry interests, the ITTO was handicapped by its exclusive institutional focus on the tropical timber trade. While at the outset, it made some sense to limit the organization's mandate exclusively to tropical timber, growing awareness of poor management practices in temperate forests suggested the need for an organization with a larger mandate that could encompass all forests. A revamped International Timber Organization (ITO) could have been established during the 1992–94 round of renegotiations (the original mandate under the International Tropical Timber Agreement ended in 1994). Instead, and despite pressure from the developing country coalition, the original scope on tropical timber was retained. The inflexibility of the developed country coalition in the face of a rapidly changing globalized world timber industry rendered the ITTO marginal in subsequent global forest policy making.

Third, the organizational form of the ITTO permitted civil society actors only to voice but not to represent their interests (Gale, 1998a). Although the organization was strongly supported by environmental organizations through the 1980s, that support declined precipitously in the 1990s, as environmental interests were sacrificed to economic interests by both state coalitions. It was the ITTO's partisan, non-transparent, failed mission to Sarawak, Malaysia in 1989–90 that precipitated the final departure of environmental NGOs. The Sarawak Mission recommended a level of cut that was well beyond any that could reasonably be regarded as sustainable, and the Mission's report created an outcry at subsequent ITTO meetings when it was reviewed (Gale, 1996).

The above analysis of the FSC, SCC/CSA and ITTO enable us to capture the essence of the ecological political economic problematic. This is as follows. Within the socionatural web, ecological and social production, transportation (display) and consumption activities are intrinsically linked to and mutually construct each other. Historically, ecological conversion of matter/energy far exceeded social conversion, and the impact of the latter on the integrity of the socionatural web was insignificant. In the modern era, however, and as a consequence of a conversion regime based on the logic of the private factory, the free market and proprietary technology (a regime fostered by the state at the national level, but which has now escaped its control), society has become a partner with nature in matter/energy conversion. The expansive logic of this conversion regime has generated a set of powerful socio-economic forces located in the state and in the marketplace, whose overriding interests lie in the perpetuation of the regime's central elements.

A minimal solution, in this context, is the ecologizing of this matter/energy conversion regime by subjecting the processes within it to the discipline of ecoinformed democratic discourse. It is that precise ecologically informed democratization that is so evident in the history, structure, ethos and practice of the FSC and so absent in the SCC/CSA and ITTO. Unsurprisingly, also, it explains why the FSC constitutes such a threat to both states and corporations and why both have mobilized to defeat this unique civil society-led experiment.

CONCLUSION

It has been argued in this chapter that all production, human and non-human, takes place in a socionatural web, a unified space of social and ecological relations. Consequently, nature and society are seamlessly interwoven and mutually construct each other. The maintenance of the integrity of the socionatural web has been the product of the operation of ecological processes in the past four billion years (that is, since life began to evolve on the planet). It is now under increasing stress as a consequence of social production, which has expanded massively in the past 300 years. The reason for the massive increase in social production lay in the discovery of a new logic of matter/energy conversion, the private factory/free market/proprietary technology regime. While this conversion regime is remarkably productive and flexible, it lacks the necessary ecological and social feedback mechanisms that enable its expansion to occur within ecosystem limits. Its two major institutional innovations – the state and the market – are structurally incapable of slowing this growth and/or altering its quality.

There are today, consequently, no guardians of the socionatural web in its entirety. Most people (living under the pressure to make ends meet, keep the factory going, improve working and pay conditions, or ensure the development and implementation of policies that facilitate the former) take an anthropocentric, parochial view. Corporate CEOs struggle to reduce taxes, lobby for flexible labour practices, maintain/increase security of investment and create efficient markets for their products via free trade and deregulation. Workers struggle both at the workplace and through party politics to safeguard salary, job security, safety, health and employment rights. Politicians, ever concerned about maintaining their relevance and legitimacy, respond to social pressure, aiming to create jobs, attract investment, maintain monetary stability and preserve the state's economic and military security. Even environmentalists have a largely parochial focus, aiming to safeguard the ecology and often ignoring socio-economic considerations. It is this parochial mentality that alienates the movement from various publics, including potential allies in the indigenous peoples' movements. Policies are developed that do not take into account the loss of livelihoods, the destruction of capital and the imposition of hardship.

In the current historical epoch, a complete transformation of the private factory/free market/proprietary technology regime seems unlikely. The regime, as it stands, is the only one that is capable of the timely delivery of the number and variety of goods that meet human needs/wants. And the desirability of alternative regimes must always be considered within that context, that is, of their capacity to deliver the goods and services that are, even without advertising, in high demand. On the other hand, it is clear that the socionatural web is being unsustainably stressed to meet the demands being placed on it and that the customary guardians of human welfare, the state and the market, are unable to discipline the logic of this dominant matter/energy conversion regime. Consequently, it is up to civil society actors, at the local, regional and global levels, using all the resources and ingenuity at their disposal, to step in and provide the necessary regulation.

The institutional structures of the FSC constitute a practical example of how civil society can make a difference. Through the FSC, the system of ecocertification and labelling is restructuring one network that composes the socionatural web: the forest products industry network. The modest goal here is not to overthrow the conversion regime in its entirety but to regulate its operation to ensure ecological sustainability. This necessitates that private ownership come with definite responsibilities; that information be provided to consumers on a product's production and processing methods; and that technology be subjected to rigorous testing to minimize the risk of ecological damage.

This is a modest agenda. After all, the conversion regime being sought through this process remains capitalist, if by that one refers to a system in which ownership of the means of production rests mostly in private hands. On the other hand, it is a modified, constrained, more reflexive form of capitalism, one that recognizes its own inability to generate the regulatory conditions for sustainability. If that is the case, then institutions such as the FSC are not merely interesting social experiments, but crucial institutions that could, if permitted, provide the kind of socio-ecological feedback that is so lacking under the dominant logic of the private factory/free market/proprietary technology regime.

In this context, a key research question is whether the institutional innovation of the FSC is possible in other issue areas. Is it possible to envision, for example, a Mining Stewardship Council (MSC), a Fisheries Stewardship Council (FSC), a Coffee Stewardship Council (CSC) and an

Agricultural Stewardship Council (ASC)? What are the conditions of the possibility of establishing these councils? These are important research questions that need to be addressed in the coming years, since progress in each of these areas could ultimately become the means for a much deeper systemic transformation.

———————————

NOTES

1. There will be an understandable tendency to want to 'reduce' these complex conversion regimes to 'capitalism', 'socialism' and 'communitarianism' respectively. I do not adopt this terminology here, because each term is laden with meanings that I consider problematic. Despite the clumsiness of the terminology at times, therefore, I prefer to keep the separate components of the three regimes in mind.
2. Although the scarcity of natural resource inputs can be reflected in the price system, this does not secure those resources against ecological degradation. Increasing prices raise the incentive to those with access to the resources to exploit them. Furthermore, while rising prices can, under certain circumstances, lead to greater production efficiencies and substitution, the logic of the system's operation offers no guarantee that the new processes and/or materials used will be ecologically benign.
3. See, for example, M'Gonigle (Chapter 1) and Agrawal (Chapter 3) on the potential role of community; and Perkins (Chapter 10) on LETS. Alperovitz (Chapter 9) provides a comprehensive review of innovations in the United States.
4. In the past year, the SCC has become even more interested in the strategic trade implications of international standards. Thus, the SCC is currently engaged in developing a Canadian Standards Strategy, which is 'designed to harness the entire standards infrastructure to promoting economic progress and social well-being'. The Strategy will set out Canada's master plan on standards, identify the roles to be played by stakeholders and 'promises competitive advantage for the Canadian economy' (SCC, 1999, p. 2). Such a chauvinistic and parochial mandate undermines the capacity of the SCC/CSA to develop standards that safeguard the socionatural web's econatural dimension, should such action conflict with the demands of economic competitiveness.

Bibliography

Abel, T.D. (1999), 'Devolution revolutions: civic environmentalism and local policy effort', Paper delivered at the Annual Meeting of the American Political Science Association, Atlanta, Georgia (September), pp. 2–5.

Aberley, D. (ed.) (1994), *Futures by Design: The Practice of Ecological Planning*, Gabriola Island, BC, and Philadelphia, PA: New Society Publishers.

Abrams, E., A. Freter, D. Rue and J. Wingard (1996), 'The role of deforestation in the collapse of the late classic Copan Maya state', in L. Sponsel, T. Headland and R. Bailey (eds), *Tropical Deforestation: The Human Dimension*, New York, NY: Columbia University Press, pp. 55–75.

Ackerman, B. and A. Alstott (1999), *The Stakeholder Society*, New Haven, CT: Yale University Press.

Adkin, L.E. (1992), 'Counter-hegemony and environmental politics in Canada', in W.K. Carroll (ed.), *Organizing Dissent: Contemporary Social Movements in Theory and Practice*, Toronto, Ontario: Garamond Press, pp. 135–56.

Adkin, L.E. (1994), 'Environmental politics, political economy, and social democracy in Canada', *Studies in Political Economy*, **45** (fall), 130–69.

Adkin, L.E. (1998a), *The Politics of Sustainable Development: Citizens, Unions, and the Corporations*, Montreal, London, New York: Black Rose Books.

Adkin, L.E. (1998b), 'Ecological politics in Canada: elements of a strategy of collective action', in R. Keil, D. Bell, P. Penz and L. Fawcett (eds), *Political Ecology: Global and Local*, London and New York: Routledge, pp. 292–322.

Adkin, L.E. (1999), 'Natural Heritage Act: Orwellian travesty', *Edmonton Journal* (25 April).

Adkin, L.E. (2000), 'The rise and fall of new social movement theory?', in A. Bakkan and E. MacDonald (eds), *Critical Political Theory*, Kingston, Ontario: McGill-Queen's University Press (forthcoming).

Agarwal, A. and S. Narain (1991), 'Global warming in an unequal world: a case of environmental colonialism', *Earth Island Journal* (spring), 39–40.

Agarwal, B. (1994), *A Field of One's Own: Gender and Land Rights in South Asia*, Cambridge: Cambridge University Press.

Agarwal, B. (1998), 'The gender and environment debate', in R. Keil, D. Bell, P. Penz and L. Fawcett (eds), *Political Ecology: Global and Local*, London and New York: Routledge, pp. 193–219.

Agrawal, A. (1994), 'I don't need it but you can't have it: politics on the commons', *Pastoral Development Network*, **36a** (July) 36–55.

Agrawal, A. (1996), 'The Community vs the Market and the State', *Journal of Agricultural and Environmental Ethics*, **9** (1), 1–15.

Agrawal, A. (1999), *Greener Pastures: Politics, Markets, and Community among a Migrant People*, Durham, NC: Duke University Press.

Agrawal, A. and S. Goyal (2001), 'Group size and collective action: third party monitoring and common pool resources', *Comparative Political Studies* (forthcoming).

Agrawal, A. and G. Yadama (1997), 'How do local institutions mediate market and population pressures on resources? Forest Panchayats in Kumaon, India', *Development and Change*, **28** (3), 435–65.

Alaska Permanent Fund Corporation (APFC) (1991), *An Alaskan's Guide to the Permanent Fund*, 4th edn, Juneau, AK: Alaska Permanent Fund Corporation.

Alcorn, J. (1981), 'Huastec noncrop resource management: Implications for prehistoric rain forest management', *Human Ecology* **9**, 395–417.

Allen, P.M. (1994), 'Evolutionary complex systems: models of technology change', in L. Leydesdorff and P. Van Den Besselaar (eds), *Evolutionary Economics and Chaos Theory*, New York, NY: St. Martin's Press.

Alliance for Responsible Trade (1997), 'Alternatives for the Americas', Washington, DC: Institute for Policy Studies.

Alperovitz, G. (1994), 'Distributing our technological inheritance', *Technology Review*, **97** (7) (October), 31–6.

Alperovitz, G., T. Howard, A. Scharf and T. Williamson (1995), *Index of Environmental Trends*, Washington, DC: National Center for Economic and Security Alternatives.

Alperovitz, G., D. Imbroscio and T. Williamson (forthcoming), *Democracy, Community, and Economic Viability in the Global Era*.

Alston, L., T. Eggertsson and D. North (eds) (1996), *Empirical Studies in Institutional Change*, Cambridge: Cambridge University Press.

Althusser, L. (1979), *For Marx*, translated by Ben Brewster, London: Verso.

Althusser, L (1984), *Essays on Ideology*, London and New York: Verso.

Altvater, E. (1993), *The Future of the Market*, London and New York: Verso.

Altvater, E. (1998), 'The new global order and the environment: defining the issues', in R. Keil, D. Bell, P. Penz and L. Fawcett (eds), *Political Ecology: Global and Local*, London and New York: Routledge, pp. 19–45.

Anderson, A. and D. Posey (1989), 'Management of a tropical scrub savanna by the Gorotire Kayapo of Brazil. Advances in Economic Botany', **7**, 159–73.

Anderson, D. and R. Grove (eds) (1989), *Conservation in Africa: People, Policies and Practice*, Cambridge: Cambridge University Press.

Anderson, K. (1987), 'A gendered world: women, men and the political economy of the seventeenth-century Huron', in H.J. Maroney and M. Luxton (eds), *Feminism and Political Economy*, London: Methuen.

Anderson, R.S. and W. Huber (1988), *The Hour of the Fox: Tropical Forests, the World Bank, and Indigenous People in Central India*, Seattle, WA: University of Washington Press.

Andrews, A. (1967), *Greek Society*, London and New York: Penguin Books.

An Tir, An Canan 'Sna Daoine (1995), 'Massive swing of opinion against superquarry', *West Highland Free Press* (26 May).

Appfel-Marglin, F. and K.P. Addelson (1997), 'A mutual learning', in T. Schroyer (ed.), *A World That Works*, New York, NY: Bootstrap Press, pp. 291–306.

Archer, M., R. Bhaskar, A. Collier, T. Lawson and A. Norrie (eds) (1998), *Critical Realism: Essential Readings*, London and New York: Routledge.

Arnold, J. (1990), 'Social forestry and communal management in India', Social Forestry Network Paper 11b, London: Overseas Development Institute.

Arthur, B. (1990), 'Positive feedbacks in the economy', *Scientific American*, **262** (February).

Arthur, C.J. (ed.) (1996), *Engels Today: A Centenary Appreciation*, Basingstoke and London: Macmillan.

Ascher, W. (1995), *Communities and Sustainable Forestry in Developing Countries*, San Francisco, CA: ICS Press.

Ash, R.F. and R. Edmonds (1998), 'China's land resources, environment and agricultural production', *The China Quarterly*, **156** (December), 836–79.

Avery, B. (1999), 'Resource firms fear shift to courts on environment', *Edmonton Journal* (10 April).

Bailey, R. and T. Headland (1991), 'The tropical rain forest: is it a productive environment for human foragers?', *Human Ecology*, **19** (2), 261–85.

Baines, G. (1991), 'Asserting traditional rights: Community conservation in Solomon Islands', *Cultural Survival Quarterly*, **15** (2), 49–51.

Balee, W. (1992), 'People of the fallow: A historical ecology of foraging in lowland South America', in K. Redford and C. Padoch (eds), *Conservation of Neotropical Forests*, New York, NY: Columbia University Press, pp. 35–57.

Balee, W. (1994), *Footprints in the Forest: Ka'apor ethnobotany – the historical ecology of plant utilization by an Amazonian people*, New York, NY: Columbia University Press.

Banerjee, S. (1984), *India's Simmering Revolution: The Naxalite Uprising*, London: Zed Books.

Banuri, T. and F.A. Marglin (eds) (1993), *Who Will Save the Forests?* London: Zed Books.

Barber, E.W. (1994), *Women's Work: The First 20,000 Years*, New York, NY: Norton.

Barker, M.L. and D. Soyez (1994), 'Think locally act globally? The trans-nationalization of Canadian resource-use conflicts', *Environment* **36** (5) (June), 12–20 and 32–6.

Bates, R.H. (1989), *Beyond the Miracle of the Market*, Cambridge: Cambridge University Press.

Baviskar, A. (1995), *In the Belly of the River: Tribal Conflicts over Development in the Narmada Valley*, Delhi: Oxford University Press.

Bebbington, A. (1996), 'Movements, modernizations, and markets: indigenous organizations and agrarian strategies in Ecuador', in R. Peet and M. Watts (eds), *Liberation Ecologies: Environment, Development, Social Movements*, London: Routledge, pp. 86–109.

Beck, U. (1992), *Risk Society*, London: Sage.

Beck, U. (1995a), *Ecological Society in an Age of Risk*, Cambridge: Polity Press.

Beck, U. (1995b), *Ecological Enlightenment*, trans. Mark Ritter, Atlantic Highlands, NJ: Humanities Press.

Beck, U. (1998), *Democracy Without Enemies*, Cambridge: Polity Press.

Beder, S. (1993), *The Nature of Sustainable Development*, Newham: Scribe.

Behr, P. (1999), 'Maryland's hostile-takeover defense', *The Washington Post* (25 February), E1.

Bell, D. (1973), *The Coming of Post-Industrial Society: A Venture in Social Forecasting*, New York, NY: Basic Books.

Benko, G. and U. Strohmayer (eds) (1997), *Space and Social Theory: Interpreting Modernity and Postmodernity*, Oxford: Blackwell.

Benton, T. (1988), 'Humanism = Speciesism?', *Radical Philosophy*, **50**, 4–18.

Benton, T. (1989), 'Marxism and natural limits', *New Left Review*, **178**, 51–86.

Benton, T. (1991), 'Biology and social science', *Sociology*, **25**, 1–29.

Benton, T. (1992), 'Ecology, socialism and the mastery of nature: a reply to Reiner Grundmann', *New Left Review*, **194**, 55–74.

Benton, T. (1993), *Natural Relations: Ecology, Animal Rights and Social Justice*, London: Verso.

Benton, T. (ed.) (1996), *The Greening of Marxism*, New York and London: Guilford.

Bhatt, C.P. (1990), 'The Chipko Andolan: forest conservation based on people's power', *Environment and Urbanization*, **2**: 7–18.

Bhattacharya, J. (1995), 'Solidarity and agency: rethinking community development', *Human Organization*, **54**, 60–69.

Biodiversity Conservation Network (BCN) (1999), *Evaluating linkages between business, the environment and local communities*: Final Stories from the Field. Biodiversity Support Program: Washington, DC.

Blaikie, P. and H. Brookfield (1987), *Land Degradation and Society*, London: Methuen.

Blaikie, P., T. Cannon, I. Davis and B. Wisner (1994), *At Risk: Natural Hazards, People's Vulnerability, and Disasters*, London and New York: Routledge.

Blau, J. (1999), *Illusions of Prosperity*, New York, NY: Oxford University Press.

Bookchin, M. (1980), *Towards an Ecological Society*, Montreal, Quebec: Black Rose Books.

Bookchin, M. (1982), *Ecology of Freedom: The Emergence and Dissolution of Hierarchy*, Palo Alto, CA: Cheshire Books.

Borda, F. (ed.) (1985), *The Challenge of Social Change*, London: Sage.

Borghese, E. (1987), 'Third world development: The role of non-governmental organizations', *The OECD Observer*, **145**.

Boserup, E. (1970), *Women's Role in Economic Development*, New York, NY: St. Martin's Press.

Bourdieu, P. (1982), *Outline of a Theory of Practice*, Cambridge: Cambridge University Press.

Bowles, S. (1999), 'Globalization and redistribution: feasible egalitarianism in a competitive world', Paper for presentation at the World Congress of the International Economic Association in Buenos Aires (August).

Bramwell, A. (1989), *Ecology in the 20th Century*, New Haven, CT: Yale University Press.

Brandis, D. (1897), *Forestry in India: Origins and Early Developments*, New Delhi: Vedam Books.

Braudel, F. (1982), *The Structures of Everyday Life*, New York, NY: Harper and Row.

Breckenridge, L.P. (1992), 'Protection of biological and cultural diversity: Emerging recognition of local community rights in ecosystems under international environmental law', *Tennessee Law Review*, **59**: 735–85.

Bromley, D. and M. Cernea (1989), 'Management of common property natural resources: overview of Bank experience', in L.R. Meyers (ed.), *Innovation in Resource Management: Proceedings of the Ninth Agriculture Sector Symposium*, Washington, DC: The World Bank, pp. 29–45.

Brookfield, H. and C. Padoch (1994), 'Appreciating agrodiversity: A look at the dynamism and diversity of indigenous farming practices', *Environment*, **36** (5): 6–11, 37–45.

Brownrigg, L. (1985), 'Native cultures and protected areas: Management options', in J.A. McNeely and D. Pitt (eds), *Culture and Conservation: The Human Dimension in Environmental Planning*.

Bryant, R. (1992), 'Political ecology: an emerging research agenda in Third-World Studies', *Political Geography*, **11** (1), 12–36.

Bryant, R. and G. Parnwell (1996), *Environment and Development in Southeast Asia*, London: Routledge.

Burda, C., D. Curran, F. Gale and M. M'Gonigle (1997), *Forests in Trust: Reforming British Columbia's Forest Tenure System for Ecosystem and Community Health*, Report 97–1, Eco-Research Chair of Environmental Law and Policy, University of Victoria, Victoria, British Columbia, Canada.

Burkett, P. (1998), 'A critique of Malthusian Marxism', *Historical Materialism*, **2**, 118–42.

Business Council for Sustainable Development (1992), *Changing Course: A Global Business Perspective on Development and the Environment*, Cambridge, MA: MIT Press.

Buttel, F.H. and W. Sunderlin (1988), 'Integrating political economy and political ecology: an assessment of theories of agricultural and extractive industry development in Latin America', Paper presented at the 46th International Conference of Americanists, Amsterdam, 4–8 July.

Callenbach, E. (1978), *Ecotopia*, London: Pluto Press.

Callicott, J.B. (1994), *Earth's Insights: A Multicultural Survey of Ecological Ethics from the Mediterranean Basin to the Australian Outback*, Berkeley, CA: University of California Press.

Cameron, B. (1994), 'The impact of free trade on women's employment', York University, Ontario, Canada.

Campbell, B. (1993), 'Globalization, trade agreements, and sustainability', in Canadian Environmental Law Association, *The Environmental Implications of Trade Agreements*, Toronto, Ontario: Ministry of Environment and Energy.

Canedy, D. (1998), 'Down payments on a dream', *Ford Foundation Report*, **29** (1) (winter), 4–7.

Capra, F. (1996), *The Web of Life: A New Scientific Understanding of Living Systems*, New York and London: Anchor Books/Doubleday.

Carney, J. (1996), 'Converting the wetlands, engendering the environment: the intersection of gender with agrarian change in Gambia', in R. Peet and M. Watts (eds), *Liberation Ecologies: Environment, Development, Social Movements*, London: Routledge, pp. 165–87.

Carroll, W.K. (ed.) (1992), *Organizing Dissent: Contemporary Social Movements in Theory and Practice*, Toronto, Ontario: Garamond Press.

Carroll, W.K. (ed.) (1997), *Organizing Dissent: Contemporary Social Movements in Theory and Practice*, 2nd edn, Toronto, Ontario: Garamond Press.

Carroll, W.K. and R. S. Ratner (1996), 'Master framing and cross-movement networking in contemporary social movements', *The Sociological Quarterly*, **37** (4), 601–25.

Casanova, J. (1994), *Public Religions in the Modern World*, Chicago: Chicago University Press.

Catton, W.R. Jr. and R.E. Dunlap (1978), 'Environmental sociology: a new paradigm', *The American Sociologist*, **13**, 41–9.

Cavanaugh, W.T. (1995), '"A fire strong enough to consume the house": the Wars of Religion and the rise of the state', *Modern Theology*, **11** (4), 397–420.

CEPAL (UN Economic Commission for Latin America and the Caribbean) (1998a), 'Capital Flows to Latin America and the Caribbean 1997', *CEPAL News*, **18** (3).

CEPAL (UN Economic Commission for Latin America and the Caribbean) (1998b), *Foreign Investment in Latin America and the Caribbean*, Santiago, Chile: United Nations.

Chambers, R. (1979) 'Rural Development: Whose Knowledge Counts?' *IDS Bulletin*, **10** (2).

Chiras, D. (1988), *Environmental Science: A Framework for Decision Making*, Menlo Park, CA: The Benjamin/Commings Publishing Company.

Ciriacy-Wantrup, S.V. and R.C. Bishop (1975), 'Common property as a concept in natural resources policy', *Natural Resources Journal*, **15**, 713–27.

Clapp, J. (1994), 'Africa, NGOs, and the international toxic waste trade', *Journal of Environment and Development*, **3** (2) (summer), 17–46.

Clarke, S.E. and G.L. Gaile (1998), *The Work of Cities*, Minneapolis, MN: University of Minnesota Press.

Clay, J. (ed.) (1988), *Indigenous Peoples and Tropical Forests: Models of Land Use and Management from Latin America*, Report # 27, Cambridge, MA: Cultural Survival.

Clugston, R.M., and T.J. Rogers (1995), 'Sustainable livelihoods in North America', *Development* **3** (September), 60–3.

Cohen, M. (1992), 'The implications of economic restructuring for women: the Canadian situation', Paper presented at the Canada in Transition Conference, the Autonomous University of Mexico, Mexico City, Mexico (27 November).

Cohen, M.G. (1996), 'New international trade agreements: their reactionary role in creating markets and retarding social welfare', in Isabella Bakker (ed.), *Rethinking Restructuring: Gender and Change in Canada*, Toronto, Ontario: University of Toronto Press.

Colborn, T., D. Dumanoski and J.P. Myers (1996), *Our Stolen Future*, New York, NY: Dutton.

Collard, A. with J. Contrucci (1988), *The Rape of the Wild*, London: The Women's Press.

Collier, A. (1994), *Critical Realism*, London: Verso.

Collins, C., B. Leonard-Wright and H. Sklar (1999), *Shifting Fortunes: The Perils of the Growing American Wealth Gap*, Boston, MA: United for a Fair Economy.

Commoner, B. (1993), 'Population, development, and the environment: trends and key issues in the developed countries', *International Journal of Health Services*, **23** (3), 519–39.

Conca, K. (1998a), 'Imagine there's no countries: a postsovereign perspective on the global South's environmental impact', Working Paper, Harrison Program on the Future Global Agenda, University of Maryland, MD <www.bsos.umd.edu/harrison>.

Conca, K. (1998b), 'The environment-security trap', *Dissent*, **45** (3) (summer), 40–5.

Cook, C. (1996), 'The divided island of New Guinea: People, development and deforestation', in L.E. Sponsel, T.N. Headland and R.C. Bailey (eds), *Tropical Deforestation: The Human Dimension*, pp. 253–71. New York, NY: Columbia University Press.

Coontz, S. and P. Henderson (1986), *Women's Work, Men's Property*, London: Verso.

Corbett, T. (1995), 'The birth of legitimacy of ecology within the global political economy', unpublished Paper, Griffith University, Queensland, Australia.

Corbridge, S.E. and S. Jewitt (1997), 'From forest struggles to forest citizens? Joint Forest Management in the unquiet woods of Jharkhand', *Environment and Planning A*, **29** (12), 2145–64.

Council on Environmental Quality (1997), *Environmental Quality, 25th Anniversary Report*, Washington, DC: US Government Printing Office.

Council on Environmental Quality (1998), *Environmental Quality: Along the American River, 26th Annual Report*, Washington, DC: US Government Printing Office.

Dahl, R.A. and E.R. Tufte (1973), *Size and Democracy*, Stanford, CA: Stanford University Press.

Dahlman, C. (1980), *The Open Field System and Beyond: A Property Rights Analysis of an Economic Institution*, Cambridge: Cambridge University Press.

Daly, H. (1973), *Towards a Steady-State Economy*, San Francisco, CA: W.H. Freeman.

Daly, H. (1991a), *Steady-State Economics*, Washington, DC: Island Press.

Daly, H. (1991b), 'Sustainable growth: a bad oxymoron', *Grassroots Development*, **15** (3), 39.

Daly, H. (1993), 'From adjustment to sustainable development: the obstacle of free trade', in Ralph Nader et al., *The Case Against Free Trade: GATT, NAFTA, and the Globalization of Corporate Power*, San Francisco and Berkeley, CA: Earth Island Press/North Atlantic Books.

Daly, H. and J.B. Cobb, Jr. (1989), *For the Common Good*, Boston, MA: Beacon Press.

Daly, H. and J.B.Cobb, Jr. (1994), *For the Common Good*, 2nd edn, Boston, MA: Beacon Press.

Daly, H. and R. Goodland (1992), 'An ecological-economic assessment of deregulation of international commerce under GATT', Washington, DC: World Bank, Environment Department.

Dauvergne, P. (forthcoming), *Unstable Corporate Environments: Loggers and Degradation in the Asia-Pacific*.

Davies, J.C. and J. Mazurek (1997), *Regulating Pollution: Does the System Work?* Washington, DC: Resources for the Future.

Dei, G.J.S. (1992), 'A forest beyond the trees: Tree cutting in rural Ghana', *Human Ecology*, **20** (1), 57–88.

Denevan, W.M. (1992), 'The pristine myth: The landscape of the Americas in 1492', *Annals of the Association of American Geographers*, **82** (3), 369–85.

Department of the Environment (DoE) (1994), *The Mineral Planning Guidance 6: Guidelines for Aggregates Provision in England and Wales*, London: HMSO.

Deth, J. van and E. Scarborough (1995), *The Impact of Values*, Oxford: Oxford University Press.

DeWitt, J. and M. Mlay (1999), 'Community-based environmental protection: encouraging civic environmentalism', in K. Sexton, A.A. Marcus, K.W. Easter and T.D. Burkhardt (eds), *Better Environmental Decisions*, Washington, DC and Covelo, CA: Island Press, pp. 353–76.

Diaw, M.C. (1998), 'From sea to forest: an epistemology of *Otherness* and institutional resilience of non conventional economic systems', Paper presented at the 7th International Association for the Study of Common Property Conference, Vancouver, British Columbia, Canada, 10–14 June.

Diwan, R. and M. Lutz (eds) (1985), *Essays in Gandhian Economics*, New Delhi: Gandhi Peace Foundation.

Dobson, A. (1998), *Justice and the Environment*, Oxford: Oxford University Press.

Dobson, A. (ed.) (1999), *Fairness and Futurity*, Oxford: Oxford University Press.

Dodwell, D. (1992), 'GATT issues warning against environmental imperialism', *Financial Times* (12 February).

Donovan, R. (1994) 'BOSCOSA: Forest Conservation and Management through Local Institutions (Costa Rica)', in D. Western and R.M. Wright (eds), *Natural Connection: Perspectives in Community-based Conservation*, Washington, DC: Island Press, pp. 215–33.

Dorm-Adzobu, C., O. Ampadu-Agyel and P.G. Veit (1991), *Religious Beliefs and Environmental Protection: The Malshegu Sacred Grove in Northern Ghana*, Center for International Development and Environment, Nairobi, Kenya: World Resources Institute (WRI).

Douglass, M. (1992), 'The political economy of urban poverty and environmental management in Asia: Access, empowerment and community based alternatives', *Environment and Urbanization*, **4** (2), 9–32.

Douthwaite, R. (1996), *Short Circuit: Strengthening Local Economies for Security in an Unstable World*, Foxhole, UK: Green Books.

Dove, M. (1982), 'The Myth of the "Communal" Longhouse in Rural Development', in C. MacAndrews and L.S. Chin (eds), *Too Rapid Rural Development*, Athens, OH: Ohio State University Press, pp. 14–78.

Dowie, M. (1995), 'Greens outgunned', *Earth Island Journal*, **10** (2) (spring), 26–7.

Dréze, J. and A. Sen (eds) (1996), *Economic Development and Social Opportunity*, Oxford: Clarendon Press.

Dryzek, J. (1987a), *Rational Ecology*, New York, NY: Basil Blackwell.

Dryzek, J. (1987b), 'Complexity and rationality in public life', *Political Studies*, **35**, 424–42.

Dryzek, J. (1997), *The Politics of the Earth (Environmental Discourses)*, Oxford: Oxford University Press.

Dudley, N., J-P. Jeanrenaud and F. Sullivan (1995), *Bad Harvest? The Timber Trade and the Degradation of the World's Forests*. London: Earthscan.

Duesenberry, J.S. (1949), *Income, Saving and the Theory of Consumer Behavior*, Cambridge, MA: Harvard University Press.

Durbin, J.C. and J.A. Ralambo (1994), 'The role of local people in the successful maintenance of protected areas in Madagascar', *Environmental Conservation*, **21** (2), 115–20.

Durning, A. (1992), *How Much is Enough? The Consumer Society and the Fate of the Earth*, New York, NY: W.W. Norton.

Easterbrook, G. (1995), *A Moment on Earth*, New York, NY: Viking.

Eckersley, R. (1992), *Environmentalism and Political Theory*, Albany, NY: State University of New York Press.

Eckholm, E. (1976), *Losing Ground: Environmental Stress and World Food Prospects*, New York, NY: W.W. Norton & Co.

Economist, The (1998), 'Small but perfectly formed' (3 January), **346**: 65–8.

Ehrlich, P. (1971), *The Population Bomb*, New York, NY: Ballantine Books.

Ehrlich, P. and A. Ehrlich (1990), *The Population Explosion*, New York, NY: Simon and Schuster.

Ehrlich, P. and A. Ehrlich (1996), *Betrayal of Science and Reason*, Washington, DC: Island Press.

Eisinger, P.K. (1991), 'The state of state venture capitalism', *Economic Development Quarterly*, **5** (1).

Ekins, P. (1995), 'Trading off the future: making world trade environmentally sustainable', in R. Krishnan, J. Harris and N. Goodwin, *A Survey of Ecological Economics*, Washington, DC: Island Press, pp. 306–11.

Elliott, C. (1999), 'Forest certification: analysis from a policy network perspective', Ph.D. Dissertation (Thèse N° 1965), Départment de Génie Rural, École Polytechnique Fédérale de Lausanne, Switzerland.

Elliott, L. (1997), *The Global Politics of the Environment*, New York, NY: New York University Press.

Elson, D. (1993), 'Gender-aware analysis and development economics', *Journal of International Development*, **5** (2).

England, R.W. and J.M. Harris (1997), 'Alternatives to Gross National Product: a critical survey', G-DAE Discussion Paper No. 5, Medford, MA: Global Development and Environment Institute.

Escobar, A. (1992), 'Imagining a post-development era? Critical thought, development and social movements', *Social Text*, **10** (2/3), 20–56.

Escobar, A. (1995), *Encountering Development: The Making and Unmaking of the Third World*, Princeton, NJ: Princeton University Press.

Esteva, G. (1987), 'Regenerating peoples' spaces', *Alternatives*, **12** (1), 125–52.

Esteva, G. and M.S. Prakash (1998), *Grassroots Postmodernism: Remaking the Soil of Cultures*, London: Zed Press.

Etzioni, A. (1996), 'Positive aspects of community and the dangers of fragmentation', *Development and Change*, **27**, 301–14.

Evans, P. (1995), *Embedded Autonomy: States and Industrial Transformation*, Princeton, NJ: Princeton University Press.

Fairservis, W. Jr. (1975), *The Roots of Ancient India*, Chicago, IL: The University of Chicago Press.

Ferber, M. and J. Nelson (1993), *Beyond Economic Man*, Chicago, IL: Chicago University Press.

Feshbach, M. and A. Friendly, Jr. (1992), *Ecocide in the USSR*, New York, NY: Basic Books.

Fischer-Kowalski, M. and H. Haberl (1993), 'Metabolism and colonisation: modes of production and the physical exchange between societies and nature', *Innovation*, **6** (4), 415–42.

Fischer-Kowalski, M. and H. Haberl (1997), 'Tons, joules and money: modes of production and their sustainability problems', *Society and Natural Resources*, **10**, 61–85.

Fischer-Kowalski, M., H. Haberl and H. Payer (1994), 'A plethora of paradigms: outlining an information system on physical exchanges between the economy and nature', in R. Ayres and U. Simonis (eds), *Industrial Metabolism*, Tokyo, New York and Paris: United Nations University.

Folbre, N. (1986), 'Hearts and spades: paradigms of household economics', *World Development*, **14** (2), 245–55.

Folbre, N. (1994), *Who Pays for the Kids?* London and New York: Routledge.

Food and Agriculture Organization (FAO) (1999), 'Status and progress in the implementation of national forest programmes: Outcome of an FAO worldwide survey', Mimeo, FAO: Rome.

Forest Stewardship Council (FSC) (1999), 'FSC Principles and Criteria', Oaxaca, Mexico: Forest Stewardship Council.

Foster, G.D. (1999), 'Transnational environment threats: tomorrow's hidden enemy', *World Watch*, **12** (3) (May/June), 7–10.

Foucault, M. (1983), 'The subject and power', in H.L. Dreyfus and P. Rabinow, *Michel Foucault: Beyond Structuralism and Hermeneutics*, pp. 208–26, Chicago, IL: University of Chicago Press.

Foucault, M. (1991), 'Governmentality', in G. Burchell, C. Gordon and P. Miller (eds), *The Foucault Effect: Studies in Governmentality, with Two Lectures and an Interview with Michel Foucault*, Chicago, IL: University of Chicago Press, pp. 87–104.

France, Commissariat général du Plan (1993), *L'économie face à l'écologie*, Paris: Éditions la Découverte/La Documentation Française.

Frank, R.H. (1985), *Choosing the Right Pond*, Oxford: Oxford University Press.

Frank, R.H. (1999a), *Luxury Fever: Why Money Fails to Satisfy in an Era of Excess*, New York, NY: Free Press.

Frank, R.H. (1999b), 'The victimless income gap?', *The New York Times* (12 April).

Freeman, R.B. (1999), 'Solving the new inequality', in R.B. Freeman (ed.), *The New Inequality: Creating Solutions for Poor America*, Boston, MA: Beacon, p. 14.

French, H. (1990), *Green Revolutions: Environmental Reconstruction in Eastern Europe and the Soviet Union*, Worldwatch Paper No. 99, Washington, DC: Worldwatch Institute.

French, H. (1993), 'Costly tradeoffs: reconciling trade and the environment', Worldwatch Institute Paper No. 113, Washington, DC: Worldwatch Institute (7 March).

French, H. (1995), *Partnership for the Planet: An Environmental Agenda for the United Nations*, Washington, DC: Worldwatch Institute.

Freund, P. and G. Martin (1993), *The Ecology of the Automobile*, Montreal, Quebec and New York, NY: Black Rose Books.

Friedmann, J. (1988), *Life-Space and Economic Space: Essays in Third World Planning*, New Brunswick, NJ: Transaction Books.

Friedmann, J. and H. Rangan (eds) (1993), *In Defense of Livelihood: Comparative Studies in Environmental Action*, West Hartford, CT: Kumarian Press.

Friends of the Earth (1996), 'The case against the Harris superquarry', Edinburgh: Friends of the Earth and Link Quarry Group.

Friends of the Earth (1999), 'Green Scissors '99', Washington, DC: Friends of the Earth.

Funtowicz, S. and J. Ravetz (1994), 'The worth of a songbird: ecological economics as a post-normal science', *Ecological Economics*, **10** (August), 197–207.

Gabriel, C. and L. Macdonald (1996), 'NAFTA and economic restructuring: some gender and race implications', in I. Bakker (ed.), *Rethinking Restructuring: Gender and Change in Canada*, Toronto, Ontario: University of Toronto Press.

Gadamer, H-G. (1994), *Truth and Method* (2nd revised edn), New York, NY: Continuum Books.

Gadgil, M. (1992), 'Conserving biodiversity as if people matter: A case study from India', *Ambio*, **21** (3), 266–70.

Gadgil, M. and R. Guha (1992), *This Fissured Land: An Ecological History of India*, Berkeley, CA: University of California Press.

Gadgil, M. and R. Guha (1995), *Ecology and Equity: The Use and Abuse of Nature in Contemporary India*, London: Routledge.

Gale, F. (1996), 'The mysterious case of the disappearing environmentalists: the International Tropical Timber Organization', *Capitalism Nature Socialism*, **7** (3) (September), 103–18.

Gale, F. (1998a), *The Tropical Timber Trade Regime*, Basingstoke, UK and New York, NY: Macmillan and St. Martin's Presses.

Gale, F. (1998b), 'Ecoforestry bound: how international trade agreements constrain the adoption of an ecosystem-based approach to BC's forests', in C. Tollefson (ed.), *The Wealth of Forests: Markets, Regulation and Sustainable Forestry*, Vancouver, British Columbia: UBC Press.

Gale, F. (1998c), 'Theorizing power in ecological economic', *Ecological Economics*, **24** (11) (November).

Gale, F. (1999), 'Greening Ricardo: Rethinking trade theory in an era of globalization', in W. Hein and P. Fuchs (eds), *Globalization and the Ecological Crisis*, Hamburg: Hochschule für Wirtschaft und Politik.

Gale, F. (forthcoming), 'Economic specialization versus ecological generalization: the trade policy implications of taking ecosystem-based management seriously', *Ecological Economics*.

Gardiner, J. (1997), *Gender, Care and Economics*, London: Macmillan.

Gare, A. (1993), 'Soviet environmentalism: the path not taken', *Capitalism Nature Socialism*, **4** (4), 69–88.

George, S. (1992), *The Debt Boomerang*, Boulder, CO and San Francisco, CA: Westview Press.

Georgesçu-Roegen, N. (1971), *Economics and the Entropy Process*, Cambridge, MA: Harvard University Press.

Gereffi, G. (1994), 'The organisation of buyer-driven commodity chains: how US retailers shape overseas production networks', in G. Gereffi and M. Korzeniewicz (eds), *Commodity Chains and Global Capitalism*, Westport, CT: Praeger.

Gereffi, G. and M. Korzeniewicz (eds) (1994), *Commodity Chains and Global Capitalism*, Westport, CT: Praeger.

Ghai, D. (1993), 'Conservation, Livelihood and Democracy: Social Dynamics of Environmental Change in Africa', *Osterreichische Zeitschrift fur Soziologie*, **18**, 56–75.

Gibson, C. (1999), *Politicians and Poachers: The Political Economy of Wildlife Policy in Africa*, Cambridge: Cambridge University Press.

Gibson, C. and S. Marks (1995), 'Transforming Rural Hunters into Conservationists: An Assessment of Community-Based Wildlife Management Programs in Africa', *World Development*, **23**, 941–57.

Giddens, A. (1991) *The Consequences of Modernity*, Cambridge: Polity Press.

Giddens, A. (1994), *Beyond Left and Right*, Cambridge: Polity Press.

Gill, S. (1995), 'Theorizing the interregnum: the double movement and global politics in the 1990s', in B. Hettne (ed.), *International Political Economy: Understanding Global Disorder*, Halifax: Fernwood Press.

Gilligan, C. (1981), *In a Different Voice: Psychological Theory and Women's Development*, Cambridge, MA: Harvard University Press.

Gills, B. and A.G. Frank (1991), '5000 years of World System history: the cumulation of accumulation', in C. Chase-Dunn and T. Hall (eds), *Core/Periphery Relations in Pre-Capitalist Worlds*, Boulder, CO: Westview.

Goodstein, E. (1995), 'The economic roots of environmental decline: property rights or path dependence?', *Journal of Economic Issues*, **29** (4) (December), 1029–43.

Gorz, A. (1989), *Critique of Economic Reason*, London and New York: Verso.

Gorz, A. (1980), *Ecology as Politics*, London: Pluto.

Gottlieb, R. (ed.) (1996), *This Sacred Earth*, London: Routledge.

Gould, S.J. (1987), *An Urchin in the Storm: Essays about Books and Ideas*, New York, NY: W.W. Norton.

Government of India (1985), *National Forest Policy*, New Delhi: Lok Sabha Secretariat.

Government of West Bengal (1996), *Status Report on Arabari Socio-Economic Project*, Calcutta, Directorate of Forests: Silviculture South Division.

Grundmann, R. (1991), 'The ecological challenge to Marxism', *New Left Review*, **187**, 103–20.

Guha, R. (1989), *The Unquiet Woods: Ecological Change and Peasant Resistance in the Himalaya*, New Delhi: Oxford University Press.

Gurung, B. (1992) 'Towards Sustainable Development: A Case in the Eastern Himalayas', *Futures*, **24**, 907–16.

Hall, V. (1999), 'Hinton still hopeful that Cheviot mine will go ahead', *Edmonton Journal* (10 April).

Hampson, C. (1990), 'Industry and the environment: a question of balance', in D.J.R. Angell, J.D. Comer and M.L.N. Wilkinson (eds), *Sustaining Earth: Response to the Environmental Threat*, London: Macmillan, pp. 108–19.

Hansen, E. and H. Juslin (1999), 'The status of forest certification in the ECE region', Geneva Timber and Forest Discussion Paper, Timber Section, Trade Division, UN-Economic Commission for Europe, Switzerland.

Haraway, D. (1990), 'A manifesto for cyborgs', in L.J. Nicholson (ed.), *Feminism/Postmodernism*, New York and London: Routledge, pp. 190–233.

Haraway, D. (1991), 'Situated knowledges: the science question in feminism and the privilege of partial perspective', in D. Haraway (ed.), *Simians, Cyborgs, and Women: The reinvention of nature*, New York, NY: Routledge, pp. 183–201.

Hardin, G. (1968), 'The tragedy of the commons', *Science*, **162**, 1243–8.

Hart, Michael (1995), 'A multilateral agreement on foreign direct investment – why now?' Ottawa, Ontario: Centre for Trade Policy and Law, Carleton University and the Faculty of Law, University of Ottawa, International Trade Law and Policy Occasional Paper 37 (December).

Hartsock, N. (1983), *Money, Sex and Power: Developing the Ground for a Specifically Feminist Historical Materialism*, New York and London: Longman.

Harvey, D. (1974), 'Population, resources, and the ideology of science', *Economic Geography*, **50** (3), 256–78.

Harvey, D. (1985), *The Urbanization of Capital: Studies in the History of Capitalist Urbanization*, Baltimore, MA: Johns Hopkins University Press.

Harvey, D. (1996), *Justice, Nature and the Geography of Difference*, Oxford: Blackwell.

Hawken, P. (1993), *The Ecology of Commerce*, New York, NY: HarperCollins Publishers.

Hayden, A. (1999), *Sharing the Work, Sparing the Planet*, Toronto, Ontario: Between the Lines Press.

Hayek, F. (1937), 'Economics and knowledge', *Economica*, February, 33–54.

Hayek, F. (1944), *The Road to Serfdom*, Chicago, IL: University of Chicago Press.

Hayward, T. and J. O'Neill (eds) (1997), *Justice, Property and the Environment*, Aldershot: Ashgate.

Hecht, S.B. and A. Cockburn (1989), *The Fate of the Forest: Developers, Destroyers, and Defenders of the Amazon*, London: Verso.

Heilbroner, R. (1985), *The Nature and Logic of Capitalism*, New York and London: W.W. Norton & Company.

Hempel, L. (1996), *Environmental Governance: The Global Challenge*, Washington, DC: Island Press.

Heskin, A.D. (1991), *The Struggle for Community*, Boulder, CO: Westview Press.

Hill, M.A. and A.J. Press (1994), 'Kakadu National Park: An Australian Experience in Comanagement', in D. Western and R.M. Wright (eds), *Natural Connections: Perspectives in Community-based Conservation*, Washington, DC: Island Press, pp. 135–160.

Hirsch F. (1976), *Social Limits to Growth*, Cambridge, MA: Harvard University Press.

Hoban, T.J. and M.G. Cook (1988), 'Challenge of Conservation', *Forum for Applied Research and Public Policy*, **3**, 100–2.

Hobbes, T. (1968), *Leviathan*, London: Penguin Books.

Hobsbawm, E. and T. Ranger (1983), *The Invention of Tradition*, Cambridge: Cambridge University Press.

Hoff, M.D. (1998), *Sustainable Community Development: Studies in Economic, Environmental, and Cultural Revitalization*, Boca Raton, FL: Lewis Publishers.

Hornborg, A. (1998), 'Towards an ecological theory of unequal exchange: articulating world system theory and ecological economics', *Ecological Economics*, **25** (1), 127–36.

Hornby, A.S. (1974), *Oxford Advanced Learner's Dictionary of Current English*, Oxford: Oxford University Press.

Howard, T. (1999), 'Ownership matters', *YES! A Journal of Positive Futures*, **9** (spring), 24–7.

Howard, T. and K. Rusch (forthcoming), 'Innovations in ownership', Washington, DC: NCESA.

Hryciuk, D. and D. Howell (1999), 'Court quashes mine approval', *Edmonton Journal* (10 April).

Hubbell, L.K. and T.M. Selden (1994), 'Central planning, internal security, and the environment', *Public Finance Quarterly*, **22** (3) (July), 291–310.

Hudson, M. (1996), 'The negative option: localization for ecological-economic harmony in an interconnected world', unpublished Paper, Faculty of Environmental Studies, York University, North York, Ontario, Canada.

Hudson, M. (1997), 'Border crossings: linking local and global struggles for sustainable livelihood through alternative trade', MES Thesis, Faculty of Environmental Studies, York University, North York, Ontario, Canada.

Huntsinger, L. and A. McCaffrey (1995), 'A Forest for the Trees: Forest Management and the Yurok Environment', *American Indian Culture and Research Journal*, **19**, 155–92.

Huq, A.M. (1985), 'The doctrine of international trade: a Gandhian perspective', in R. Diwan and M. Lutz (eds), *Essays in Gandhian Economics*, New Delhi: Gandhi Peace Foundation, pp. 166–74.

Hyde, W.F., D.H. Newman and R.A. Sedjo (1991), *Forest Economics and Policy Analysis: An Overview*, Washington, DC: The World Bank.

Ilahaine, H. (1995), 'Common property, ethnicity, and social exploitation in the Ziz villey, southeast Morocco', Paper presented at the IASCP conference.

Inglehart, R. (1997), *Modernization and Postmodernization: Cultural, Economic, and Political Change in 43 Societies*, Princeton, NJ: Princeton University Press.

Ives, J.D. and B. Messerli (1989), *The Himalayan Dilemma: Reconciling Development and Conservation*, London: Routledge.

Jackson, C. (1993), 'Women/nature or gender/history? A critique of ecofeminist "development"', *Journal of Peasant Studies*, **20** (3), 389–419.

Jackson, C. (1994), 'Gender analysis and environmentalisms', in T. Benton and M. Redclift (eds), *Social Theory and the Global Environment*, London: Routledge, pp. 113–49.

Jackson, J.H. (1993), 'World trade rules and environmental policies: congruence or conflict?', in D. Zaelke, P. Orbuch and R.F. Housman (eds), *Trade and the Environment*, Washington, DC and Covelo, CA: Island Press.

Jackson, T. (1996), *Material Concerns: Pollution, Profit and Quality of Life*, London and New York: Routledge.
Jagannathan, N.V. (1987), *Informal Markets in Developing Countries*, New York, NY: Oxford University Press.
Jancar, B. (1987), *Environmental Management in the Soviet Union and Yugoslavia*, Durham, NC: Duke University Press.
Jewitt, S. (1995), 'Europe's others? Forestry policies and practices in colonial and postcolonial India', *Environment and Planning D: Society and Space*, **13**, 67–90.
Jodha, N.S. (1998), 'Community management of the commons: re-empowerment process and the gaps', Paper presented at the 7th International Association for the Study of Common Property Conference, Vancouver, British Columbia, Canada (10–14 June).
Johnston, R.J. (1996), *Nature, State and Economy: A Political Economy of the Environment*, Chichester and New York: John Wiley & Sons.
Johnstone, N. (1995), 'Trade liberalization, economic specialization, and the environment', *Ecological Economics*, **14** (3), 165–73.
Kaplan, R.D. (1994), 'The coming anarchy', *The Atlantic Monthly* (February), 44–76.
Katzenstein, P.J. (1985), *Small States in World Markets*, Ithaca, NY: Cornell University Press.
Keck, M. and K. Sikkink (1998), *Activists Beyond Borders: Advocacy Networks and International Politics*, New York, NY: Cornell University Press.
Keil, R., D. Bell, P. Penz and L. Fawcett (eds) (1998), *Political Ecology: Global and Local*, London and New York: Routledge.
Kempton, W.M., J. Boster and J. Hartley (1995), *Environmental Values in American Culture*, Cambridge, MA: MIT Press.
Kettel, B. (1998), 'Women, environment and development: from Rio to Beijing', in R. Keil, D. Bell, P. Penz and L. Fawcett (eds) (1998), *Political Ecology: Global and Local*, London and New York: Routledge, pp. 220–39.
Khor, M. (1993), 'Free trade and the Third World', in R. Nader (ed.), *The Case Against Free Trade*, San Francisco and Berkeley, CA: Earth Island Press.
Kiss, Agnes (ed.) (1990), *Living with Wildlife: Wildlife Resource Management with Local Participation in Africa*, Washington, DC: The World Bank.
Krugman, P. (1995), 'Globalization and the inequality of nations', Working Paper No. 5098, Cambridge, MA: National Bureau of Economic Research (April).
Krugman, P. (1996), *The Self-Organizing Economy*, Cambridge, MA: Blackwell.
Kuehls, T. (1996), *Beyond Sovereign Territory*, Minneapolis, MN: University of Minnesota Press.
Kuhn, T.S. (1970), *The Structure of Scientific Revolutions*, 2nd edn, Chicago, IL: University of Chicago Press.
Kuiper, E. and J. Sap (1995), *Out of the Margin: Feminist Perspectives on Economics*, London: Routledge.
Kuttner, R. (1998), 'Rampant bull: social security and the market', *The American Prospect*, **39** (July–August), 30–6.
Lane, R. (1993), 'Does money buy happiness?' *The Public Interest*, **113** (fall), 56–65.
Lang, T. and C. Hines (1993), *The New Protectionism: Protecting the Future Against Free Trade*, London: Earthscan Publications.
Latour, B. (1987), *Science in Action*, Cambridge, MA: Harvard University.
Laxer, G. (2000), 'Surviving the Americanizing New Right', *Canadian Review of Sociology and Anthropology*, **37** (1), 55–75.

Leach, M. (1991), 'Engendering environments: understanding natural resource management in the West African Forest Zone', *Institute of Development Studies Bulletin*, **22**.

Leff, E. (1995), *Green Production*, New York and London: Guilford Press.

Leff, E. (1996), 'From ecological economics to productive ecology: perspectives on sustainable development from the South', in R. Costanza, S. Olman and J. Martinez Alier (eds), *Getting Down to Earth: Practical Applications of Ecological Economics*, Washington, DC: Island Press, pp. 77–90.

Lélé, S.M. (1991), 'Sustainable development: a critical review', *World Development*, **19** (6), 607–21.

Les Verts (1994), *Le Livre des Verts: Dictionnaire de l'Écologie politique*, Paris: Éditions du Félin.

Les Verts (1995), *Oser l'Écologie et la Solidarité (plateforme de Dominique Voynet pour l'élection présidentielle de 1995)*, Paris: Les Verts (mars).

Les Verts (1999), *Réinventer L'Europe (programme des Verts pour les élections européennes du 13 juin 1999)*, Paris: Les Verts.

Levin, R. and D. Weiner (eds) (1997), *'No More Tears . . . ': Struggles for Land in Mpumalanga, South Africa*, Trenton, NJ and Asmara, Eritrea: Africa World Press.

Leydesdorff, L. and P. Van Den Besselaar (eds) (1994), *Evolutionary Economics and Chaos Theory*, New York, NY: St. Martin's Press.

Li, T.M. (1996), *Images of community: Discourse and Strategy in Property Relations. Development and Change*, **27** (3), 501–28.

Lichtenberg, J. (1995), 'Consuming because others consume', *Report from the Institute for Philosophy & Public Policy*, **15** (4) (special issue, fall), 23–8.

Lieten, G.K. (1992), *Continuity and Change in Rural West Bengal*, New Delhi: Sage Publications.

Light, A. (ed.) (1998), *Social Ecology after Bookchin*, New York, NY: The Guilford Press.

Lipietz, A. (1987), *Mirages and Miracles: the Crises of Global Fordism*, London: Verso.

Lipietz, A. (1989), *Choisir L'Audace,* Paris: Editions la Découverte.

Lipietz, A. (1993), *Vert Espérance (L'avenir de l'écologie politique)*, Paris: Éditions La Découverte.

Lipietz, A. (1995), *Green Hopes: The Future of Political Ecology*, trans. Malcolm Slater, Cambridge: Polity Press.

Lipietz, A. (1996), *La Société en Sablier: Le partage du travail contre la déchirure sociale*, Paris: Editions la Découverte.

Lipietz, A. (1999), 'Tiers-secteur écologiquement et socialement utile', *Vert Europe* (Magazine d'écologie politique des verts français et européens), **2** (mars).

Lipschutz, R.D. with J. Mayer (1996), *Global Civil Society and Global Environmental Governance*, Albany, NY: SUNY Press.

Louge, J. (1998), 'Rustbelt buyouts: why Ohio leads in worker ownership', *Dollars & Sense* (September/October), 34–5.

Lovejoy, A. (1974), *The Great Chain of Being*, Cambridge, MA: Harvard University Press.

Lovelock, J. (1988), *The Ages of Gaia: A Biography of Our Living Earth*, Oxford and New York: Oxford University Press.

Lovins, A.B., L.H. Lovins, and P. Hawken (1999), 'A road map for natural capitalism', *Harvard Business Review* (May–June), 145–58.

Low, M. (1997), 'Representation unbound: globalization and democracy', in K.R. Cox (ed.), *Spaces of Globalization: Reasserting the Power of the Local*, New York and London: Guilford Press, pp. 245–74.

Lowi, T., C. Sunstein, J. Savitz, M. Wilson and E. Weltman (1999), *Boston Review*, **24** (5) (October/November).

Lynch, O.J., and K. Talbott (1995), *Balancing Acts: Community-Based Forest Management and National Law in Asia and the Pacific*, Washington, DC: World Resources Institute.

Macgregor, S. (1996), 'Sustainable for whom? Feminist perspectives on sustainability', unpublished Paper, Faculty of Environmental Studies, York University, North York, Ontario, Canada.

Mackenzie, F. (1998), '"The cheviot, the stag . . . and the white, white rock?" Community, identity and environmental threat on the Isle of Harris', *Environment and Planning D: Society and Space*, **16**, 509–32.

MacNeill, J., P. Winsemius and T. Yakushiji (1991), *Beyond Interdependence: The Meshing of the World's Economy and the Earth's Ecology*, New York, NY: Oxford University Press.

Magnusson, L. and J. Ottosson (eds) (1997), *Evolutionary Economics and Path Dependence*, Cheltenham, UK and Brookfield, US: Edward Elgar.

Mahon, R. (1991), 'From "bringing" to "putting": the state in late twentieth-century social theory', *Canadian Journal of Sociology*, **16** (2), 119–44.

Maltz, A. (1995), 'Commentary on the Harris superquarry inquiry', *Journal of Law and Religion*, **11**, 793–833.

Mamdani, M. (1996), *Citizen and Subject: Contemporary Africa and the Legacy of Colonialism*, Princeton, NJ: Princeton University Press.

Manning, A. (1996), 'The ecology of Scotland', Public Lecture, Edinburgh City Chambers, Edinburgh, Scotland.

Marks, S. (1984), *The Imperial Lion: Human Dimensions of Wildlife Management in Central Africa*, Boulder, CO: Westview Press.

Martin and Abercrombie, QCs (1995), 'Final submission to the public enquiry on behalf of Redland Aggregate Limited'.

Marx, K. (1978), 'The German ideology', in R.C. Tucker (ed.), *The Marx-Engels Reader*, 2nd edn, London and New York: W.W. Norton & Company.

Matzke, G.E. and N. Nabane (1996), 'Outcomes of a community controlled wildlife program in a Zambezi valley community', *Human Ecology*, **24** (1), 65–85.

McCay, B.J. and J. Acheson (eds) (1989), *The Question of the Commons: The Culture and Ecology of Communal Resources*, Tucson, AZ: The University of Arizona Press.

McDade, L. (ed.) (1993), *La Selva: Ecology and Natural History of a Neotropical Rainforest*, Chicago, IL: University of Chicago Press.

McGee, T.G. (1997), 'Globalization, urbanization and the emergence of sub-global regions: a case study of the Asia-Pacific region', in R.F Watters and T.G. McGee (eds), *New Geographies of the Pacific Rim: Asia Pacific*, Bathurst, NSW: Crawford Publishing.

McIntosh, A. (1995), 'Public inquiry on the proposed Harris superquarry: witness on the theological considerations concerning superquarrying and the integrity of creation', *Journal of Law and Religion*, **XI**, 774.

McIntosh, A., A. Wightman and D. Morgan (1994), 'Reclaiming the Scottish Highlands: Clearance, conflict and crofting', *The Ecologist*, **24** (2), 64–70.

McKean, M. (1992), 'Success on the commons: A comparative examination of institutions for common property resource management', *Journal of Theoretical Politics*, **4** (3), 247–82.

McManus, P. (1996), 'Contested terrains: politics, stories, and discourses of sustainability', *Environmental Politics*, **5** (1), 48–73.

Meadows, D. and others (1992), *Beyond the Limits: Global Collapse or a Sustainable Future*, London: Earthscan.

Meadows, D. and others (1974), *The Limits to Growth: A Report for the Club of Rome's Project on the Predicament of Mankind*, New York, NY: Universe Books.

Mellor, M. (1992), *Breaking the Boundaries: Towards a Feminist Green Socialism*, London: Virago.

Mellor, M. (1995), 'Materialist communal production: getting from "there" to "here"', in J. Lovenduski and J. Stanyer (eds), *Contemporary Political Studies*, Belfast: Political Studies Association.

Mellor, M. (1996), 'The politics of women and nature: affinity, contingency or material relation?', *Journal of Political Ideologies*, **1** (2), 147–64.

Mellor, M. (1997a), *Feminism and Ecology*, Cambridge, UK and New York, NY: Polity and New York University Presses.

Mellor, M. (1997b) 'Women, nature and the social construction of "economic man"', *Ecological Economics*, **20** (2), 129–40.

Meyer, W.B., and B.L. Turner II (eds) (1994), *Changes in Land Use and Land Cover: A Global Perspective*, Cambridge: Cambridge University Press.

M'Gonigle, M. (1998a), 'Structural instruments and sustainable forests: a political ecology approach', in C. Tollefson (ed.), *The Wealth of Forests: Regulation, and Sustainable Forestry*, Vancouver, British Columbia: University of British Columbia Press.

M'Gonigle, M. (1998b), 'The dialectic of centre and territory', Treatment paper prepared for the Transdisciplinary Virtual Workshop 'From Centre to Territory: Theorizing and Practicing Strong Sustainability: An Ecological Political Economy (EPE) Perspective', University of Victoria, Victoria, British Columbia (March–April).

M'Gonigle, M. (1999a), 'The political economy of precaution', in C. Raffensperger and J. Tickner (eds), *Protecting Public Health and the Environment: Implementing the Precautionary Principle*, Washington, DC: Island Press.

M'Gonigle, M. (1999b). 'Ecological economics and political ecology: towards a necessary synthesis', tenth anniversary analysis article, *Ecological Economics*, **28**, 11–26.

M'Gonigle, M. (1999c), 'Reconstituting sovereignty as reclaiming territory: new (old) approaches to human security', Plenary Presentation, Canadian Council of International Law, Annual Conference, Ottawa, Ontario, October.

M'Gonigle, M. (2000), 'A new Naturalism: is there a (radical) truth beyond the (postmodern) abyss?', *Ecotheology*, **8**, 8–39.

Mies, M. (1986), *Patriarchy and Accumulation on a World Scale: Women in the International Division of Labour*, London: Zed Books.

Mies, M. (1999), *Patriarchy and Accumulation on a World Scale: Women in the International Division of Labour*: 2nd edn, London: Zed Books.

Mies, M. and V. Shiva (eds) (1993), *Ecofeminism*, London and Delhi: Zed Books and Kali.

Milani, B. (1999), *Designing the Green Economy for a Post-Industrial Transition*, Lanham, MD: Rowman and Littlefield.

Milbrath, L.W. (1996), 'Becoming sustainable: changing the way we think', in D. Pirages (ed.), *Building Sustainable Societies*, Armonk, NY: M.E. Sharpe, pp. 275–98.

Miliband, R. (1969), *The State in Capitalist Society*, London: Weidenfeld and Nicolson.

Mishra, S. (1994), 'Women's indigenous knowledge of forest management in Orissa (India)', *Indigenous Knowledge and Development Monitor*, **2** (3).

Mitchell, J. (1997), 'Nowhere to hide: the global spread of high-risk synthetic chemicals', *World Watch*, **10** (2), (March/April), 27–36.

Mitlin, D. (1992), 'Sustainable development: a guide to the literature', *Environment and Urbanization*, **4** (2), 111–24.

Mokhiber, R. and R. Weissman (1998), 'Petitioning to revoke the Charter of Unocal', *Liberal Opinion Weekly* (28 September).

Moore, D. (1996), 'Marxism, culture, and political ecology: Environmental struggles in Zimbabwe's Eastern Highlands', in R. Peet and M. Watts (eds), *Liberation Ecologies: Environment, Development, Social Movements*, New York, NY: Routledge.

Morrison, R. (1995), *Ecological Democracy*, Boston, MA: South End Press.

Murdock, B.S. and K. Sexton (1998), 'Community-based environmental partnerships', in K. Sexton, A. Marcus, T.D. Burkhardt and K.W. Easter (eds), *Better Environmental Decisions: Strategies for Governments, Businesses, and Communities*, Washington, DC and Covelo, CA: Island Press, pp. 377–400.

Murphree, M.W. (1993), *Communities as Resource Management Institutions*, London: International Institute for Environment and Development.

Murphy, A. (1996), 'The sovereign state system as political-territorial ideal: historical and contemporary considerations', in T.J. Biersteker and C. Weber (eds), *State Sovereignty as Social Construct*, Cambridge: Cambridge University Press.

Myers, P. (1998), 'Livability at the ballot box: state and local referenda on parks, conservation, and smarter growth, election day 1998', Discussion Paper, State Resource Strategies, for The Brookings Institution Center on Urban and Metropolitan Policy (January 1999), <www.srsmyers.org/srsmyers/elections.htm>.

Nader, R. (ed.), *The Case Against Free Trade*, San Francisco and Berkeley, CA: Earth Island Press.

Nanda, M. (1991), 'Is modern science a western, patriarchal myth?', *South Asia Bulletin*, **11**, 32–61.

National Association of State Development Agencies (NASDA) (1998), *Directory of incentives for business investment and development in the United States: A state by state guide*, 5th edn, Washington, DC: National Association of State Development Agencies, CD-ROM.

National Center for Employee Ownership (NCEO) (1997), 'A brief introduction to employee ownership', Oakland, CA: NCEO.

National Congress for Community Economic Development (NCCED) (1995), 'Tying it all together: the comprehensive achievements of community-based development organizations', Washington, DC: NCCED.

National Congress for Community Economic Development (NCCED) (1999), '1998 Census of CDCs', Washington, DC: NCCED (October 15), <www.ncced.org/>.

National Cooperative Bank (1998), 'A day in the life of cooperative America', Washington, DC: National Cooperative Bank (October).

Naughton-Treves, L. (1997), 'Wildlife versus farmers: Vulnerable places and people around Kibale National Park, Uganda', *Geographical Review*, **87** (1), 462–88.

Naughton-Treves, L. and S. Sanderson (1995), 'Property, politics and wildlife conservation,' *World Development*, **23** (8), 1265–75.

Nelson, J. (1993), 'The study of choice or the study of provisioning? Gender and the definition of economics', in M. Ferber and J. Nelson (eds), *Beyond Economic Man*, Chicago, IL: Chicago University Press.

Nelson, J. (1996), *Feminism, Objectivity and Economics*, London: Routledge.

Neumann, R.P. (1996), 'Local challenges to global agendas: conservation, economic liberalization, and the pastoralists' rights movement in Tanzania', *Antipode*, **27** (4), 363–82.

Newmark, W.D. (1996), 'Insularization of Tanzanian parks and the local extinction of large mammals', *Conservation Biology*, **10** (6), 1549–56.

New York Times (1999), 'Work, work and more work', (11 September), A15.

Nikijuluw, V. (1994) 'Indigenous fisheries resource management in the Maluku Islands', *Indigenous Knowledge and Development Monitor*, **2** (2).

Norgaard, R. (1995), 'Sustainable development: a co-evolutionary view', in R. Krishnan, J.M. Harris and N. Goodwin (eds), *A Survey of Ecological/Economics*, Washington, DC and Covelo, CA: Island Press.

North, D. (1990), *Institutions, Institutional Change, and Economic Performance*, Cambridge: Cambridge University Press.

Northcott, M.S. (1996), *The Environment and Christian Ethics*, Cambridge: Cambridge University Press.

Norton, B.G. (1989), 'The cultural approach to conservation biology', in D. Western and M.C. Pearl (eds), *Conservation for the Twenty-First Century*, pp. 241–6.

Nozick, M. (1993), *No Place Like Home*, Ottawa, Ontario: Canadian Council for Social Development.

O'Brien, M., S. Penna and C. Hay (eds) (1999), *Theorising Modernity: Reflexivity, Environment and Identity in Giddens' Social Theory*, London and New York: Longman.

O'Connor, J. (1976), 'What is political economy?', in D. Memelstein (ed.), *Economics: Mainstream Readings and Radical Critiques*, 3rd edn, New York, NY: Random House.

O'Connor, J. (1988), 'Capitalism, nature, socialism: a theoretical introduction', *Capitalism Nature Socialism*, **1** (fall).

O'Connor, J. (1994), 'Is sustainable capitalism possible?', in M. O'Connor (ed.), *Is Capitalism Sustainable?* New York, NY: Guilford Press.

O'Connor, J. (1998), *Natural Causes: Essays in Ecological Marxism*, New York, NY: The Guilford Press.

Oelschlaeger, M. (1994), *Caring for Creation: An Ecumenical Approach to the Environmental Crisis*, New Haven, CT: Yale University Press.

O'Hara, S. (1997), 'Toward a sustaining production theory', *Ecological Economics*, **20** (2) (February), 141–54.

Olson, M. (1965), *The Logic of Collective Action: Public Goods and the Theory of Groups*, Cambridge, MA: Harvard University Press.

Olson, M. (1984), 'What we lose when the rich go on the dole: tax deductible llamas hurt the economy more than welfare cadillacs', *The Washington Monthly* (January).

Orr, D.W. (1999), 'The ecology of giving and consuming', in R. Rosenblatt (ed.), *Consuming Desires: Consumption, Culture and the Pursuit of Happiness*, Washington, DC and Covelo, CA: Island Press, pp. 137–54.

Orvis, J. (1998), 'Interview by the National Center for Economic and Security Alternatives (NCESA) staff with Julie Orvis of the Institute for Community

Economics (ICE)', Washington, DC: National Center for Economic and Security Alternatives (June).

Ostrom, E. (1987), 'Institutional arrangements for resolving the commons dilemma: some contending approaches', in B.J. McCay and J.M. Acheson (eds), *The Question of the Commons: The Culture and Ecology of Communal Resources*, Tucson, AZ: University of Arizona Press, pp. 250–65.

Ostrom, E. (1990), *Governing the Commons: The Evolution of Institutions for Collective Action*, Cambridge: Cambridge University Press.

Ostrom, E. and E. Schlager (1995), 'The formation of property rights', in S. Hanna, C. Folke and K. Maler (eds), *Rights to Nature*, Washington, DC: Island Press.

Ostrom, E., L. Schroeder and S. Wynne (1993), *Institutional Incentives and Sustainable Development: Infrastructure Policies in Perspective*, Boulder, CO: Westview Press.

Oxford Forestry Institute (1991), 'Pre-project report on incentives in producer and consumer countries to promote sustainable development of tropical forests', ITTO PPR 22/91, Yokohama: ITTO.

Panchak, P. (1998), 'The future manufacturing', *Industry Week*, **247** (17) (21 September), 96–105.

Parker, E. (1993), 'Fact and fiction in Amazonia: The case of the Apete', *American Anthropologist*, **95**, 715–23.

Parry, D. and B. Campbell (1992), 'Attitudes of rural communities to animal wildlife and its utilization in Chobe Enclave and Mababe Depression, Botswana', *Environmental Conservation*, **19** (3), 245–52.

Peet, J. (1992), *Energy and the Ecological Economics of Sustainability*, Washington, DC, and Covelo, CA: Island Press.

Peet, R. and M. Watts (1996), 'Liberation ecology: development, sustainability, and environment in an age of market triumphalism', in R. Peet and M. Watts (eds), *Liberation Ecologies: Environment, Development, Social Movements*, London: Routledge, pp. 1–45.

Peluso, N. (1992), *Rich Forests, Poor People: Resource Control and Resistance in Java*, Berkeley, CA: University of California Press.

Peluso, N. (1993), 'Coercing conservation: the politics of state resource control', *Global Environmental Change*, **4** (2), 199–217.

Peluso, N. (1995), 'Whose woods are these? Counter-mapping forest territories in Kalimantan, Indonesia', *Antipode*, **27** (4), 383–406.

Peluso, N. (1996), 'Fruit trees and family trees in an anthropogenic forest: Ethics of access, property zones and environmental change in Indonesia', *Comparative Studies in Society and History*, **38**, 510–48.

Pepper, D. (1984), *The Roots of Modern Environmentalism*, London: Routledge.

Perkins, P.E. (1996a), 'Building communities to limit trade', *Alternatives*, January, 10–15.

Perkins, P.E. (1996b), *NAFTA and Environmental Regulation: The Ontario Experience*, unpublished Paper.

Perkins, P.E. (1997), 'What is sustainable trade?' in D. Gupta and N. Choudhry (eds), *Studies in Globalization and Development*, Dordrecht: Kluwer, pp. 273–298.

Perkins, P.E. (1999), 'Trade, transition paths, and sustainable economies', *Canadian Journal of Development Studies*, **XX** (3), 594–608.

Perlin, J. (1991), *A Forest Journey: The Role of Wood in the Development of Civilization*, London and Cambridge, MA: Harvard University Press.

Perrow, C. (1984), *Normal Accidents: Living with High-Risk Technologies*, New York, NY: Basic Books.

Perry, J.A. and R.K. Dixon (1986), 'An interdisciplinary approach to community resource management: Preliminary field test in Thailand', *Journal of Developing Areas*, **21** (1), 31–47.

Peters, P. (1983), 'Gender, development cycles and historical process: a critique of recent research on women in Botswana', *Journal of Southern African Studies*, **10** (1), 100–22.

Peters, P. (1987), 'Embedded systems and rooted models: the grazing lands of Botswana and the commons debate', in B.J. McCay and J.M. Acheson (eds), *The Question of the Commons: The Culture and Ecology of Communal Resources*, Tucson, AZ: University of Arizona Press, pp. 171–94.

Peters, P. (1994), *Dividing the Commons: Politics, Policy and Culture in Botswana*, Charlottesville, VA: University of Virginia Press.

Peterson, D.J. (1993), *Troubled Lands: The Legacy of Soviet Environmental Destruction*, Boulder, CO: Westview.

Plumwood, V. (1993), *Feminism and the Mastery of Nature*, London: Routledge.

Plumwood, V. (1995), 'Nature, self and gender: feminism, environmental philosophy, and the critique of rationalism', in R. Elliot (ed.), *Environmental Ethics*, Oxford: Oxford University Press.

Poffenberger, M. (ed.) (1990), *Keepers of the Forest: Land Management Alternatives in Southeast Asia*, West Hartford, CT: Kumarian.

Poffenberger, M. (1994), 'The Resurgence of Community Forest Management in Eastern India', in D. Western and R.M. Wright (eds), *Natural Connections: Perspectives in Community-based Conservation*, Washington, DC: Island Press, pp. 53–79.

Poffenberger, M. (1996), 'Strengthening community forest management in Ghana', in M. Poffenberger (ed.), *Communities and Forest Management*, Washington, DC: IUCN, pp. 28–33.

Poffenberger, M. and B. McGean (eds) (1996), *Village Choices, Forest Choices: Joint Forest Management in India*, Delhi: Oxford University Press.

Polanyi, K. (1944), *The Great Transformation*, Boston, MA: Beacon Press.

Posey, D. (1984), 'A preliminary report on diversified management of tropical forest by the Kayapo Indians of the Brazilian Amazon', *Advances in Economic Botany*, **1**, 112–26.

Posey, D. (1985), 'Indigenous management of tropical forest ecosystems: The case of the Kayapo Indians of the Brazilian Amazon', *Agroforestry Systems*, **3**, 139–58.

Pouchepadass, J. (1995), 'Colonialism and environment in India: comparative perspective', *Economic and Political Weekly*, **19** (August), 2059–67.

Poulantzas, N. (1976), 'The capitalist state: reply to Miliband and Laclau', *New Left Review*, **95**.

Power, T.M. (1996), *Lost Landscapes and Failed Economies*, Washington, DC and Covelo, CA: Island Press.

Powers, R. (1991), *Far from Home: Life and Loss in Two American Towns*, New York, NY: Random House.

Princen, T. (1997), 'The shading and distancing of commerce: When internalization is not enough', *Ecological Economics*, **20**, 235–53.

Princen, T. and M. Finger (1994), *Environmental NGOs in World Politics*, London: Routledge.

Prugh, T., R. Costanza and H. Daly (1999), *The Local Politics of Global Sustainability*, Washington, DC and Covelo, CA: Island Press.

Public Employees for Environmental Responsibility (PEER) (1999), 'Murky waters: official water quality reports are all wet, an inside look at EPA's implementation of the Clean Water Act', PEER Report No. 27, Washington, DC: PEER, May.

Pujol, M. (1992), *Feminism and Antifeminism in Early Economic Thought*, Aldershot: Edward Elgar.

Putterman, L., J.E. Roemer and J. Silvestre (1998), 'Does egalitarianism have a future?', *Journal of Economic Literature*, **36** (2) (June), 861–902.

Quinlan, A.J. and S.B. Greenberg (1997), 'Re: the national environmental impact in 1996', A report to the League of Conservation Voters and the Sierra Club (30 January).

Rajasekaran, B. and D.M. Warren (1994), 'IK for socioeconomic development and biodiversity conservation: The Kolli hills', *Indigenous Knowledge and Development Monitor*, **2** (2).

Raju, G., R. Vaghela and M.S. Raju (1993), *Development of People's Institutions for Management of Forests*, Ahmedabad, India: Viksat, Nehru Foundation for Development.

Rangan, H. (1997a), 'Property vs. control: the state and forest management in the Indian Himalaya', *Development and Change*, **28** (1), 71–94.

Rangan, H. (1997b), 'State-lands, petty commodity extraction, and sustainable rural development in South Africa', Paper presented in the panel on 'Issues in African Agriculture' at the annual meeting of the Association of American Geographers, Dallas-Fort Worth, TX (April 1–5).

Rangan, H. (1997c), 'Indian environmentalism and the question of the state: problems and prospects for sustainable development', *Environment and Planning (A)*, **29** (12), 2129–43.

Rangan, H. (forthcoming), *Of Myths and Movements: Rewriting Chipko*, London: Verso Press.

Rangan, H. and M.B. Lane (1998), 'Indigenous peoples and forest management: comparative analysis of institutional approaches in Australia and India', Paper presented at the 7th International Association for the Study of Common Property Conference, Vancouver, British Columbia, Canada (10–14 June).

Raval, S. (1994), 'Wheel of life: Perceptions and concerns of the resident peoples for Gir National Park in India', *Society and Natural Resources*, **7**, 305–20.

Rawls, J. (1983), *A Theory of Justice*, Harmondsworth: Penguin.

Redclift, M. (1987), *Sustainable Development: Exploring the Contradictions*, New York, NY: Methuen.

Redford, K. and J. Mansour (eds) (1996), *Traditional Peoples and Biodiversity Conservation in Large Tropical Landscapes*, Arlington, VA: The Nature Conservancy, Latin America and Caribbean Division.

Rees, W. (1992), 'Ecological footprints and appropriated carrying capacity: what urban economics leaves out', *Environment and Urbanization*, **4** (2), 121–30.

Rees, W. (1996), 'Ecological footprints of the future', *People & the Planet*, **5** (2).

Rees, W. and M. Wackernagel (1994), 'Ecological footprints and appropriated carrying capacity', in A. Jansson, M. Hammer, C. Folke and R. Costanza (eds), *Investing in Natural Capital: The Ecological Economics Approach to Sustainability*, Washington, DC and Covelo, CA: Island Press.

Reich, R. (1999), 'Foreward', in R. Freeman, *The New Inequality: Creating Solutions for Poor America*, Boston, MA: Beacon Press, pp. viii–ix.

Reilly, W.K (1990), 'The green thumb of capitalism', *Policy Review* (fall), 16–21.

Reynolds, L.T. (1994), 'Institutionalizing flexibility: a comparative analysis of Fordist and Post-Fordist models of third world agro-export production', in G. Gereffi and

M. Korzeniewicz (eds.), *Commodity Chains and Global Capitalism*, Westport, CT: Praeger.

Ribot, J. (1996), 'Participation without representation: Chiefs, councils, and forestry law in the West African Sahel', *Cultural Studies Quarterly*, **20** (3), 40–4.

Ribot, J. (1998), 'Theorizing access: forest profits along Senegal's charcoal commodity chain', *Development and Change*, **29** (2), 307–41.

Ribot, J. (forthcoming), 'Decentralization, participation, and representation: administrative apartheid in Sahelian forestry', in P. Peters (ed.), *Development Encounters*, Cambridge, MA: Harvard University Press.

Richards, P. (1985), *Indigenous Agricultural Revolution: Ecology and Food Production in West Africa*, Boulder, CO: Westview Press.

Robbins, P. (1996), 'Nomadization in western Rajasthan: An institutional and economic perspective', Mimeo, 27 pp.

Roberts, W. and S. Brandum (1995), *Get a Life! How to Make a Good Buck, Dance Around the Dinosaurs, and Save the World While You're At It*, Toronto, Ontario: Get a Life Publishers.

Robinson, J.G. and K. Redford (eds) (1991), *Neotropical Wildlife Use and Conservation*, Chicago, IL: The University of Chicago Press.

Robinson, M. (1995), 'Towards a new paradigm of community development', *Community Development Journal*, **30** (1), 21–30.

Rodriguez, F. (undated), 'Inequality, redistribution and rent-seeking', College Park, MD: Department of Economics, University of Maryland, mimeo.

Rodriguez, F. (1998), 'Essays on redistribution, development, and the state', Ph.D. Dissertation, Cambridge, MA: Harvard University.

Rodrik, D. (1998), *Has Globalization Gone Too Far?* Washington, DC: Institute for International Economics.

Rodrik, D. (1999), *The New Global Economy and Developing Countries: Making Openness Work*, Baltimore, MD: Johns Hopkins University Press.

Roemer, J.E. (1998), 'Why the poor do not expropriate the rich: an old argument in new garb', *Journal of Public Economics*, **70**, 399–424.

Roosevelt, A. (1989), 'Resource management in Amazonia before the conquest: Beyond ethnographic projection', *Advances in Economic Botany*, **7**, 30–62.

Rosen, C. (1998), 'An overview of ESOPs, stock options, and employee ownership', Oakland, CA: NCEO.

Ross, D. (1995), 'Council rejects superquarry', *Glasgow Herald* (6 June).

Rouner, L.S. (ed.) (1991), *On Community*, Notre Dame: University of Notre Dame Press.

Rowell, A. (1996), *Green Backlash: Global Subversion of the Environmental Movement*, London and New York: Routledge.

Ruggie, J.G. (1993), 'Territoriality and beyond: problematizing modernity in international relations', *International Organization*, **47** (1), 139–74.

Sabel, C., A. Fung and B. Karkkainen (1999), 'Beyond backyard environmentalism', *Boston Review*, **24** (5) (October/November), 4–11.

Saberwal, V. (1996), *You can't grow timber and goats in the same patch of forest: Grazing policy formulation in Himachal Pradesh, India, 1865–1960*, prepared for presentation at the workshop on Agrarian Environments: Resources, Representations and Rule in India, Program in Agrarian Studies, New Haven, CT: Yale University, May 2–4, 1997.

Sachs, C. (1996), *Gendered Fields*, Boulder, CO: Westview.

Sachs, W. (1989), 'A critique of ecology: the virtue of enoughness', *New Perspectives Quarterly* (spring), 16–19.

Sachs, W. (1992), 'Von der Vereitlung der Reichtümer zur Verteilung der Risiken', *Universitas*, **9**, 887–97.
Sachs, W. (1993), 'Global ecology in the shadow of "development"', in W. Sachs (ed.), *Global Ecology: A New Arena of Political Conflict*, London and Atlantic Highlands, NJ: Zed Books.
Sachs, W., S. George, I. Illich and A. Ross (1997), 'Slow is beautiful', *New Perspectives Quarterly*, **14** (1) (winter), 4–10.
Sachs, W., R. Loske, M. Linz et al. (1998), *Greening the North: A Post-Industrial Blueprint for Ecology and Equity*, London: Zed Books.
Sagan, S.D. (1993), *The Limits of Safety*, Princeton, NJ: Princeton University Press.
Sagoff, M. (1988), *The Economy of the Earth*, Cambridge: Cambridge University Press.
Sale, K. (1985), *Dwellers in the Land: the Bioregional Vision*, San Francisco, CA: Sierra Club.
Salleh, A. (1995), 'Nature, woman, labour, capital: living the deepest contradiction', *Capitalism, Nature, Socialism*, **6** (1), 21–39.
Sanday, P. (1981), *Female Power and Male Dominance*, Cambridge: Cambridge University Press.
Sanderson, S. (1994), 'Political-Economic institutions', in W.B. Meyer and B.L. Turner II (eds), *Changes in Land Use and Land Cover: A Global Perspective*, Cambridge: Cambridge University Press, pp. 329–56.
Sandilands, C. (1992), 'Ecology as politics: the promise and problems of the greens', in W.K. Carroll (ed.), *Organizing Dissent: Contemporary Social Movements in Theory and Practice*, Toronto, Ontario: Garamond Press, pp. 157–73.
Sandilands, C. (1997), 'Is the personal always political? Environmentalism in Arendt's Age of "the Social"', in W.K. Carroll (ed.), *Organizing Dissent: Contemporary Social Movements in Theory and Practice*, 2nd edn, Toronto, Ontario: Garamond Press, pp. 76–93.
Saxena, N.C. and V. Ballabh (eds) (1995), *Farm Forestry in South Asia*, New Delhi: Sage.
Schlager, E. and E. Ostrom (1992), 'Property rights regimes and natural resources: A conceptual analysis', *Land Economics*, **68** (3), 249–62.
Schmidheiny, S. (1992), *Changing Course: A Global Business Perspective on Environment and Development*, Cambridge, MA: The MIT Press.
Schor, J.B. (1991), *The Overworked American*, New York, NY: Basic Books.
Schor, J.B. (1998), *The Overspent American*, New York, NY: Basic Books.
Schor, J.B. (1999), 'What's wrong with consumer society? Competitive spending and the "New Consumerism"', in R. Rosenblatt (ed.), *Consuming Desires: Consumption, Culture and the Pursuit of Happiness*, Washington, DC and Covelo, CA: Island Press, pp. 37–50.
Schroyer, T. (ed.) (1997), *A World That Works: Building Blocks for a Just and Sustainable Society*, New York, NY: Bootstrap Press.
Schwindt, R. (1996), *Chopping Up the Money Tree: Distributing the Wealth from British Columbia's Forests*, Vancouver, British Columbia: The David Suzuki Foundation.
Sclove, R. (1997), 'Research by the People', in T. Schroyer (ed.), *A World That Works*, New York, NY: Bootstrap Press, pp. 278–290.
Scott, J.C. (1987), *Weapons of the Weak: Everyday Forms of Peasant Resistance*, New Haven, CT: Yale University Press.
Scott, J.C. (1998), *Seeing Like a State*, New Haven, CT: Yale University Press.

Scottish Office (SO) (1994), *National Planning Policy Guidelines: Land for Mineral Working*, Edinburgh: Environmental Department, Scottish Office.

Segal, J.M. (1995), 'Rising consumption, unchanging needs', *Report from the Institute for Philosophy and Public Policy*, 15 (4) (fall).

Segal, J.M. (1999), *Graceful Simplicity*, New York, NY: Henry Holt and Company.

Sen, A.K. (1990), 'Gender and cooperative conflicts', in I. Tinker (ed.), *Persistent Inequalities: Women and World Development*, New York, NY: Oxford University Press, pp. 123–49.

Sen, G. (ed.) (1992), *Indigenous Vision: People of India. Attitudes to the Environment*, New Delhi: Sage Publications.

Shackley, M. (1998) 'Designating a protected area at Karanambu Ranch, Rupununi Savannah, Guyana: Resource management and indigenous communities', *Ambio*, 27 (3), 207–10.

Shapiro, I. and R. Greenstein (1999), 'The widening income gulf', Washington, DC: Council on Budget and Policy Priorities (4 September), <www.cbpp.org/9-4-99tax-rep.htm>.

Shapiro, M. (1993), 'Capitalism compounds Moscow's ecological mess', *Washington Post* (21 May).

Shifting Fortunes (1999), 'A scholar who concentrates . . . on concentrations of wealth', *Too Much* (winter).

Shiva, V. (1989), *Staying Alive: Women, Ecology and Development*, London: Zed Books.

Sierra Club of Canada, Prairie Chapter (1999), 'Statement regarding the Cardinal River Coals Ltd. Cheviot Mine proposal', <www.sierraclub.ca/prairie/cheviot2.html> (15 April).

Simon, J. (1994), 'More people, greater wealth, more resources, healthier environment', *Economic Affairs*, 14 (3), 22–9.

Simons, H.C. (1948), *Economic Policy for a Free Society*, Chicago, IL: University of Chicago Press.

Singleton, S. and M. Taylor (1992), 'Common property, collective action and community', *Journal of Theoretical Politics*, 4 (3), 309–24.

Sinha, S., S. Gururani and B. Greenberg (1997), 'The "New Traditionalist" discourse of Indian environmentalism', *Journal of Peasant Studies*, 24 (3), 65–99.

Sirianni, C. and L. Friedland (1997), 'Civic innovation & American democracy', *Change*, 29 (January/February) (1), 14–23.

Sivaramakrishnan, K. (1995), 'Colonialism and forestry in India: Imagining the past in present', *Comparative Studies in Society and History*, 37 (1), 3–40.

Sivaramakrishnan, K. (1996), *Forests, politics and governance in Bengal, 1794–1994*, Vols. 1 & 2, PhD thesis, New Haven, CT: Yale University.

Smith, A. (1776 [1986]), *The Wealth of Nations: Books I–III*, London and New York: Penguin Books.

Smith, D. (1995), '"Politically correct": an ideological code', in S. Richer and L. Weir (eds), *Beyond Political Correctness: Toward the Inclusive University*, Toronto, Ontario: University of Toronto Press, pp. 23–50.

Sobell, V. (1990), 'The systemic roots of the East European ecological crisis', *Environmental Policy Review*, 1, 1–10.

Société Générale France (1999), 'Focus: reducing work week in France: a preliminary assessment', *Société Générale France Monthly Economic Report* (10 June).

Society for the Promotion of Wastelands Development (SPWD) (1993), *Joint Forest Management Update 1993*, New Delhi: SPWD.

Someshwar, S. (1993), 'People versus the state? Social forestry in Kolar, India', in J. Friedmann and H. Rangan (eds), *In Defense of Livelihood: Comparative Studies on Environmental Action*, West Hartford, CT: Kumarian Press, pp. 182–208.

Soja, E. (1989), *Postmodern Geographies*, London: Verso.

Soysal, Y.N. (1994), *Limits of Citizenship: Migrants and Postnational Membership in Europe*, Chicago, IL: University of Chicago Press.

Sponsel, L.E., T.N. Headland and R.C. Bailey (eds) (1996), *Tropical Deforestation: The Human Dimension*, New York, NY: Columbia University Press.

Standards Council of Canada (SCC) (1998), *Annual Report 1997–98*, Ottawa, Ontario: Standards Council of Canada <www.scc.ca/report/97-98/growing.html>.

Standards Council of Canada (SCC) (1999), 'Canadian Standards Strategy', Ottawa, Ontario: Standards Council of Canada <www.scc.ca/canstrategy/css_e.htm>.

Stauber, J. and S. Rampton (1995), *Toxic Sludge is Good for You!* Monroe, ME: Common Courage Press.

Steininger, K. (1994), 'Reconciling trade and environment: towards a comparative advantage for long-term policy goals', *Ecological Economics*, **9**, 23–42.

Stumm, T.J. (1997), 'Revenue generation and expenditure implications of municipal non-utility enterprises', *Journal of Public Budgeting, Accounting and Financial Management*, **8** (4) (winter), 498–515.

Switzer, J.V. (1997), *Green Backlash: The History and Politics of Environmental Opposition in the U.S.*, Boulder, CO: Lynne Rienner.

Taga, L.S. (1976), 'Externalities in a command society', in F. Singleton (ed.), *Environmental Misuse in the Soviet Union*, New York, NY: Praeger Publishers, pp. 75–100.

Taylor, M. (1982), *Community, Anarchy and Liberty*, Cambridge: Cambridge University Press.

Taylor, P.J. and F.H. Buttel (1992), 'How do we know we have global environmental problems? Science and the globalization of environmental discourse', *Geoforum*, **22** (3), 405–12.

Tendler, J. (1975), *Inside Foreign Aid*. Baltimore, MD: Johns Hopkins University Press.

Thurow, L.C. (1980), *The Zero-Sum Society: Distribution and the Possibilities for Economic Change*, New York, NY: Basic Books.

Tietenberg, T. (1997), *Environmental Economics and Policy*, Reading, MA: Addison-Wesley.

Timmerman, P. (1998), 'It's not easy being green', in R. Keil, D. Bell, P. Penz and L. Fawcett (eds), *Political Ecology: Global and Local*, London and New York: Routledge, pp. 325–35.

Tiwary, M. (1998), 'Participatory forest management in West Bengal: ground-breaking triumph or dilemma in the "commons"?', Paper presented at the Workshop on Participatory Natural Resource Management, Oxford, England (April 6–7).

Tokar, B. (1997), *Earth for Sale: Reclaiming Ecology in the Age of Corporate Greenwash*, Boston, MA: South End Press.

Townsend, K. (1993), 'Steady-state economies and the command economy', in H. Daly and K. Townsend (eds), *Valuing the Earth: Economics, Ecology, Ethics*, Cambridge, MA: MIT Press, pp. 275–296.

Tully, J. (1994), 'Aboriginal property and western theory: Recovering middle ground', *Social Philosophy and Policy*, **11** (2), 153–80.

Tully, J. (1995), *Strange Multiplicities: Constitutionalism in an Age of Diversity*, Cambridge: Cambridge University Press.

Twyman, C. (1998), 'Rethinking community resource management: Managing resources of managing people in Western Botswana?', *Third World Quarterly*, **19**, 745–70.

Underwood, D.A. (1998), 'The institutional origins of crisis for economy and ecology', *Journal of Economic Issues*, **32** (2) (June), 513–22.

United Nations Environmental Programme (UNEP) (1999a), *Global Environment Outlook – 2000*, London: Earthscan.

United Nations Environmental Programme (UNEP) (1999b), 'Press release: the Global Environmental Outlook – 2000 report', Nairobi, Kenya (15 September).

Upton, C. and S. Bass (1995), *The Forest Certification Handbook*, London: Earthscan.

US Bureau of Economic Analysis (1995), *Regional Projections to 2045: Volume 1, States*, Washington, DC: Bureau of Economic Analysis (July).

US Census Bureau (1998), *Statistical Abstract of the United States: 1998*, 118th edn, Washington, DC: US Government Printing Office, 307 and 451.

US Census Bureau (1999), 'Historical income tables – families, Table F–2: share aggregate income received by each fifth and top 5 percent of families (all races), 1947 to 1998', Washington, DC: US Census Bureau (11 November), <www.census.gov/hhes/income/histinc/f02.html>.

Van der Stichele, M. (1997), *Globalisation, Marginalisation, and the World Trade Organisation*, Amsterdam: The Transnational Institute.

Vermeer, E.B. (1998), 'Industrial pollution in China and remedial policies', *The China Quarterly*, **156** (December), 952–85.

Vlachou, A. (1994), 'Reflections on ecological critiques and reconstructions of Marxism', *Rethinking Marxism*, **7** (3), 112–28.

Wackernagel, M. and W. Rees (1996), *Our Ecological Footprint*, Gabriola Island, BC: New Society Publishers (New Catalyst Bioregional Series).

Wall, Glenda. (1999), 'Science, nature, and the nature of things: an instance of Canadian environmental discourse, 1960–1994', *Canadian Journal of Sociology*, **24** (1) (winter).

Walter, E., C. McKay and M. M'Gonigle (1999), 'Fishing around the law: the Pacific Salmon Management System as a structural infringement of aboriginal rights', Report 99–1, Eco-Research Chair of Environmental Law and Policy, University of Victoria, British Columbia.

Wang, C. (1999), 'China's environment in the balance', *The World & I*, **14** (10) (Oct), 176–84.

Wapner, P. (1996), *Environmental Activism and World Civic Politics*, Albany, NY: SUNY Press.

Ward, K. (ed.) (1990), *Women Workers and Global Restructuring*, Ithaca, NY: ILR Press, Cornell University.

Waring, M. (1989), *If Women Counted*, London: Macmillan.

Warwick, H. (1995), 'Mountain Resistance', *Resurgence*, **169**, 28–9

Weiner, D.R. (1988), *Models of Nature: Ecology, Conservation, and Cultural Revolution in Soviet Russia*, Bloomington, IN: Indiana University.

Welford, R. and R. Starkey (eds) (1996), *The Earthscan Reader in Business and the Environment*, London: Earthscan.

Wells, M. and K. Brandon (1992), *People and Parks: Linking Protected Area Management with Local Communities*, Washington, DC: The World Bank, WWF and USAID.

Wernick, I.K. and J.H. Ausubel (1995), 'National materials flows and the environment' *Annual Review of Energy and Environment*, **20**, 463–92.

Western, D. (1994), 'Ecosystem Conservation and Rural Development', in D. Western and R.M. Wright (eds), *Natural Connections. Perspectives in Community-based Conservation*, Washington, DC: Island Press, pp. 15–52.

Western, D. and R.M. Wright (eds) (1994), *Natural Connections: Perspectives in Community-based Conservation*, Washington, DC: Island Press.

Wiewel, W. and J. Persky (1994), 'The growing localness of the global city', *Economic Geography*, **70** (2) (April), 129–44.

Williams, G. (1997), 'State, discourse, and development in India: the case of West Bengal's Panchayati Raj', *Environment and Planning A*, **29** (12), 2099–112.

Williamson, J.G. and P.H. Lindert (1980), *American Inequality: A Macroeconomic History*, New York, NY: Academic Press.

Williamson, T. (1998), 'What Comes Next? Proposals for a Different Society', Washington, DC: National Center for Economic and Security Alternatives.

Willis, J. (1998), 'The 32-hour cure: shortening the work week would create more jobs and foster sustainability', *Alternatives Journal*, **24** (2) (spring).

Wilson, J., J. Acheson, M. Metcalfe and P. Kleban (1994), 'Chaos, complexity and community management of fisheries', *Marine Policy*, **18** (4), 291–305.

Wisner, B. (1990), 'Harvest of Sustainability: Recent Books on Environmental Management', *Journal of Development Studies*, **26**, 335–41.

Wood, E.M. (1995), *Democracy against Capitalism: Renewing Historical Materialism*, Cambridge: Cambridge University Press.

World Bank (1991), *The Forest Sector*, Washington, DC: World Bank.

World Bank (1992), *World Development Report*, Washington, DC: World Bank.

World Commission on the Environment and Development (WCED, the Brundtland Commission) (1987), *Our Common Future*, New York, NY: Oxford University Press.

Worth, R. (1999), 'Asleep on the beat', *The Washington Monthly*, **31** (1) (November), 36–41.

WRI (World Resources Institute) (1999), *World Resources 1998–1999*, New York, NY: Oxford University Press.

Yearley, S. (1991), *The Green Case*, London: Harper Collins.

Yoon, C.K. (1999), 'Few Federal checks exist on the growing of crops whose genes are altered', *New York Times* (3 November).

York, G. (1999), 'A way of life is dying with the reindeer', *The Globe and Mail* (4 March) A15.

Young, O. (ed.) (1997), *Global Governance: Drawing Insights from the Environmental Experience*, Cambridge, MA: MIT Press.

Zerner, C. (1994), 'Through a green lens: The construction of customary environmental law and community in Indonesia's Maluku Islands', *Law and Society Review*, **28** (5), 1079–122.

Index